HOW
TENNIS
INVENTED
EVERYTHING

HOW
TENNIS
INVENTED
EVERYTHING

Christian Howgill

Fulham Folios

Fulham Folio Press

Fulham Folios

Fulham Folio Press full address and contact details can be found
at their website on www.fulhamfoliopress.com

© Copyright Christian Howgill 2021

Christian Howgill has asserted his right under the Copyright, Designs and Patents
Act, 1988 to be identified as the author of this work

This is a First Edition manuscript

First published in Great Britain by Fulham Folio Press in 2021

www.fulhamfoliopress.com

A CIP catalogue record for this book is available from The British Library

Hardback ISBN 978-1-5272-9519-3

Typeset in 11/17pt Palatino
by RefineCatch Limited, www.refinecatch.com

Printed and bound in Great Britain by Clays Ltd, Elcograf S.p.A.

CONTENTS

WITH SPECIAL THANKS TO

There are obviously many people who have helped me gather the stories and mostly I have credited them within the relevant stories themselves, but I must pay special tribute to several people who aided and abetted me with their editorial skills.

The biggest thank you must go to Jill Daamen, who not only proofread the third and final draft of the book but also copy edited it. How she did it all in the time constraints given, I don't know, especially as she was not only editing several other projects at the time but also in high demand as one of London's most elite on-set physiotherapists, whose client list is just about every Hollywood film star who comes to London.

I must also thank Iain Johnstone, who proofread the second draft. As a renowned film critic and highly esteemed writer himself, he came up with many creative suggestions and was incredibly encouraging and supportive. Incidentally, do check out his own tennis book, *Wimbledon 2000*, an ingenious and suspenseful novel set around two twins separated at birth who unwittingly both grow up to be professional tennis players.

Many thanks also to Tim Pike, who proofread the very first draft with his usual meticulous attention to detail. Tim is never one to mince his words – he prefers to save that for the tennis courts of west London!

"... tennis uses the language of life.
Advantage, service, fault, break, love,
the basic elements of tennis are those
of everyday existence, because every
match is a life in miniature."
Andre Agassi

INTRODUCTION

For those of you thinking that the title of the book may lean a little towards hyperbole, permit me to explain. The book is designed to appeal to the fragile ego of tennis players everywhere. It's dedicated to anyone who has known the humiliation of being handed a bagel by someone we had presumed an inferior adversary, whose name we have tried to forget but whose face keeps coming back to haunt us in the wee small hours of the night as we relive the memory of that duffed backhand volley we dumped into the net that would have won us the first game of the set and changed the whole balance of the match.

And, although all the stories here are based on fact, I would prefer you to regard the title with a healthy dose of poetic licence, because this book was written as a balm to soothe the soul of players everywhere, while reminding us what a great game tennis is.

My hope is that the book will reveal some truths about the game, long since lost in the shadows of time, and illustrate how it enriches not just the lives of those of us who play it, but also those poor lost beings who have never felt the joy of a crisply struck backhand as it whizzes past a hapless opponent and lands just inside the baseline for a clean winner.

Now, obviously, I don't want you to think that given the book's title, I am a man prone to exaggeration, or that I am a man who, even though my line calls be true, may revert to alternative facts from time to time for the sake of a good story.

So for all those Doubting Thomases, I can assure you that, even if some of the conclusions may have been greased a little to fit the conceit of the book, the astounding facts that follow are all based on well researched and previously documented facts by authors, scholars, historians and academics far more learned than I.

This then is a book for all, to make us see how tennis has influenced the world in ways we never realised and that in reality, even if tennis may not have actually invented *everything*, it has certainly shaped our lives in many surprising ways.

So prepare to be seduced by a delicious feast of tennis titbits, the digestion of which will allow you to discover how this humble game of ours invented everything from early language to the modern washing machine; how it first invented banking and then caused the global financial crisis; how it helped England win the 1966 football World Cup; and how it can lay claim to some of the greatest shifts in history ever recorded, from the death of kings to the birth of democracy and back again.

But before I engage you in a big hitting, best of five sets championship tournament match through tennis history, all I ask is that you open your heart, sit back and prepare to suspend any lingering cynicism and forgive me on one or two of the more tenuous conclusions. Look upon it not so much as an academic history, but more of a love letter to the game of tennis.

THE PRE-MATCH WARM-UP

Allow me to set the scene properly for you, as I ready myself to serve up the first chapter.

Let the stadium fill, sense the crowd hush and the drama build, a quick glance to the serve clock to see how many seconds I have left before the chair umpire takes umbrage and issues a warning – 5 seconds left.

Just enough time to wipe the sweat from my brow, tweak the strings on my racket, fiddle with my grip, tap the dust from the sole of my shoe, correctly align my water bottles, check my towels are positioned properly, flip my hair back behind my ear, tug at my shorts, loosen my collar, look up to check everyone's ready and bounce the ball of rhetoric a few more times than is strictly necessary just to crank up the tension.

Let the game begin …

SECTION 1

THE FINANCIAL SECTOR

I'm going to open with a blistering first serve straight down the 'T' explaining how tennis invented banking, not only because it's particularly relevant to us in these precarious times, but for the much simpler reason that this was the very first fact that I stumbled upon which made me realise that tennis had given the world so much more than just a ball game.

TENNIS INVENTS BANKING

The story of how I stumbled across the idea that tennis invented banking came to me quite by accident from a flippant remark made way back in 2008. The date is relevant and if you flinched subconsciously when you saw that date but can't remember why, let me refresh you.

2008 was the year that the world found itself in the middle of the biggest financial meltdown since the Great Depression and the Wall Street crash of 1929. In financial terms and in media coverage, the situation was very similar to the Corona Virus pandemic of 2020, but mercifully without the horrific loss of life. The 2008 crash was being splashed across every newspaper around the world, and TV channels were streaming 24-hour live coverage of the plummeting global share prices as we all watched on in open-mouthed horror. It was total turmoil and within days thousands of jobs were gone, hundreds of financial institutions vanished, and even the normally rock-steady residential property market saw prices collapse overnight. Speculation was rife, but everyone was blaming the fat cat banks at the time, as huge investment companies, financial institutions and centuries old banks crumbled faster than an Arctic glacier.

The financial crisis was all everyone was talking about and it was all too depressing, so I thought I would take refuge in a cosy little haven away from it all and slipped into the viewing gallery of the Real Tennis courts at The Queen's Club.

Real Tennis is different from the game of Lawn Tennis that most of us know today. Real Tennis is played indoors against walls and over roof-topped courts, and is where the modern game of Lawn Tennis stems from. But for the purposes of this book and to avoid confusion, let's use a little poetic licence and group them all together as tennis for the moment.

So, anyway, there I was in the Real Tennis viewing gallery, or

3

Dedans as it's sometimes called, trying to escape all the banking meltdown mayhem. Nothing much was going on, there was just a solitary member on court having a Real Tennis lesson from one of the coaches – the perfect respite from the financial wipe-out going on in the real world.

A few minutes later I was joined by Howard Angus, who was then the Head Coach at Queen's and one of the greats of the game having been crowned Real Tennis World Champion three times in a row in the late '70s. So who better than he to sit and chat with about the intricacies of Real Tennis?

Howard was regaling me with how the sport used to be all about gambling and he explained how they used to divide up the money and all the different terms used. That was when I quipped back at him, *"Ah, so it was tennis that invented banking and landed us in the middle of this whole friggin' current financial crisis that we find ourselves in now!"*

Howard stopped mid track, *"Well, possibly,"* he replied in hushed tones, *"but I wouldn't go shouting that from the rooftops around here!"* He was right of course. We were in a tennis club surrounded by many members who worked in the industry and we were currently being sponsored by a bank. We laughed conspiratorially like naughty schoolboys before parting ways and getting back to work.

But it was that chance remark that sparked off a chain of thought which started life as a simple tea towel, expanded into a series of greeting cards before finally morphing into the book you see before you now. So what was it that Howard had said that led me to quip that tennis had invented banking?

Let's start with the basics.

Most of us are familiar with the banking terms *gross profit* and *net profit*. *Gross profit* meaning the total sum of all the sales; and *net profit* is the gross profit minus all the overheads and expenses incurred to get there. But few of us know the precise origins of either.

That's nothing to be ashamed of, because even those working in banking struggle to explain where the two expressions come from. One or two of the more erudite financiers educated in the classics may defer to the basic origins of the word *gross* and mutter something about it being derived from the Latin *Grossus*, or the French *Gros*, meaning *full, large, thick, fat*, etc. ... This goes some way to explaining its etymological roots but falls short of clarifying how it found its way into the banking world.

Interestingly, though, when it comes to *net profit* not a single banker has ever been able to give me even the basic etymology, let alone how it came to be an everyday banking term. For reference's sake then, and for those moments when you find yourself surrounded by a room full of bankers and stumped for any interesting banter, you could casually drop into the conversation that the word *net* stems from the Old Norse, Dutch and Saxon words *net*, and probably the German word *netz*; the Latin verb *nitidus*, and more recently from the French, *net*, all of which mean *elegant, tie off, capture, sharpen, neat* or *trim*.

That's all good and fine, and excellent ammunition to fight back with when a banker is regaling you with stories of the latest Libor interbank lending rates, but none of that really explains how either of these words came to be used in the modern banking sense, and more importantly, how tennis was involved? Well, as luck would have it, the explanation is as neat and elegant as a Federer drop-shot. Both the *gross* and *net* profit terms stem from an earlier form of this grand old game, what we now call Real Tennis, or Court Tennis which we mentioned earlier.

In medieval times, almost all sports, including golf, football, cards and dice were played for money and tennis was no exception. Debtors' prisons were full of tennis players whose forehand returns were not as big as their mouths and whose serves were as feeble as their wallets.

In those days the two players would each wager their stake before the game. A designated Marker would be appointed to keep track of the score and act as an independent referee to cut down on any cheating or disputed line calls. As the name suggests, the Markers would literally mark up the score in chalk at the side of the court, so there could be no arguments or challenges to the score later on.

Before the game started, each player would hand the Marker their individual stake, which would then become the wager to be awarded to the winner of the match. This was called the *gross*, as it contained the *full, untrimmed* stake. But, before the match began, the players had to pay the Marker for his services, so this fee was deducted from the *gross* and the balance was placed under net where it could be safely seen throughout the match, thus the remaining balance became known as the *net profit*.

Hence the difference between *gross* profits and *net* profits and the true explanation of how tennis invented banking. It's a shameful secret that the tennis world has kept under wraps for several hundred years, guarding it more fiercely than the hiding place of the Holy Grail itself, after all tennis is a highly respected game and we have our reputation to think of, so remember what Howard told us about this, keep schtum and don't tell anyone.

TENNIS INVENTS THE WORLD'S FINANCIAL CRISIS

As if inventing banking wasn't enough shame for the game of tennis to bare, there is yet more ignominy to pile upon it, as the noble game also hijacked another major mainstay of the financial world. Tennis may well have been able to live down that it was responsible for the birth of banking if only it hadn't then gone on to cause the biggest financial crisis the world has ever seen. Oops!

Most people take the view that the aforementioned global financial crisis of 2008 was all the fault of the sub-prime market in America, avaricious stock market speculators, greedy bankers, grasping brokers, gluttonous hedge fund managers and the weak, ineffectual politicians who regulate them.

Well, of course, to a certain extent you are right, but how did it all start? Most experts agree that it was all down to a few slightly dodgy American speculators who first decided to wrap up some no-hope loans into another bundle of only slightly less dodgy loans, that were then coated in loans that looked a bit safer, and then surrounded with yet more loans that looked slightly more sturdy in appearance, rather like a rotten nest of Russian dolls.

Surely tennis, that homespun, elegant game of the English gentlemen, couldn't possibly be implicated in such a heinous scandal? Well, unfortunately, yes it is because if you go back far enough, one could actually say that just about every financial crisis in history could be well and truly blamed on tennis. Hard as it may be for any racket waving sports fan to live with this fact, but the origins of our glutinous and volatile financial markets can indeed be traced directly back to our beloved game to about five hundred years ago.

Throughout much of northern Europe, early 15th-century farmers used to plant miles and miles of hedges around their land, which served a multitude of purposes. Firstly, to mark out their territory as boundary lines, providing a tangible sign of ownership to warn off thieves and trespassers. Secondly, it served not only to keep their livestock in but also to keep other livestock from wandering in and eating their valuable crops. And thirdly, they found that the fields with the good sturdy hedges around them gave far higher yields as they were also better protected from the elements.

Over the years the methodology of using hedges this way turned the noun of a hedge into a verb, leading to the phrase *"to hedge"* something, meaning to use that something as a barrier or a safeguard. Consequently, the expression quickly spread to the world of tennis, where gambling was prevalent and the term was used by anyone who wanted to safeguard their original bet. They did this by placing other wagers at different odds, or even wagers on several players rather than only one, a practice that came to be known as *"hedging your bets"*.

This eventually led to a whole new market sector, the hedge fund. It's an almost identical system that hedge fund managers use today as they bet on the stock market. They *hedge* their bets by offsetting them against other stocks and options, causing massive swings and fluxes in the highly unpredictable and speculative options market, often placing money they haven't even got on future options, in the hope that one or the other will come up trumps and that they'll never actually have to fork out for the duff ones when they become due. Unfortunately, when they see that one option is about to fail, they might take out an option on another stock, in the hope that it covers their original loss, and then if that one looks set to be a bad investment as well, they try to cover them both in another bigger speculative option and the whole rotten Russian doll analogy springs to mind again.

Suddenly, you can see how this innocent tennis gambling tactic slowly unfolded into the American sub-prime market of mortgage-backed securities, which gave rise to the deepest global banking crisis the world has ever seen, laying waste to some of the biggest names in finance.

So, 2008 may have remained all sweet in the tennis world for the Bryan Brothers, but it was game, set and match for Lehman Brothers. Sweet returns for Johnnie Mac but set point for Freddie Mac. Fannie Mae but didn't, while Rafa certainly did. Things couldn't have been serener for Williams but Merrill got lynched. Federer was crowned king, but the Royal Bank of Scotland was dethroned. It was OMG for AIG and ASBOs for HBOS.

Tch! Tennis, you have a lot to answer for!

TENNIS INVENTS NEW FINANCIAL MARKET SECTOR

Whilst still in the world of banking and high finance, it's worth noting that just after Spencer Gore had won the very first Wimbledon Championships in 1877, he was asked what he thought of this new-fangled game of Lawn Tennis.

Gore replied that he thought the game lacked enough variety to ever rank as one of the great sports, and he predicted that it would never catch on.

So, not content with tennis inventing banking, net profits, gross profits, hedge funds and the world's biggest ever financial crisis, we also have Spencer Gore's comments which seem to have unwittingly spawned another fruitful new business sector for the world of high finance – the Futures Market.

Looking at my impoverished investment portfolio, I think my financial advisor may well be a descendant of the not-so-prescient Mr Gore.

TENNIS INVENTS THE HANDICAPPING SYSTEM

Anyone who has played club tennis will be familiar with the tennis handicapping system, which issues handicaps appropriate to each player's differing competitive level to even out the game, just as they do in golf and horse racing.

For instance, a common tennis handicap would be for the better player to start 30–0 down, or to be limited to only one serve. But in the old days, before the rules were officially regulated, other more eccentric handicaps were often allocated, especially when high financial wagers were involved.

Among the more bizarre was one issued in 1844 by the Englishman Charles Taylor, who knew that his tennis skills were vastly superior to those of the annoyingly boastful Italian swagger head, Signor Ricardo. Taylor was so confident that he wagered a large sum that he could beat the chesty, jumped-up Italian blaggard even whilst riding on his horse.

Ricardo accepted the challenge but, before the game could be played, the horse had to be fitted with special tennis shoes so as not to wreck the court. They tried using felt shoes, but found them to be too slippery and dangerous for the horse, so they eventually shod the beast in some specially designed leather ones which offered the perfect amount of grip-to-softness ratio. And so the challenge was set.

Taylor's tennis skills may well have outclassed those of the Italian upstart, but the Roman rogue's skill at judging a good bet was far superior. The wily Itie beat the equine-bound Taylor in straight sets, trousered his winnings, and rode off into the Tuscan sunset with a very smartly shod stallion, laughing all the way to *la banca*.

TENNIS INVENTS MORE MAD HANDICAPPING SYSTEMS

Such crazy betting was commonplace in those days; in Peter Seddon's book, *Tennis's Strangest Matches*, he records that Charles Delahaye wagered a large sum on a match whilst wearing a full dress uniform of the French National Guard, including armour, helmet and chainmail gloves. He had the racket in his right and his musket, with full bayonet attached, in his left.

Louis Labbé once played an entire match whilst carrying another man on his shoulders. Such was the confidence of another young Frenchman Ray Masson that he laid down a challenge match in which he had to jump in and out of a barrel in between each shot.

In more recent times at The Queen's Club in London, I once organised a tennis match where the writer, broadcaster and comedian Tony Hawks played the entire match whilst still attached to a domestic refrigeration unit. Not just any fridge, of course; it was the one he had hitch-hiked his way round Ireland with, turning the whole adventure into a bestselling book, *Round Ireland with a Fridge*.

Tony may have lost the match, but he won the hearts of all the spectators who had gathered to watch the match. And on the up-side, at least he had some ice-cool refreshments on hand to drown his sorrows.

TENNIS INVENTS LOSING YOUR SHIRT

We have established that in the early days of tennis, gambling was rife, to a dangerous degree in fact, so much so, that tennis has a good claim to giving rise to the populist saying *"He lost his shirt on it"*.

Indeed, in the 12th century, the Duke of Burgundy recorded a particularly bad run of form in the tennis gambling stakes. First off, he lost a substantial amount of money to the Duke of Bourbon, then he lost even more to William de Lyon, before finally losing again to Guy de Trimouille – and all in consecutive games. Being unable to pay the mounting debts, he was forced to hand over his girdle as part payment. Presumably, the Duke was compelled to leave with his tail between his legs both literally and metaphorically.

Sadly it seems that wandering the land bereft of suitable trouser-holding-up equipment didn't deter the young Duke from gambling on the steadiness of his forehand again. For shortly afterwards, he was once again unable to pay another tennis gambling debt and was forced to part with his girdle yet again, this time to the Comte d'Eu. The girdle was recorded as being worth 80 francs, which is the equivalent of several thousands of pounds in today's money, so it seems that the Comte d'Eu did rather well.

Following the Brexit vote, it seems Britain will have to pay the equivalent of many billions of girdles to the European Union as well. In fact, I wouldn't be surprised if Boris Johnson also refers to them as something similar to Les Comtes d'EU.

SECTION 2

THE ROYAL CONNECTION

Horse racing is often referred to as the sport of kings, but long before the royals became besotted with our equine friends, the moniker belonged to another sport much more worthy of the title, tennis.

Kings and queens from across Europe, especially Britain and France, were regularly bewitched and beguiled by the game's elusive charms. So much so, that on many occasions their devotion to the sport has changed the course of history.

So let's take a look at some of the more notable examples.

TENNIS INVENTS HISTORY – AND A BIG PLOP OF IRONY

James I of Scotland was totally smitten with his tennis but little did he realise that his devotion would not just cost him his crown but his life.

James used to play almost daily in the monastic cloisters at Perth, which was by all accounts a lovely court except for one tiny flaw. It had an open drain in the corner, which served as part of the monastery's main sewer system for the monks' holy ablutions.

Now, although I'm sure the good monks didn't ablute during His Maj's actual game, the drain hole itself did prove to be a blessed problem. The sovereign's forehand would occasionally go awry and more oft than not, a stately tennis ball would plop down the royal plop hole.

Hallowed and pure as the monks holy lavations may be, it is certainly not something that a reigning monarch wants to go rummaging around in just before having to save a break point on his serve during the crucial seventh.

On top of all that, historical records show that tennis balls in those days were hideously expensive and, painful as it is to lose a service game, that is nothing compared to the pain felt by a Scotsman at the sight of money, quite literally, going down the drain.

So, the canny wee Jimmy jammed the john by having a huge stone paving slab placed over the hole so that no-one could be privy to his privy no more. With the closet closed, everyone was happy; the monks continued to ablute freely and James continued to play his errant forehands safe in the knowledge that they would no longer end up in the monks' end-ups.

Job done, so to speak. What could possible go wrong? Well, quite a lot apparently, because the royal duties of a king were not limited to drain-hole repair. Being king meant that you had to fight off uprisings, pacify rebels, keep the nobility on side, reform taxes, impose law, maintain order, placate all your various wives, service your many mistresses, survive kidnappings, pay ransom monies, bribe dissenting officers, explore new territories, defeat pirates, set up spy networks, invent new torture methods, make the Scots believe you were at war with the English, tell the English you were at war with the French, tell the French you were at war with the Dutch, and make the Dutch think you were at war with the Spanish, and all the while trying to convince the Swiss that you were perfectly neutral.

All of which wasn't easy, and James upset a lot of people trying to pull off this delicate balancing act. Most notable amongst the grumbling grouses was a group of Scottish nobility who decided that King James wasn't devoting enough time to thoroughly detesting the English and so, in 1437, they mounted a murderous coup against him.

They stormed the royal palace and eventually had the retreating James cornered in his bedroom chambers. James was trapped. As the rebels beat down his door, desperate courtiers levered up the wooden flooring of his bathroom and lowered him down into the drains of the royal cludgie so that he could escape through the underground sewage system, surely giving a whole new meaning to the phrase *"he was only going through the motions"*.

James made good his escape all the way to the end of the sewer, only to find the exit blocked by the very same stone he had ordered to be placed there at the far corner of the tennis court. James pushed and he shoved with all his royal might but he couldn't shift it.

Irony just doesn't seem to be a strong enough word to define his highness's right royal predicament. If ever the phrase *"up shit creek without a paddle"* found itself out of work and looking for a suitable sentence to give itself worthy employment, then this surely must be the occasion. But poor old King James, not only did he not have a paddle, he didn't even have the proverbial canoe!

Eventually, the rebels got wind of his whereabouts, quite literally probably, flushed him out of his cubby hole, and put him to the sword.

Tennis has claimed the lives of several kings throughout history but surely there can be none more ironic than that of James I, who was, quite literally, killed at his own convenience.

TENNIS INVENTS MORE HISTORY

You would have thought that the royals would have got the message about the perils of tennis to those born of blue blood but, unfortunately, the fatal attraction didn't end with death of King James. For there is yet another dramatic death of a king caused by the game. Don't get too upset though, it was only a French one.

Louis X was a very keen tennis player, his love of the game bordered on obsession. In fact, he became so aggrieved when he was unable to play during winter or when it rained that he ordered the construction of several indoor courts. They were built in Paris around the end of the 13th century and are thought to be the very first indoor tennis courts ever constructed.

In due course, this design spread to royal palaces across Europe and the style and layout of Louis' courts still form the basis of all the indoor Real Tennis courts that we know today.

Unfortunately, though, it wasn't long before the royal tennis curse struck again. It was in June 1316 at Vincennes, Louis was having a very hard-fought match and is recorded as sweating so profusely that his attending courtiers started to grow increasingly concerned at his pallor and tried to get him to rest a while. But the devoted tennis fan was having none of it and ploughed on.

When the game eventually ended, Louis was gasping for breath and excessively thirsty. Not having any of the nicely refrigerated modern electrolyte-based rehydration drinks to hand, Louis chose what in those days was the next best thing, and gulped down *"a copious quantity of cooled wine"*.

The over-exertion followed by the excessive quantities of wine was not a good combo because, as the evening air cooled, the King started to develop a severe chill. Concerned courtiers took him to his chamber to rest but it was to no avail, and later that evening Louis took a turn for the worse and died.

And yet, the blue blooded numbskulls still didn't take heed of the royal tennis curse because Louis was not the last king to be killed off by the game. In spite of the fact that the game had slaughtered half his ancestry, Charles VIII was also a big fan of the game and decided to try and break the curse and also took up tennis. A sport that, if you were of royal lineage, proved to be less of a ball game and more like Russian Roulette.

The year was 1498, just two and a half years after his famous retreat from Italy – good to know he learned *something* from the Italians while he was there – and Charles found himself on a small tennis court in Amboise. The records show that he was concentrating so hard on watching the ball that he completely failed to notice a load-bearing stone lintel above the entrance to the court, and ran head first into it. When it comes to a human skull colliding with a three-ton stone lintel, then there was only ever going to be one winner.

Courtiers attended to the bruising of the Crown's crown, but with no MRI scanner nearby, probably due to Government cutbacks, the attending doctors were totally oblivious to the subdural haematoma slowly growing inside the royal bonce. A few hours later, Charles fell into a lethal coma and died.

Since the entire brood of Charles's offspring had unfortunately all died before him, probably from playing tennis, the throne passed to his father's second cousin, the Duke of Orléans who was crowned King Louis the XII.

Obviously learning from his predecessor's fate, and from what happened to his unfortunate namesake Louis X, all being killed by the game, King Louis XII decided to give this whole tennis thing a rather wide berth, opting instead for less dangerous pastimes like archery, jousting and going to war with the English.

An interesting addendum to that story is that, simply because of all the contemporary written records that make account of his death,

Louis X was actually the first named tennis player ever to be recorded as playing the game.

I'm sure His Maj would have preferred to be remembered for his fiscal reforms, or as the first king to abolish slavery, or as the king who granted equality to all, but hey, when you're royal and you take up tennis, then there's really only ever going to be one outcome.

TENNIS INVENTS THE SMUTTY DOUBLE-ENTENDRE

Shakespearean historians will tell you that the bard often wrote quite lascivious prose to amuse the bawdy crowds who stood in the central auditorium, but not many remember that one of the earliest recorded gags was about the innocent game of tennis.

This passage, from *Henry V* refers to the incident we touched upon earlier earlier, where the French ambassador brings the young king *"a tun of treasure"* from the young French Dauphin, and when the King asks what this fantastic haul of treasure was, Exeter replies:

Exeter: *Tennis balls, my liege.*
King Henry: *We are glad the Dauphin is so pleasant with us;*
              His present and your pains we thank you for:
              When we have match'd our racquets to these balls,
              We will, in France, by God's grace, play a set
              Shall strike his father's crown into the hazard.
              Tell him he hath made a match with such a wrangler
              That all the courts of France will be disturb'd with
              chases.

But this rhetoric is mild compared to the far more salacious efforts recorded in Drayton's evocative poem *The Ballade of Agincourt*, written in 1606, which begins with the famous line, *"Fair stood the wind for France"*.

The poem soon descends into the vernacular to appeal to the masses, when he also recalls the Henry V incident of being mockingly sent the tennis balls. The King's answer is given thus:

King Henry: *... I'll send him Balls and Racquets if I live,*
              That thy such Racquet shall in Paris see,

When over lyne with Bandies I shall drive,
As that before the Set be fully done,
France may (perhaps) into the Hazard runne.

Apart from the obvious pun on the word *balls*, this passage is often cited by the literary critic, Marshall, as offering one of the first examples of the two variants of the word *racket* meaning both *commotion* as well as a *tennis racket*.

It also plays on the word *Hazard*, meaning the wall that juts out in a Real Tennis court as well as the more commonly used meaning of *risky*, or *dangerous*.

Not one to miss out on a cheap laugh, Drayton also shows us his linguistic skill with another early pun on the word *bandy*. This is an old Real Tennis term, meaning *"to rally back and forth"*, but is also now used to mean *"to put someone down, or intentionally spread malicious gossip"*.

So, almost a full set of tennis puns for young Drayton, many of which we still use today. Not the most erudite humour by today's standards, but remember in those days more sophisticated humour like satire would have resulted in them being beheaded, so they had to make do with a bevy of naughty puns, slapstick and nob gags. Which is pretty much my excuse as well, and I'm sticking to it.

TENNIS INVENTS RAIN STOPS PLAY

Charles IX was the son of King Francis II and Catherine de Medici, a premeditated combination of royalty and wealth previously unparalleled as they were two of the wealthiest and best-connected families in the world. So to say that Charles was born with a silver spoon in his mouth doesn't do the expression justice. And, as King Francis II and Catherine de Medici were both absolutely tennis-mad, I think it's safe to say that Charles was not just born with a silver spoon in his mouth but also with a 24-carat gold racket protruding from his royal let-them-eat-cakehole.

And it wouldn't have been strung with common old catgut, *"Mon dieu! Non!"* It would've been strung with a mix of duodenal digestive systems extracted from the royal deer, the finest bison, imported elks, along with some specially selected Wagyu Kobe beef that had most likely been hand massaged by the King's own private masseuses.

Renowned for his impatience, foul temper and ruthlessness, Charles had been playing tennis almost before he had learned enough words to have his chef hung, drawn and quartered for serving the wrong kind of brioche with his foie gras.

There is an account that he was once disturbed in the middle of a game of tennis to be informed that a group of Huguenot rebels were mounting an assassination attempt on him. He was told that the rebels had already killed one his most loyal friends and that they were gaining ground on the palace and getting close to the court where he was playing. Charles was said to have been so aggrieved at being forced to abandon his game that he stormed off court cussing and swearing.

In a vile fit of temper, the foul-mouthed monarch hurled his racket to the ground, smashing it to pieces and breaking some of those very exclusive colonic strings. Bold be the umpire who deducted a point penalty for racket abuse on this occasion!

Still fuming, Charles reluctantly fled to safety but was so incandescent with rage that he ordered the immediate slaughter of 4,000 Huguenots as revenge. I must say, I feel a bit like that when I lose my serve as well.

History doesn't record whether this fit of pique was because he was annoyed at the death of his friend or because they interrupted his tennis game when he was a break up. Either way, it seems a bit harsh but, hey, it's good to be king.

Charles though was also a huge fan of puns, so he may have been slightly cheered to know that this was the first and only ever recorded incident of reign stops play!

TENNIS INVENTS OLDEST BALL

In terms of function, Westminster Hall is often a bit neglected as a building in that it serves as little more than a giant corridor these days, but when it was built it was one of the biggest and most impressive buildings in the world. In terms of location, it is the grand old building that stands to the far right of The Houses of Parliament, in fact if you were any further right you'd be Nigel Farage.

First commissioned in 1097 by King William II, the son of William the Conqueror, Westminster Hall would have been the centre piece of his home, Westminster Palace. Although it has undergone many changes since that time, the actual walls of Westminster Hall still survive to this day.

But the building itself holds several unanswered mysteries. The first conundrum is the fact that throughout history architects have failed to work out how on earth they managed to support such a large expanse of roof. Typically, Norman construction methods would use central pillars to support a roof structure of that size, but recent archaeology digs revealed that no such supports were ever in place. It seems that the wooden timbers defy all logic in being able to bear such a huge weight-to-load ratio. But, bewildering as that is, it pales in significance when it comes to the Hall's other mystery.

This second conundrum may be smaller in scale but it is of greater concern to those of us who are more tennis-centric. Because, equally baffling to historians is the fact that during a renovation of the roof beams in 1920, they discovered, stuck mischievously into the rafters, a tennis ball that dates back to somewhere between 1450 and 1500, making it by far the oldest tennis ball ever found.

This means that a ball struck in the Middle Ages didn't come back down to earth for over five centuries, which qualifies it as officially the longest timed lob in tennis history. I have a friend called Will Robson who specialises in lobbing, and he does it so high and so frequently that we are officially obliged to inform Air Traffic Control whenever he is playing, but even he would have to play second fiddle to this one.

The real mystery, of course, is how on earth it got there, as there are no official records of tennis ever having been played there. But, if history has taught us anything, it's that official records never tell the whole story. Unless there was a visiting dignitary or a matter of state involved, there would be no reason to document the fact that the King or his family decided to play a game of tennis in Westminster Hall. It was his private palace and so no record would have been kept of a game of tennis.

All things considered, the Hall was the perfect place to play. It was incredibly large, it was warm, it was dry, and it certainly would've saved the royals having to saddle up their entire entourage, grab the next gilded carriage and ride several miles to the nearest court. And as there were no rules on court sizes in those days, then you could just string a rope across the centre and, hey presto, you have the world's first ever indoor tennis court!

But there is still mystery of whose ball it could have been. It could have belonged to any of the royal households from the Yorkist dynasty of Edward and Richard to one of the Tudor Henrys. Personally, my money is on Henry VIII – not only is he well documented as a keen player of the game but also because, let's face it, when you've got six wives, you would need to take a little recreational time out for yourself occasionally.

What we do know is, that whoever hit the ball into the rafters would have lost the point, and, if it was indeed Henry VIII, then we know that he had a foul temper and didn't like to lose, so, who knows what the ramifications were? If he'd been having a bad day, then that might just have been the straw that broke the camel's back, pushed him over the edge, and, if the rhyme about his wives is right, *"Divorced, beheaded, died, divorced, beheaded, survived"*, then maybe it was not the only spherical object that was lost that day.

All we know for certain is that the Westminster ball is heralded as the oldest surviving leather-skinned pillock left anywhere in the world, unless, of course, you count Donald Trump.

SECTION 3

POLITICS

There is a neat cross-over in the 18th century when tennis goes from being the sport of kings, and embodying privilege, to becoming the improbable saviour of the people, a flag bearer for everything from freedom and equality, all the way through to inventing democracy itself.

Sound unlikely? Read on …

TENNIS INVENTS DEMOCRACY

OK, I understand that the concept of democracy being invented by tennis may give rise to some spluttering objections from various far flung corners of the globe. Granted, the Ancient Greeks could certainly lay claim to a basic form of democracy a couple of thousand years earlier.

But as there are not too many Ancient Greeks still around to voice their objections, and in the absence of a suspiciously large wooden horse outside my front door, I shall move the discussion on to favour my own country. Here in England you could argue that, in 1215, the Magna Carta established the ground rules for much of the Parliamentary democracy that we enjoy today.

On the other hand, you could also argue that both of those early stabs at it were not true democracies because, much like several other earlier attempts, they were very limited in who was actually allowed to vote and who wasn't. Limiting the votes to only the privileged few, the nobles, the elite, and the more learned, leaving the vast majority of citizens without a vote, which didn't really progress the good name of democracy that we know and love today. We needed something that would give democracy a helping hand. We needed something that would give it integrity. We needed tennis.

Which brings us neatly to the truest, purest form of early democracy. A democracy that is so deeply indebted to tennis that the word *"tennis"* is even incorporated into the name of the title deed.

Let me take you back in time. It's France. It's 1789.

It's the French Revolution ...

The Revolution overthrew the monarchy and, although in the short term it may have led to years of bloodshed and political turmoil, it finally culminated in establishing a republic. Inspired by liberal and radical ideas, the French Revolution profoundly altered the course, not just of modern democracy but of modern history.

33

It triggered the global decline of the rule of monarchy and dictatorships, replacing them with republics and democracies around the world. In fact, this single event is often cited by historians as one of the most pivotal cultural events in human history.

So how did tennis come to play such a crucial role that it even had its name incorporated into the title?

It all started because Louis XVI was ruthlessly hunting down the rebels who kept meeting up in secret to gather support against him. The group's aim was to form a National Assembly to conduct the nation's affairs and they wanted it to consist of the people, not the ruling elite. It was to be *"of the people, by the people, for the people"*.

The French King, though, didn't really fancy the idea of losing his fine lifestyle, his royal palaces or even his very regal head, all of which he had become inordinately fond of, so he ordered the closure of the State Rooms where the rebels used to meet and sent the troops in to stop any further gatherings.

The rebels, though, got wind of the soldiers' imminent arrival and, being similarly fond of keeping their own heads attached to their torso, fled to the only other building that was big enough to fit them all, the Tennis Court.

Indeed, it was here that the burgeoning National Assembly first took refuge, the very tennis court that is depicted in Jacques-Louis David's famous painting of this historic meeting that captures the decisive moment where the rebels all swear allegiance to what is now known as *"The Tennis Court Oath"*.

David's painting shows nearly 600 rebels, including the likes of the great Robespierre himself, crammed into the court. They were hanging from the rafters, windows, galleries, rooftops and dedans, swearing *"never to separate, and always to reassemble, whenever circumstances required, until the constitution of the Kingdom of France and the freedom of its people was complete"*.

The Tennis Court Oath played an absolutely decisive role in the

French Revolution. It was so much more than just an act of revolution, the importance and integrity of it was constantly referred to by the rebels throughout the years of carnage that followed, and it always brought them back together and gave them the strength to fight on. The assertions of political authority and social philosophy that *The Tennis Court Oath* stood for went far beyond its original objective, and it is often hailed by historians as the true beginning of modern democracy.

It's a story that often leaves people open mouthed in astonishment when I tell it, but having regaled it to a friend of mine a few years ago, they looked at me, obviously impressed that the sport he loved so much had played such a vital part in the history of democracy, but there was a subtext of slight perplexity to his expression.

"So, this Robespierre fellow," he enquired. *"If he was really such a great man, why did they call him The Tennis Court Oaf?"*

TENNIS INVENTS THE SECRET SERVICE

Spying on our enemies has been part of human nature since before *Homo Sapiens* could even talk, but the first mention of an officially sanctioned state secret service dates back to Queen Elizabeth I. She started it for a very good reason – her life depended on it.

When Elizabeth began her reign, Britain was savagely divided by religion. Elizabeth was Protestant, whilst Mary, whom many believed was the true heir to the throne, was Catholic. To make matters worse, Britain was surrounded by Catholic nations and plots to dethrone Elizabeth and restore Mary as the rightful heir were erupting from every corner of the globe on an almost daily basis. Bloodshed, treachery and dastardly deeds of dirty double-crossing were rife. There was only one thing she could rely on to save her, of course, and that was tennis.

Being very aware of the imminent dangers lurking in every nook of the palace, Elizabeth set up a secret network of spies, not just across the country but across the world, in an international security effort that was to herald one of Britain's greatest ever exports – espionage.

But where to start? A cursory glance at the history books, or as we know it today, Wikipedia, would suggest that Sir Francis Walsingham, Elizabeth I's Secretary of State, was England's first spymaster. Walsingham set in place a lavish network of spies, planting them both here and abroad. He set up carefully structured procedures, with vast teams of agents trained in all areas of espionage, many of which are still in operation today, from inventing codes, sending secret messages, intercepting enemy communications, forging signatures, breaking into sealed letters and re-sealing them undetected, to setting up their own team of code breakers.

Intriguingly, according to historian Stephen Alford's book, *The Watchers: A Secret History of the Reign of Elizabeth I*, it suggests that Walsingham is credited with having written the first ever handbook

36

for spies, *The Book of Secret Intelligences*. Alford asserts that the book would have had all the codes and protocols that a spy would need to operate undercover. How to forge documents, break into locks, how to write and decipher codes and how to escape again unnoticed.

In the world of espionage, this book is legendary and the source of much speculation amongst historians. Although the official story is that it is long lost, many conspiracy theorists suggest that it contains just too much information ever to be let out. Hardly a year passes without a rumour emerging of someone claiming to have seen the fabled tome everywhere from Buckingham Palace to The Vatican. Uh-oh. Tom Hanks, you'd better dust down your Robert Langdon corduroy jacket, I sense another Dan Brown book on the way.

But, despite Walsingham's obvious claim to be England's first spymaster general, most historians would say that Elizabeth had already formed an earlier secret service, using another trusted ally, William Cecil, who later became Lord Burghley. It seems that long before Walsingham, Cecil had been overseeing the gathering of intelligence for the Queen for many years before that, using only her most trusted men, among them John Dee, Robert Dudley and Thomas Howard, the Duke of Norfolk.

These men were able to travel freely and spy amongst their Catholic counterparts with more ease than most, because there was one thing that was even more important to the English nobility than their religious allegiances, and that was money. Religious alliances changed with each new monarch, so religious beliefs were often feigned in order to gain patronage rather than genuinely felt. It's a bit like being a member of the Liberal Democrats.

Money, though, spoke louder than any monarchy or faith. And what was played for money? Tennis. Big money. So it was tennis that enabled these men to go about their covert existence without arousing suspicion. Just as today, the game of tennis cut across culture, race and creed. These players went from court to court, and country to country, playing the great game, for even greater stakes than their opposition realised.

Although all these men were totally loyal to Elizabeth, they would often fight dangerously amongst themselves to try and gain further favour from the Queen. And once again, tennis plays a pivotal role in the story. Intriguingly, both Dudley and the Duke are handsomely portrayed in various grandiose oil paintings, sometimes with a sword, occasionally with a tennis racket but nearly always with a handkerchief hanging from their sword belt.

Now, that might not mean anything to us today, other than perhaps they were suffering from a nasty bout of man flu, but in those days to portray yourself with a handkerchief hanging from your sword belt was not an indication of a weakened immune system; oh no, it was far more shocking. It was a brazen sign of outright salaciousness of the highest order.

In those days, a lady might give a handkerchief to a man to show her affection for him, and it would be delicately scented in her own bespoke perfume. This would act as both as an *aide-mémoire* for him of her sweetly fragranced self, and also serve as a visual signal to warn off other potential suitors that this man was taken, so back off.

Remnants of this old tradition still exist today in old movies and cartoons, when the fair maiden will *"accidentally"* drop her handkerchief for her hero to pick it up. So, you see, a well-placed handkerchief was said to represent a visible token of affection to a woman with whom you were close to, but not yet married to.

Hence, the provocative nature of such a scandalous gesture being openly portrayed in a portrait. It would be the equivalent today of a celebrity Tweeting a picture of themselves in bed, but with someone obviously hidden under the sheets next to them, maybe only a naked royal leg sticking out the side giving only the merest hint of who it might be.

It was widely speculated at the time that the handkerchiefs

depicted in the aforementioned portraits were depicting a memento of the Queen herself. Tantalisingly, the handkerchiefs of both these men are said to show only partial snippets of embroidery on them that may, or may not, be interpreted as belonging to the Queen. Elizabethan scandals didn't get much bigger than this. Hanky-gate was the talk of the town.

Incidentally, it is also believed to be the derivation of the phrase, *hanky-panky*. But let us not get too distracted by the bawdy innuendo of fragrant patches of embroidered linen and return to this escalating battle of egos between Dudley and the Duke. A feud that is rumoured to have reached a climax during an infamous tennis match, as recounted by the Earl of Atholl when he met the English ambassador, Thomas Randolph, in Scotland in March 1565.

He wrote:

> *"That early the Duke's grace and my Lord of Leicester were playing at tennis, the Queen beholding of them, and my Lord Robert being hot and sweating took the Queen's napkin out of her hand and wiped his face, which the Duke seeing said that he was too saucy, and swore that he would lay his racket upon his face; where up rose a great trouble and the Queen offended sore with the Duke."*

This public act of such obvious effrontery nearly cost the Duke his life. He was exiled from the country and ordered to try and earn back her majesty's respect by becoming an undercover agent to spy on any potential uprisings that may be stirring abroad.

Not too bad a punishment you might think, but this was a job that was considered so fraught with danger that it was as good as a death sentence and the Duke was not expected to return.

However, it seems that the Duke was as skilled at espionage as he was at courting, because he didn't just survive his days as an undercover tennis playing spook, he excelled at it. So much so that he was able to win back favour with his Queen and reignite their bond. No doubt he liked his mead shaken, not stirred.

Encouraged by the success of her agents, Elizabeth decided to expand her network of spies. Known as *"The Watchers"*, they travelled the length and breadth of the globe, tennis racket in one hand, code book in the other, seeking out possible dissenters in their furtive battle to protect the Crown.

None of the opposition players who were unfortunate enough to play these undercover spies ever realised that the stakes that they were playing for were far higher than the monies wagered on the tennis game.

They knew that one loose shot could lose them a fortune, but none of them realised that one loose word could cost them their life.

TENNIS INVENTS DIPLOMACY

Having invented democracy, tennis kind of sat on its laurels for a bit. It became a bit self-satisfied and no doubt dined out on the fact a little too often and became a bit fat on the proceeds. It probably thought that giving the world democracy was sufficient endowment for a ball game.

Fast forward a couple of centuries, and the now balding tennis was sitting in front of the fire, comfy slippers on, listening to Radio 4, when it caught a glimpse of its bulging middle-aged belly and thought, *"Hmn, maybe it's time I got down to the gym, got back into shape and invented something new in the political world"*.

Sure enough, almost two centuries after inventing democracy, tennis was back, only this time it was going to have a crack at the world of diplomacy.

It was the spring of 1971. The Cold War had been raging for a quarter of a century and diplomatic tensions between the East and the West were at their very frostiest and with no sign of a thaw. In fact, no official American delegation had been invited to China since the Communist takeover in 1949. How on earth was it possible then that, a few months later, President Nixon himself would land in Beijing for a landmark meeting that was to change Sino-American relations forever?

Well, only one thing could make that possible, of course – tennis. Or, to be more precise, the condensed-down, indoor Victorian version of the game, that we now know better as table tennis.

The event that sparked this ground-breaking thaw in diplomatic relations took place twelve months earlier and without a diplomat in sight, and owed its origins to a chance encounter between two men competing against each other in the World Table Tennis Championships and was to give rise to a whole new phrase in international relations – Ping-Pong Diplomacy.

41

Here's what happened. An American table tennis player had been on the practice courts at the World Table Tennis Championships in Japan and missed his team bus back to his hotel, and so surreptitiously snuck on to the bus of the Chinese players, as he'd seen that they were all staying at the same hotel.

After a frosty 15 minutes of obeying strict international protocol whereby nobody was allowed to speak or interact with anyone from the opposing nations, one of the Chinese team went over and handed him a peace offering of a silk scarf depicting the famous Huangshan Mountains. Using the on-board interpreter, the two athletes got talking and realised that their so-called deadly enemies were actually just ordinary, really nice, genuine human beings and they got on really well with each other.

When the bus arrived back at the hotel, journalists saw the two players chatting together and were so astonished that they took photos of this rare meeting of nations. Such was the scarcity of such an occurrence that the photos dominated news headlines around the world.

When Mao Zedong saw it, he realised immediately that punishing the players for breaking protocols would be terrible PR and spotted an opportunity. He invited the American team to stop off on an all-expenses paid visit to China on their way back home after the World Championships. The visit was cleared, and so it happened that the American team spent a week in China playing exhibition matches, touring the Great Wall, visiting the Summer Palace and attending the state ballet. Again, it made headlines around the world and 15 American table tennis players had suddenly become the most important international diplomats of their time.

Nixon, sensing a shift in diplomatic alliances and wanting to make the most of this new-found goodwill, announced that the US was easing its travel ban and lifted trade embargos on China. Shortly after this, he also secretly sent Secretary of State Henry Kissinger to

Beijing to try and arrange an even bigger coup – a Presidential visit to China.

The gamble paid off and seven months later, in February 1972, President Nixon touched down in Beijing to set off one of the biggest tectonic shifts of diplomacy in world history. The Chinese Premier Zhu En-lai summed up its importance: *"Never before in history has a sport been so effectively used as a means of international diplomacy."* President Nixon himself defined it simply as *"the week that changed the world"*.

In February 2002, during a state visit to China, President George W. Bush recalled the Ping-Pong diplomacy incident to President Jiang Zemin reminding him that *"Thirty years ago this week, President Richard Nixon showed the world that two vastly different governments could meet on the grounds of common interest and in a spirit of mutual respect"*.

Time magazine hailed it as *"The ping that was heard around the world"* and, as it turned out, it was a ping that went on to diffuse the bitter pong of the Cold War forever.

Of course, then Trump picks up his phone and one tweet later, half a century of diplomatic protocol is blown to hell in all four corners of the globe.

Oh dear. I'm not sure that even tennis can save the world now.

TENNIS UNINVENTS DIPLOMACY

The Tribune Book of Open Air Sports was written in 1887 by an American called Henry Hall, a man who seems to have had all the diplomatic skills of a young Donald Trump. He dismissed all Englishmen as unable to compete with American sportsman *"because Americans are full of fire and intense action. No hit is too hard, no shot too violent, and no bat is too rigorous"*.

Englishmen, on the other hand, he derides are

> *"too solid and patient, and are built more to endure. They prefer tools and machinery to do their work for them. They are governed too much by tradition, and put much useless matter, money and time into their work. Probably because their forefathers of titled personages have always done things that way. Baseball is the announcement of our athletic youth, whereas tennis is for those circles which like a more gentle and graceful sport."*

How did a career in the Diplomatic Corp pass Mr Hall by? I think if Donald Trump was ever re-elected and was looking for a new Secretary of State – and let's face it when wasn't he? – then I'm sure some of Hall's descendants would meet with his approval.

TENNIS INVENTS AN AMERICAN PRESIDENT

OK, so this one is a tale of patriotism and commercialism so finely blended and intertwined that it could only happen in America.

At the turn of the last century, an American meat-packing company, helpfully called The Schwartzchild and Sultzberger Meat Packing Company of Chicago, noticed that they were selling a lot of their waste at a very low price to a company that made tennis racket strings from the off-cuts of their unwanted offal. They noticed that this other company was selling the strings at a rather tasty profit and quite rightly thought that they might be better off by keeping the gut and making the strings themselves.

They quickly realised that their current name, The Schwartzchild and Sultzberger Meat Packing Company of Chicago, was a bit of a mouthful and not exactly catchy as a brand name. So, they decided to look for a name that was shorter and had a little more gravitas.

After much discussion, they decided that it would be a good idea to use a name that already had a good brand association and was already well trusted and respected. They decided to name their new company after their popular and much respected president, Woodrow Wilson. And so the Wilson tennis brand was born. At first, they just produced the strings but were so successful that they started to venture into other areas of the sport like rackets, balls and clothing. And the rest, as they say, is history.

Hmn, let's hope we won't be seeing the Trump tennis racket strings any time soon. Although, come to think of it, they'd probably be able to generate great spin.

HOW TENNIS WON THE SECOND WORLD WAR

Writers are always granted a little *"poetic licence"* when penning their works and there are several instances when writing this book where I have fairly shamelessly stretched a couple of the stories in order to fit the constructs of the book's title. Overall, when I did this, it was for fun and to make a point, but when it comes to the gruesome horrors both sides inflicted on each other during the Second World War, then there is no room for glibness. I know I need to tread lightly and be careful not to trivialise the facts simply to create a little slice of tennis entertainment.

The episode I am about to recount to you is a case in hand. There were hundreds of battles in the Second World War that epitomised both the horrors of war and the bravery of individual men in equal measure. The Burma Campaign saw more than its fair share of these grisly episodes, but none more so than a fiercely fought battle that raged for many gruelling weeks at Kohima, a battle that many historians think changed the entire balance of the war. It is known simply as *the Battle of the Tennis Court.*

In the early part of 1944, the Japanese army was making huge advances into North East India, clocking up victories almost daily as they swept deeper into Allied territory. They were doing it with such speed that it sent alarm bells all the way back to central Allied Command who became increasingly concerned that they could lose the territory completely.

The Burma Campaign was at breaking point and the momentum was with the Japanese army. All the Japanese needed to tip the balance in their favour was to take a small, but strategically critical, garrison nestled in the hills of Kohima. The garrison stood at the top of a long wooded hill on a high ridge just west of the village.

For hundreds of years it had been a picture-perfect postcard vision of an idyllic little village. All that was about to change forever.

Kohima held only a couple of small garrisons of men, but they were given the utterly ridiculous order to hold out against the overwhelming might of the advancing Japanese Army until reinforcements could be sent. What followed was not just a horrific massacre but also a show of almost inconceivable gallantry in the face of sustained attacks by an enemy who vastly outnumbered them. Witnesses describe the events that followed as some of the most bloody and bitter fighting the Burma Campaign had ever seen, and by far the fiercest of this was the hand-to-hand combat that took place on the small plateau just above the Deputy Commissioner's bungalow, on which stood his beloved tennis court.

It was the location of the Kohima garrison that made it so valuable. It was a strategically crucial ridge which was about a mile long and about 400 yards wide, with a series of hills and gullies that ran alongside the road from Imphal to Dimapur which was a major lifeline for the region. If the Allies lost this, the supply line for the whole of the North East would dry up and the consequences of that would be catastrophic for the entire war effort. The Japanese knew the importance of Kohima and made it their priority to take it.

Although the garrison was in a key position, there was a problem – there was only one narrow road leading in and out, and on 6 April 1944 this road fell into the hands of the seemingly unstoppable Japanese army. The little tennis court garrison was stranded, cut-off and alone. It consisted mainly of British, Nepalese and some local Indian soldiers. The 1st Assam Regiment were dug in at the Ridge, with the centre defended by the 4th Battalion Queen's Own Royal West Kent Regiment, and the north west of the Ridge, known as Hospital Spur, was defended by the 3rd Assam Rifles.

The north east of the Ridge was where the Deputy Commissioner Charles Pawsey's Bungalow stood, guarded by a small group of British and Ghurkha troops from the local Depot; alongside it, taking centre stage, stood the tennis court.

47

The Japanese knew that they greatly outnumbered the Allied forces and were very much aware that reinforcements were on the way, so they stormed in fast and hard to press home their advantage and wipe out the garrison quickly. Most of the positions fell almost immediately as the Allies lost all their vantage positions and were driven back toward the last defensive trenches just by the tennis court, which was managing to hold its ground against the odds, and for one very good reason.

The Allies had one small but crucial advantage over the invading Japanese ground troops – a massive Mark 3 Bren gun positioned just above the tennis court. It could fire 500 rounds per second to a distance of 600 yards and far outclassed anything the Japanese had brought with them. This caused the Japanese to suffer huge losses as they were mown down before they could get close enough for their own weapons to come into range.

Astonishingly, this didn't seem to deter the Japanese at all and they just kept coming. For two long days the Japanese continued to attack, only to be cut down by this monstrously efficient killing machine that just laid waste to wave after wave of charging Japanese, who suffered huge casualties and great loss of life as the Bren gun ruthlessly cut down vast swathes of them.

Major Boshell, who was positioned just behind the tennis court, described it as being like a suicidal pigeon shoot. Survivors said it was sickening to be a part of, and even worse to watch, but it was a do or die situation.

After repelling the marauding Japanese for two more days, suddenly, disaster struck the Allied defenders. The Bren gun ran out of bullets and the Allies only advantage was lost. The Japanese, sensing their chance, mounted a ferocious attack. Even though their main gun was out, every man on the tennis court stood his ground and fought to the last until they were totally overrun, and were either shot or bayonetted to death by the Japanese.

The invaders had won and the Battle of the Tennis Court was over. But somebody had forgotten to tell this to the 4th Battalion Queen's Own Royal West Kent Regiment, who decided to mount one last effort and ridiculously tried to counter attack. This took the Japanese by surprise and after many bloody hours, the Allies had taken back control of the area, and, far from being over, the Battle of the Tennis Court had only just begun.

Infuriated by the setback, the Japanese commander ordered his men to storm the tennis court every 30 minutes, hoping that this relentless tactic would just wear the Allies down. The bloodshed went on for another three days. But the Allies had now dug deep weapon pits and trenches both sides of the tennis court and, with the ridge above them sheltering them from being attacked from above, managed to hold out for a further two days.

The Japanese twice sensed that they had won an advantage when the front trenches ran out ammunition and looked like being overrun again but, on both occasions, Supply Sergeant Williams from the rear weapons pit managed to break through the hail of bullets and artillery fire to resupply them.

So the battle went on.

By 12 April though, the men hadn't slept or eaten for days on end and were on the verge of collapse. B Company of the Royal West Kents were sent in to the trenches around the tennis court to relieve them. Their first night there, the Japanese changed tactics and instead of storming in every 30 minutes, suddenly stopped and did nothing at all.

The Brits were confused. But the Japs had a plan. They took off their heavy boots and advanced silently through the shrubbery. It was so successful that they managed to breach the forward positions and almost overran the front trenches. The Allies were only alerted when Lieutenant Hogg cried out a warning, even as he was being stabbed in the back. He further managed to alert the rest of his men by unloading 25 rounds into his assailant.

Throughout the night and all through the next day, this brutal assault went on. The tennis court was again the focus of the battle and it was nothing less than a blood-soaked carnage throughout. With the two sides positioned at opposite ends of the court exchanging gunfire at point blank range, repelling raids, men locked in hand-to-hand combat, as a volley of bullets tore about them, lobbing grenades back and forth to each other throughout the night.

When dawn broke the following day, it revealed a blood-drenched playing surface littered with mutilated corpses and mangled body parts. The Allied troops braced themselves for the next attack but, instead, an eerie stillness hung in the air. What was even more disconcerting was that the day passed without any further Japanese attacks. The Allied troops were perplexed. Was it another trick? A psychological tactic? It certainly worked, because the Allies were as jumpy as hell. Most of them were so jittery and on edge that they spent the day drifting in and out of consciousness, jumping at the slightest sound.

It was only later that they found out that it wasn't a tactic at all. The Japanese had been called back because the British 2nd Infantry Division had turned up and were trying to take back the vital Dimapur supply road just outside Kohima, so the Japanese were forced to turn their attentions to defending their rear position instead. The Tennis Court garrison had two days of respite with hardly any serious attack, but then on 17 April, sensing that they were losing control of the Dimapur road position, the Japanese realised there was only one thing left to do. To throw all their efforts into one last attack on the tennis court which would then give them the prime defensive position needed to repel the British reinforcements behind them and then counter attack.

All Japanese troops just suddenly stormed the garrison. They easily overwhelmed the first trench, took the second trench, ploughed on and then took the Deputy Commissioner's bungalow and even secured the Allies Supply Depot, leaving only the tennis court trenches, now dangerously isolated. The Allies held off sustained attacks on the tennis court all through the night and into the next day, resisting wave after wave of enemy onslaughts. There was a small respite when the British 2nd Division and the 161st Indian Brigade managed to break through to help even out the balance of power, but the onslaught was unremitting and the body count continued to rise as advantages were gained and lost by the minute.

But then, above the crack of gunfire, over the screams of death, there was a distant rumble. It grew a little louder, then the source was revealed. A line of Allied tanks from XXXIII Corps rolled into view, the Japanese were done. Forced from their positions by solid steel, the Deputy Commissioner's bungalow, the Supply Depot, the far Ridge and the two other positions were one by one recaptured, until eventually the tanks rolled up to the side of the tennis court to be greeted by huge cheers. Cheers from men who, five minutes before, didn't even think they had enough puff to even muster another breath yet alone cheer.

Many of the Japanese soldiers, though, didn't believe in surrender and retreated to a small position to the west just out of range of the tanks and continued to mount sporadic battles for several more weeks.

It wasn't until on 10 May when a huge giant appeared. A great M3 Grant tank with its vast turret and massive 75 mm gun rumbled up the ridge. It trundled ominously towards the tennis court and then stopped. It just sat there silently on the hill for a while. Then, with a quiet creaking of heavy metal, its menacingly powerful gun turret started to turn. It juddered to a halt facing towards the remaining enemy positions.

When it let loose with its 75 mm main armament shells they easily reached into the Japanese bunker positions and just literally blew them away. The Japanese knew the game was up. The last of the Japanese resistance started to crumble and finally, after almost two months of blood-soaked fury, the Battle of the Tennis Court was over.

Supply Sergeant Williams, the man who repeatedly risked his life to get ammunitions to the front positions, was just one of a whole swathe of medals later awarded to the men who fought there.

By 15 May, as fresh troops from the British and Indian army began to reinforce the area, the Japanese began to withdraw from the region altogether. With Allies now fully realising the strategic importance of the position, they heavily fortified it with tanks, guns and troops from far and wide. With the crucial cover of the tennis court ridge now properly secured, the Allies felt free to press forward their advantage. The momentum had now shifted in the Allies' favour and they began an advance that was to lead to the eventual recapture of Burma itself.

The story of how a small garrison that held out against the might of the Japanese army that vastly outnumbered them has never gained the notoriety and attention that it deserved. It has been compared to the legendary story made famous by the epic 1964 film *Zulu* depicting the heroics of a small band of British soldiers marooned at a field hospital outpost who held out against the onslaught of 4,000 Zulu warriors at the Battle of Rorkes Drift. But, without a Hollywood film to bolster its profile, the Battle of the Tennis Court may remain just another footnote lost amongst the many tales of bravery that filled the war. It is said that one of the main reasons that so few people have ever heard of this battle was because those that did survive it were so traumatised that they couldn't even talk about it.

What we do know is that The Battle of the Tennis Court proved to be the crucial turning point in securing Kohima, which in turn proved to be the turning point of the entire Burma Campaign and so the war itself. Earl Louis Mountbatten, the Supreme Allied

Commander, described it as, *"Probably one of the greatest battles in history. It was marked as the High Water Mark of the campaign. In effect it turned the tide in the Battle for Burma."* He saluted the bravery of the British and Indian Allied Forces that held out there as *"just pure, naked, unparalleled heroism"*.

The tennis court at Kohima still exists and is meticulously maintained to this day. All the lines are still clear and crisp as the day it was first laid but, out of respect, nobody has ever played tennis on it again. Instead, they built a cenotaph in the middle of the court, standing as a ghostly but noble memorial to those, of all nations, who fell. It bears a very simple inscription:

The Battle of the Tennis Court
4 April – 15 May 1944

SECTION 4

RELIGION

They say the three topics one should never talk about at social occasions are politics, religion and sex. Well, I've already picked at a few political peccadilloes, so let's break the second cardinal sin by leaping headlong into a few tennis transgressions that centre around the second taboo, religion ...

TENNIS INVENTS THE PATRON SAINT OF ENGLAND

Now, I'm sure if you live in the UK you are well aware that the Patron Saint of England is Saint George, a gallant knight of old, often depicted on horseback famously slaying a dragon. But what you may not know is that he is not actually English at all, but Italian. Eh? What? Yep, and to top it all, St George never even visited our shores and never slayed a dragon.

To make matters worse, he should never have been appointed as our patron saint at all as that honour was already taken by Saint Edmund, a far more worthy soul and one who had originally been royally ordained as the patron saint of England about 500 hundred years earlier.

Unfortunately though, Edmund's influence began to wane when Richard III chose to adopt Saint George as the protector of his army whilst on his famous crusades. The success of Richard's endeavours convinced King Edward III to create a special honour and in 1350 he formed the Order of the Garter in Saint George's name. The cult of Saint George was further enhanced by King Henry V when his exhausted and greatly outnumbered troops pulled off a truly astonishing victory over the vastly superior French army in what many academics call the greatest land battle in history, the Battle of Agincourt.

And, if that wasn't enough to consign Saint Edmund's fate to the dustbins of history, then Shakespeare made sure that nobody would ever forget Saint George, by writing one of his most celebrated lines when he recreated the scene of King Henry V addressing his troops before the fight. Shakespeare famously finishes the king's pre-battle speech with the rousing call of, *"Cry God for Harry, England and Saint George!"* The line went on to become one of the most quoted battle cries of all time. Poor old Saint Edmund, he never stood a chance.

And this was a real shame, because, certainly as far as credentials go, King Edmund is a much better fit to be the patron saint of England. First off, he was actually English, born and bred. He was also a legendary Anglo Saxon king, a heroic warrior and as English as roast beef and beer. That's the slightly warm beer, of course, none of this ice-cold Austro-Germanic pseudo American Pilsner nonsense.

Edmund was an inspiring king and a charismatic leader, during his reign he was universally adored throughout the land but he was venerated even more after his death as England's beloved patron saint. He had his own shrines, cathedrals, statues, commemorative feast days and monuments erected in his honour up and down the country, and his legend and status only grew in importance over the years.

For five centuries, foreign dignitaries from around the globe would journey thousands of miles to worship at his reliquary. All the subsequent kings of England would flock to his shrine to yield homage to him, dedicate prayers and pay their respects to him, or ride out to secure blessings from him before a royal marriage. Entire armies would march hundreds of miles just to pray to him before going to war.

Edmund was so revered as a national figurehead that it almost surpassed his formal position of a saint and grew to a status more closely associated to that of a God. And the missing link that can tie the whole theory together to finally prove all this and which would restore Edmund as our true patron saint, is, as I'm sure you've already guessed, tennis.

Although most kings and queens of England seemed to love or play tennis, we don't know whether Edmund was a keen player or not, as written records from that period at all are practically non-existent. If he did play it was more likely to resemble the Jeu de Paume style of game.

What we do know is that Edmund was born in 841 AD and is said to have ruled over East Anglia for 14 years and is remembered as an absolutely model king, kind, considerate and brave. Characteristics that are borne out by the manner of his death, which ultimately led to his martyrdom and canonisation as a saint.

In 869, Edmund was caught off-guard by a sudden Viking invasion. He and his men fought bravely but they were vastly outnumbered and he was eventually captured by the bloodthirsty invaders, bound to a tree and tortured in front of his men in an attempt to make him give up the throne and publicly denounce Christianity.

The heroic Edmund steadfastly refused to be broken in front of his men and remained defiant. Incensed by his obstinacy, the Vikings upped the stakes and started to fire arrows, one at a time, into the less vital parts of his body in an attempt to break him. But still Edmund refused to crack and remained true to his faith, forcing the increasingly riled Vikings to eventually give up on the torture. Instead, the enraged Vikings opted to just savagely behead him. The brutal Danish invaders then took away his lopped off head and discarded it into the woods for the wolves to eat.

This was not a random act of barbarism but a very specific act of violation because, having been unable to successfully break him with torture him in life, the Vikings were hoping to make him suffer for eternity in hell. The reason was, that, in those days, it was believed that if a body was not buried whole then it could never rest in peace and could not enter into the kingdom of heaven.

But there is a mythical tale that says the monks, still loyal to their beloved king, went searching for the head. Legend has it that the monks were guided by ghostly cries of *"Here!"* echoing from the depths of the forest.

When the monks located the source of the cries, they found a huge, lone wolf standing guard over the severed head of the king, as if protecting it from predators. When the monks moved in, the wolf stood back to allow the monks to reclaim it. The lupine legend goes on to say that the wolf even followed the men back to town and stayed with them until the head was re-united with Edmund's body. The fabulous fable says that the wolf patrolled the tomb for many years and, to this day, the locals will swear that on a clear night the cry of a lone wolf can still be heard echoing around the grounds of the ruined abbey at Bury St Edmunds.

Of course, with the body and head united and whole again, it meant that the king could now rest in holy peace and could ascend to heaven. It also allowed the king to be canonised and anointed as a true Christian saint. For many years, he was known as Edmund the Martyr before being royally ordained as the first ever Patron Saint of England, from whence, a shrine and cathedral were built at Bury to honour him.

This brought great wealth to the town because when subsequent kings and subjects would come to pay their respects to the shrine, each would bring more gifts, build new shrines, erect grander cathedrals, bestow ever more lavish offerings to him, and the town grew rich and prospered enormously from it. In fact, Edmund's bones remained on display at the abbey until the dissolution of the monasteries by Henry VIII in the 16th century.

And, although it was generally believed that the long lost body of the revered 9th century king is still hidden somewhere in the old market town, complete mystery surrounded the exact location of it. Until that is, in 2017, when historian professor Francis Young put forward a new theory which is where tennis comes into play.

It was always widely accepted that the monks had taken the body and buried it in their own private graveyard, but the exact location of that has always been disputed. But Professor Young believes he has now identified both the exact point of the monk's old cemetery and the burial site of King Edmund's body. The site in question is the town's very own tennis courts.

The heritage group in charge of the abbey's old ruins is hoping to excavate the area as soon as possible. Discovery of the royal remains would undoubtedly spark off a similar surge of media interest to that generated when King Richard III's body was exhumed from underneath a car park in Leicester. Richard was later interned back into Leicester Cathedral prompting a huge turn of fortune for the city. Almost overnight the city became a hot spot for just about everything; tourism started to boom; the economy picked up; and the whole city became a cultural hotspot.

Suddenly Leicester started winning every sporting event from the snooker World Championships to the Rugby Championships and the Anglo-Welsh Cup; And, most famously of all, of course, what many pundits are still calling the greatest sporting achievement in history – Leicester Football Club limping out of the relegation zone in 2015 to becoming Premier League Champions in 2016 and then they captured the greatest prize in British football, winning the FA Cup in 2021 for the first time in history.

I'm sure the citizens of Bury St Edmunds would be hoping for something similar. And, if these sacred tennis courts do eventually prove to be the resting place of one of England's most adored kings, it will surely renew calls once again to re-instate Edmund as the true and original Patron Saint of England.

I am particularly fond of this period of English history, not because it was so turbulent and historically significant – I just love the names they attributed to all their kings. Today we just give them numerical references, like Queen Elizabeth II, King Henry VIII, or Edward the VII, but in those days you were named after your character or some well-known deed or accomplishment.

Probably the most famous ones are William the Conqueror, Edward the Confessor, Ethelred the Unready, Edward the Exiled, Ethelweard the Chronicler, Edward the Elder, and Ethelred the Obscure, can't think why we haven't heard of him before now. There was even one called Edmund the Ironside, who presumably was a king with brilliant detective skills who trundled around in some sort of wheeled chariot.

For ruling monarchs of that period, being of a humble disposition was obviously not considered a great virtue for a king to have, as witnessed by a flurry of several rather self-aggrandising names that some of the more puffy-chested monarchs chose to adorn themselves with, like Alfred the Great, Richard the Lionheart, and there was even the modestly monikered Edmund the Magnificent. And one particularly memorable one, King Cnut, whom most people remember for trying to defy the tide from coming in, gave himself the name of Cnut the Great. I remember Cnut well, because he got me thrown out school one day when I suggested that perhaps Cnut was just dyslexic.

Although I get the impression that not all the sovereign heads of state had quite got the hang of this self-glorifying nickname thing. For instance, I can't help feeling that Charles the Simple may not have quite grasped the concept; either that, or maybe it was true and he just wasn't the brightest candle in the chandelier.

Another one of my favourites was Edwig the Nameless, who didn't actually have a nickname at all, hence the made-up moniker that I have just attached to him. The real reason I wanted to mention him was because he lost his crown for running off with one of the most celebrated women of her time, and one of the earliest known women to have ever been awarded her very own nickname.

The only reason that this early feminist isn't still portrayed as an early forerunner of Women's Rights activism, is probably because of the name they gave her, Ethelgifu the Strumpet. So maybe while we are considering the patronage of Saint Edmund, perhaps we should also deliberate the virtues of honouring Ethelgifu as the Patron Saint of Celebrity. She was after all, a celebrity pioneer in her own right, a sort of early incarnation of the Kardashians.

TENNIS INVENTS SANTA CLAUS

From the patron saint of England to the patron saint of generosity – good old Saint Nicholas, or Father Christmas himself. Almost every country has its own incarnation of Santa and of how he came about.

Historians believe that the closest historical match to Santa was a 3rd-century monk called Saint Nicholas. Born to wealthy parents in Demre, Anatolia, now the territory of modern Turkey. Nicholas was raised as a Christian from an early age and was brought up to be very respectful, benevolent and charitable. Unfortunately, Nicholas's parents died when he was very young, but it did leave him exceptionally wealthy.

It is said that Nicholas took pity on some young friends of his, three impoverished sisters who didn't have enough money to offer dowries to potential husbands. When Nicholas heard that all three were going to be forced into prostitution to survive, he decided to help but, not wanting them to feel indebted to him, he decided to help them surreptitiously. In the dark of night he crept onto the roof of their house and dropped three bags of gold down their chimneys, each one containing enough money for a decent dowry, ensuring that they could each find a good husband.

This simple act of kindness filled Nicholas with such an overwhelming feeling of wellbeing that he decided to devote the rest of life to similar random acts of kindness. Driven by his Christian love for others and aided by his enormous wealth, he soon came to the attention of the church. Nicholas quickly rose through the ecclesiastical ranks culminating in him being appointed as Bishop of Myra. This was considered a highly prestigious position because Myra, that we know better as Myrrh, was one of the gifts of the Three Wise Men, and is thought to be the origin of what links Nicholas to Christmas.

For 7,000 years, Anatolia was one of the world's largest trading hubs and later became a major route frequented by pilgrims that passed from Venice and Constantinople to the Holy Land in neighbouring Palestine, so news of Saint Nicholas and his benevolent deeds quickly started to spread throughout the surrounding regions. When the Dutch got to hear about the legend of St Nicholas, they quickly adopted him into their own mythology and he became known as Sinter Klaas and they made him their patron saint. At the time, the Dutch were a great seafaring nation and one of the world's largest traders, so news of the Sinter Klaas legend quickly spread in pace and popularity throughout the world.

His fame was further helped by the fact that belief in the Pagan gods of old was starting to wane. And so it was that Sinter Klaas was soon adopted as the Patron Saint of the sea by other sea faring nations as well, replacing the old Pagan god of the sea, Poseidon.

In fact, the iconography of both St Nicholas and Poseidon bore a striking resemblance to each other and for many years were interchangeable. The likeness also matched an even older saint, called Odin. Odin is believed by many historians to be the original source of the Father Christmas legend, even if his name was later usurped by Nicholas. Odin was the Pagan god of Yule, who was known as *Jólfaðr*, which means *"Yule Father"*. Interestingly, pretty much every Father Christmas, that features in a multitude of stories from a multitude of nations across the globe, bears a striking resemblance to him.

For instance, Odin had a flying horse that had eight legs for extra speed, similar to our modern Santa in that he has eight flying reindeer instead, thought to be a legacy dating back to his Dutch roots. Some Nordic countries also had a similar figure called Kristkind, an angel-like saint who was believed to deliver presents to well-behaved children.

The legend of Santa's elves is also thought to have stemmed from Scandinavia, as Kristkind had a jolly elf named Jultomten who helped him to deliver gifts in a sleigh drawn by eight goats.

In Germany, they favoured a more genial figure called Kris Kringle, in France it was Père Noël, and in Italy it was a woman called La Befana who flew around on a broomstick.

In Russia it was an elderly woman called Baboushka, whom they believed had given the Three Wise Men the wrong directions to Bethlehem so that they couldn't find Jesus. She was said to be so filled with remorse when she realised what she'd done that she spent the rest of her life riding around Russia gifting presents to young children in the hope that one of them turned out to be the baby Jesus and that she would be forgiven. A story that an ex-girlfriend of mine said she found almost believable, right up to the bit where there were men asking for directions!

But no matter which country you visit, the Saint Nicholas figures all adhere to one characteristic; they were renowned for their generosity and benevolence, especially to well-behaved children. So, St Nicholas was almost like a mini God for children, with incentives for them to behave in order for them to be rewarded at the end of the year, in much the same way that the adult Gods offer the reward of heaven. This probably greatly aided his popularity amongst parents as it served as a very useful way of controlling your kids, long before our more modern control system – threatening to take away their smart phones!

But back in the 3rd century, it is believed that it was these early Dutch traders who were most influential in bringing their interpretation of Sinter Klaas to the big trading cities like London and New York.

As their communities grew, many of the Dutch traders stayed in these big exciting cities and integrated into the community, marrying, settling down and adopting the country as their home. Over the centuries all the various St Nicholas legends became entwined to give us the amalgam we now know as Santa Claus.

Just about every image of St Nicholas, even the earliest we can find, depicts him as a kind looking and wise old man sporting a long white beard and this is the one feature that has endured through the centuries. Some of these early images of Santa Claus depict him as an old-fashioned saint wearing white robes. Later he was portrayed wearing a green suit, which relates to when he was known as Sinter Klaas in Holland, where the Santa Claus name is first thought to have originated.

One of the great modern myths about Santa Claus is that his red robes were first attributed to him by Coca-Cola who wanted to change the colour of Santa's suit from green to red to match the colour of their brand. But this is not true. Although Coca-Cola were quick to latch on to the legend, using him relentlessly in their Christmas campaigns, and were certainly influential in cementing that imagery, they don't tell the whole story, as depictions of Santa in red had been around for nearly a century before that.

In reality, the iconic red outfit was already starting to grow in popularity thanks mainly to a series of artworks by Thomas Nast, but also many other artists like Alexander Anderson, Clement Moore, Norman Rockwell and finally, of course, the artist we love and like the best, Tom Browning, who was one of the first artists to ever draw Santa off-duty, relaxing in his summer down-time and playing, how did you guess, a game of tennis, of course.

Browning depicted St Nick all decked out in tennis gear that wasn't Wimbledon white but in bright red, even wearing a very sporty red tennis sweater. Thus ensuring that the now-famous trademark Santa colour of red was to endure to this day.

It's reassuring to know that even Santa Claus thinks tennis is the best pastime. You know you've really made it as a sport when Santa Claus believes in you.

TENNIS INVENTS A MONASTERY

This story comes from a manuscript that is believed to contain the earliest recorded reference to the game of tennis. It dates from 1219, but the tale it tells refers to events that took place in around 1150, which makes it incredibly significant in terms of the timelines of tennis history.

It has long been acknowledged that tennis was popularised in the cloisters of monasteries, but there is a wonderful legend gifted to us by the monks of Marienstatt in Germany that suggests we got it the wrong way around and that, in fact, it is a certain demonic game of tennis that led to a monastery being founded.

As a preface to what you are about to read, remember we are talking about medieval times when they believed in goblins, witches, demons and burning people at the stake. It was a period in history when people thought dreams were actually futuristic visions, and where evil spirits and deities appeared for reasons of great holy divinity. And, on that cautionary note, I will begin my tale.

And so it was that in 1219, a monk called Caesarius of Heisterbach from the Holy Order of St Bernard wrote a book entitled *Dialogues Miraculorum*, which translates as *Miraculous Tales*. In the book, he recounts the story of a young clerk in Paris who, as legend would have it, was a bit of a thickie. A knucklehead of such staggering proportions and so lacking in intelligence that he was constantly getting overlooked for promotion, despite his earnest endeavours and hard work ethic.

One day, this rather dim-witted clerk was approached by a man who we later find out was actually an emissary from hell and working for Satan. This devilish rogue sold the daft clerk a magic stone that he was assured would give him great intelligence and earn him promotion to the higher echelons of society that the idiot so desperately aspired to.

Indeed, either the stone really was magic, or the placebo effect kicked in, because the dippy young clerk soon found he was able to acquire new skills. He progressed with such ease that he promptly established himself as the perfect pupil and swiftly rose through the ranks at work.

Unfortunately, in the midst of all this, the clerk was taken ill and afflicted with a severe fever. The malaise took such a deadly turn that the clerk fell into a coma so virulent that many of the attending medics believed him to be in the throes of death. The clerk described his near death experience as like *"floating towards the light, being carried by a band of fiendish imps who whisked him away to a hellish place, full of dark valleys that steamed with poisonous vapours"*. Or Croydon, as we call it in England.

The tale takes a bizarre twist when the clerk describes how a malevolent band of demons then form into two teams and start to play tennis, using him as the ball, and his soul as the prize. He recalls the nightmare in some detail, describing their hands as having claws as sharp as nails as they hurl him around. He recounts the ordeal as *"so tortured that no martyrdom imaginable could compare"*. Although, to be fair, Piers Morgan hadn't yet been born.

Caesarius, the man credited as the author of the clerk's tale, was a monk from the Abbot of St Bernard who had heard the story from a man called Hermann who had originally heard the story from the young clerk himself.

After hearing the story, Hermann had a vision from the Virgin Mary who instructed him where he should build a monastery. Hermann dutifully built the abbey, which still stands to this day, and is known as the Marienstatt Monastery.

So what began as a satanic game of hallucinatory tennis eventually led to the forming of a brand new holy order. An ironic turn of events as it is normally monastic cloisters that lay claim to inventing tennis, and this is certainly the only record of the legend being reversed.

Before this story came to light, the first mention of tennis was thought to have been written by John Beleth in 1165 in a work entitled *Summa de Ecclesiasticis Officiis*, which documents the formal duties of the monks. It is here that we find the first mention that the monks would often play tennis in the cloisters as a means of relaxing. A detail later supported by many subsequent documents that state that monastic cloisters were often used as tennis courts.

Although many archaeological finds suggest that games with tennis-like qualities may well have existed long before that, perhaps even 3,500 years ago, these are the earliest written texts. Unless, of course, you have stumbled across the Tennis Emporium's more dubious version of history, which is blasphemously outlined in the next instalment. So if you're a delicate soul of a sensitive disposition, then I suggest you skip the next section or risk your soul suffering a similar fate to that of our dim-witted clerk …

TENNIS INVENTS JESUS

Now hold on, I know what you're thinking, but before I'm struck down by a thunderbolt from the heavens, or chased out of town by torch carrying villagers and cast out into the wilderness as a blasphemous heathen, let me just explain.

There is a wonderful story written into one of the famous medieval Mystery Plays that alludes to a rather different version of the Magi than the one to which we are more accustomed to hearing in the Bible. The play still has the Three Wise Men coming to visit the Virgin Mary in a stable after the birth of Jesus, but suggests that they didn't bring the traditional gifts of gold, frankincense and myrrh, but actually brought him three very different gifts consisting of fruit, poultry and a tennis ball!

So, Three Very Wise Men indeed then, to give him a sporting profession to fall back on in case the whole Son of God thing didn't pan out for him. It could also explain why we know so little about Jesus's early life, because they only gave him a ball but no racket, forcing him then to make a racket when he was older. There is certainly plenty of Gospel evidence to support that, as several of the Disciples mention that Jesus was a very proficient carpenter. Suddenly it all makes sense!

More scurrilous evidence to corroborate that Jesus may have been born into tennis comes from the Tennis Emporium who sell a greeting card and poster featuring several pertinent quotes from the Bible that hint that maybe tennis was a bigger influence in the Christian world than we originally thought, and even suggest that Jesus himself might have enjoyed the odd game …

To illustrate the point, here is a selection of the Tennis Emporium's *Bible* quotes below, so you can form an unbiased, non-denominational, universal, non-sectarian, ecclesiastical free, all-inclusive, non-heretical, non-iconoclastical, interdenominational, non-secular, modern ecumenical opinion of your very own, but, be it on your own conscience to look at them and may your soul remain untainted by their sacrilege ...

> *"Better one day in your courts than a thousand elsewhere."* (Psalm 84:1)
> *"Serve wholeheartedly."* (Ephesians 6:7)
> *"Love is not proud, it does not boast."* (Corinthians 13:1)
> *"When you're enraged – let loose a volley."* (Habakkuk 3:0)
> *"He came to pass."* (Luke 12:3)
> *"My soul yearns, even faints, for the courts."* (Psalm 84:2)
> *"Even as he faces death, Jesus serves ..."* (New Testament IV)

TENNIS INVENTS MEDIEVAL PANTOMIME VILLAIN

In the 1970s, Ilie Nastase and Jimmy Connors were the two bad boys of tennis. They shocked the tennis world when they questioned the line judges, argued with the referees and threw temper tantrums wherever they went. But, as it turned out, these bad boys were just the warm-up act for the real pantomime villain who was about to burst onto the scene.

It was 1977, and a 17-year-old kid, playing his first-ever Wimbledon, stunned tennis fans with a dashing display of artistry that, against all odds, swept him into the quarter-finals. The kid won the first set and the second went to a tie-break and he lost it – in every sense. The kid was so upset that he slammed his racket into the ground with fury. After all, the loss couldn't have been his fault. The racket must have been culpable.

It was at this moment that a sound emanated from the stands of Wimbledon Centre Court that had never been heard before. The crowd booed. Undeterred, the kid shoved the racket under his foot and, straining every sinew in his body, tried to break it in two. The Wimbledon crowd had never seen such a display of petulance and their displeasure grew. They booed even louder.

The kid looked up at the crowd. He'd never been booed before. He was shocked but somehow undeterred. He kind of liked the attention. The Wimbledon crowd had never booed at anyone before either. They kind of liked it too. This was new territory for everyone. But the kid was tough, he wasn't having court etiquette dictated to him by a bunch of toffee-apple-nosed English dandies, sitting in their stuffed shirts, quaffing Pimm's, whilst waving their strawberries and cream at him.

If anything, the crowd's tactics just inflamed him further. Wanting to make sure the fans knew that he didn't care, he defiantly kicked the racket away in disgust and it flew away to the side. The boos grew louder and mounted to a horrified roar of disapproval.

The kid, of course, was a young John McEnroe who revelled in provoking the crowds and stoking up the atmosphere. He lapped it up, breathed it all in and used it as fuel to spur him on to greater things. McEnroe went on to win the match and the Super-Brat moniker was born.

These days when he performs on the Legends' circuit, he jokes that it is written into his contract that he has to contest line-calls, lose his temper, and throw tantrums. And when he does, guess what, the crowds don't boo, they cheer.

But, long before Johnny Mac, Nasty and Connors perfected the art of on-court outbursts, there was an earlier gang of marauding villains even more determined to drag down the good name of tennis, and these guys were from about six centuries earlier.

The parish registry of Ottery St Mary in Devon, England, records that there were several aspiring young super-brats who had all been freely availing themselves of the monastic cloisters and causing more of a rumpus than Nastase, McEnroe, Connors, Kyrgios and Attila the Hun combined.

The parish archives leave no room for uncertainty as to the cause of this filthy fracas, namely *"an evil game called Tenys, whose players inveterately voice vain, heinous, and blasphemous words"*, as well as *"utter senseless curses that give rise to squabbles, disputes, brawls, and battles"*.

The damning account dismisses the ruffians as playing *"unlawful games"* which are *"distracting, thoughtless, reprehensible and dastardly insults to God and Majesty"*.

Of course, if players behave badly today, they are deducted points, fined, and, very occasionally, disqualified. But the local church of Ottery St Mary didn't seem to want to settle for such feeble recourse. They were so inflamed by the scoundrelous tennis players that they quite overlooked their sacred vows to turn the other cheek, and, deciding not to opt for the more ecclesiastically accepted line of forgiveness, decided to opt for one of the less charitable proverbs, and wanted an eye for eye. The parish record shows that they demanded the tennis players involved must face a *"strict and immediate excommunication"*.

Well thank goodness that the clergy no longer serve as the regulators of tennis, or else we would have been robbed of countless memorable on-court meltdowns. McEnroe would have been excommunicated a long time ago and the tennis world would have lost not just one of its most gifted exponents of the game but also one of its most esteemed commentators, and that's a sacrilege under any religion.

SECTION 5

PUBLIC SCANDALS

Most sports at some point have brushed up against the long arm of the law or had a few run-ins with unfavourable publicity, and tennis is no exception. But, like any great champion who finds themselves up against the wall, tennis has always found a way to break back.

It was Phineas T. Barnum, the 19th-century American circus owner who is usually credited with first coining the phrase *"there's no such thing as bad publicity"*. I also like writer Brendan Behan's appendum to that, when he added, *"unless it's your obituary"*. Although my favourite quote of his was when the irascible Irishman berated his psychiatrist for dismissing him as a writer with a drinking problem. The author admonished the psychiatrist by retorting that he was actually *"a drinker with a writing problem"*.

While none of the following scandals have derailed the great game too much, it's still worth looking back at some the more notable shamings that have beset the sport.

TENNIS INVENTS BRITAIN'S BIGGEST EVER SPY SCANDAL

Checkpoint Charlie, encrypted messages, hidden microfilm, secret drop-off points, exploding cigars, cigarette lighters that are really cameras, pens disguised as guns, poisoned umbrella tips – I'm sure anyone who has ever watched a Bond film is familiar with many tools of the spying trade. But there's an omission from this exclusive list and it is a tool that broke open the biggest spy scandal ever to have rocked Britain's illustrious spy-ridden history – a tennis racket.

In 1967, Britain was swinging, London was the hippest coolest city in the world; peace, love and understanding pervaded every corner of the land; the Fab Four were topping the charts and Cool Britannia was conquering the world. All seemed fab and groovy. But underneath all that glittering Summer of Love there was a diplomatic storm simmering. It grew into a scandal of international proportions and one that still reverberates through the corridors of power to this very day.

For there was another four about to rock the world, a four not quite so fab as John, Paul, George and Ringo. They were Philby, Blunt, Burgess and Maclean, the four most notorious agents ever to have been recruited by the Soviet Union. Although, at the time, we knew of only three, but rumours abounded that there was another mole in the British Secret Service who was yet to be revealed. He was dubbed *"The Fourth Man"* by the tabloids but, of course, it was tennis that was instrumental in finally unmasking the identity of the Fourth Man. Here's how it happened.

The late, great *Sunday Times* journalist Phillip Knightley would often claim that his tennis racket was the most useful tool he had in his journalistic arsenal.

He was a member at The Queen's Club and would frequently regale us with accounts of how his tennis racket facilitated him to break many of his best stories, and how it helped him gain access to sources that were closed to other, less racketed, journalists.

By simply hanging out at various prestigious tennis clubs around the world, Phillip managed to secure unscheduled tennis matches with ambassadors; Soviet cultural attachés; high ranking diplomats; foreign ministers; local parliamentarians; several top aides inside the United Nations peacekeeping forces; Egyptian naval commanders; and, most ingeniously, even an Israeli general a few days before the Six-Day War broke out.

Naturally, after the impromptu tennis matches, they would retire to the clubhouse bar, relax, have a few drinks and before long they would be exchanging impassioned views, never suspecting that in actual fact they were conducting interviews with one of England's most esteemed investigative journalists.

Perhaps most famously of all was the stunning *Sunday Times* interview with Kim Philby. Amazingly, Phillip managed to secure access to the notorious MI6 agent for an entire week's worth of interviews finally confirming Philby as the infamous Fourth Man who had actually been working for the KGB for the past thirty years. Secret footage of Philby, filmed as he gave a private talk in Russia, showed him freely admitting that his upper-class background had made it easy for him to wear his double-agent mask. He claimed his love of tennis, Wimbledon, the MCC, cricket and all things English had played a pivotal role in deflecting any suspicion all those years.

Phillip would often tell how, when he first met Philby, he was very difficult to get to know and it was extremely hard to get him to open up and talk about anything. So, Phillip tried his old tried and tested trick – to talk about their mutual love of tennis. Sure enough, Phillip soon won Philby's confidence by letting him chat about tennis which, in turn, helped break down the barriers between them. After that, Philby started to talk more freely and Phillip had an exclusive on the biggest spy scandal in British history. The fruits of which Knightley not only managed to eschew for his famous *Sunday Times* exposé but also later turned into the bestselling book, *Master Spy: The Story of Kim Philby*.

So, a handy tip for any budding secret agents, if you ever find yourself asked to go and spy for Queen and country, tell "Q" to forget the Aston Martin with built-in ejector seat, the exploding cigar, the gun disguised as a pen and the wristwatch that turns into a saw – just pack your tennis racket.

TENNIS INVENTS THE WARDROBE MALFUNCTION

For many of us the term *"wardrobe malfunction"* first entered the public domain in 2004 during half-time show at the Super Bowl when Justin Timberlake politely excused Janet Jackson's accidental exposure of her breasts as *"a wardrobe malfunction"*.

Many such occasions have been recorded since then, and some unseemly showbiz pundits even went so far as to harshly accuse Miss Jackson of purposely manufacturing the exposing of her assets in order to foster some cheap publicity. I'm sure the fact that she had also just released a new album was pure coincidence and totally unrelated to the incident of the poorly functioning wardrobe.

But, as always, it is tennis that has one of the earliest wardrobe malfunctions on record, and one that far precedes the aforementioned Nipple-gate. Let me take you back to 1891 in Stuttgart, Germany, to a tennis court scenically set by the banks of the River Neckar.

Harry Greene and his younger brother Conyngham had been locked in a particularly gripping set of tennis, so riveting that a group of passing rowers pulled up to the riverbank to try and get a better view of the game. Unfortunately, the excitement of the match proved too much for the rowers to bear, as the boat capsised tossing them into the water.

Without hesitation, young Conyngham abandoned his game to go to the aid of the overboard oarsmen, diving straight into the river to save them. The newspapers of the time were full of praise for young Conyngham's heroics and commended him for his unhesitating act of bravery.

I am sure that it was indeed an unquestionable act of gallantry by the courageous Conyngham, and suggestions that he was about to lose his serve to his sibling rival and saw the rescue as an easy out are totally unfounded. Either way, Conyngham's stoic efforts paid dividends and all the soggy rowers were brought safely back to shore. Unfortunately, when Conyngham returned to dry land to resume the game, his trousers could be considered to be malfunctioning in the wardrobe department.

His white linen summer flannels, although most excellent attire for a game of tennis, proved be less useful for water-themed activities. The light-weight trousers were so sodden and wet, rendering them completely transparent and totally unfit for purpose. Having exhibited the courage of a commando in his rescue, he was now also exhibiting that he was also going commando elsewhere, the sodden linen revealing that he had omitted the luxury of any under garments.

Much affronted by what was so blatantly on display, the ladies in the park ran screaming from the scene of the crime. So widely reported was the scandal that poor young Conyngham was ousted from society. The incident caused so much outrage that, not only was our fallen hero banished from the area, but, just to be on the safe side, even the game of tennis itself was banned from being played throughout the entire district.

I would love to say that this inaugural wardrobe malfunction was a more genuine slip up than Miss Jackson's as he had nothing to promote, but it has recently come to my attention that Conyngham was also a budding singer with an up-coming concert, so the jury remains out. Much like various parts of Miss Jackson and Conyngham's anatomy.

TENNIS INVENTS FIRST PUBLIC OUTING OF A CELEBRITY

Tennis disputes over whether an *"out!"* call was a good or bad one are certainly nothing new. The Greek writer Athenaeus Nokratios quotes an even earlier writing from the poet Antiphanes, who records a ferocious argument over a disputed line call during a game of Episkyros on whether the ball was in or out that dates back over 2,000 years.

In these enlightened times, we are also very aware that the term to *out* someone can mean something completely different. If you're not au fait with the expression of *outing* someone, it means to publicly expose them as being homosexual when they would rather not let it be known.

And tennis, of course, has one of the first and most public examples. In the 1930s, long before Boris Becker came along, there was another German ace, the delightfully named Baron Gottfried Alexander Maximilian Walter Kurt Von Cramm. But for the sake of brevity and rain forests around the world, let's just call him Von Cramm. Von Cramm was not only the holder of one of Germany's swankiest surnames, but as Germany's first international tennis star he was also one of their biggest celebrities.

In the late 1930, Von Cramm was to play a singles match against America in the finals of the Davis Cup. After the first two days, the match stood level at two games apiece with Von Cramm to play Don Budge in the deciding rubber.

In those days, the Davis Cup was the biggest event in tennis, much more important than even the Grand Slams or Olympics are today; it was revered more as if it were the Tennis World Cup. The final was a sell-out crowd to be played on Wimbledon Centre Court and attended by everyone from Queen Mary to ministers and officials.

Don Budge even received a call from the American President to

82

wish him luck. Von Cramm also got a call from his president. Only this was no ordinary phone call. His president was no ordinary official, it was Adolph Hitler.

Hitler told Von Cramm in no uncertain terms that he had to win the match to prove German superiority of the Aryan race to the watching world. Von Cramm was left a little perturbed by the call but stepped out onto Centre Court under no doubt as to what he had to do, or heaven only knew what the consequences would be.

Von Cramm went on to play what is often considered as one of the greatest Davis Cup deciding singles finals of all time. There was a slight problem though. He narrowly lost it in the fifth and final set, handing the cup to America.

Hitler went ballistic and never forgave him. But such was Von Cramm's celebrity status around the world that Hitler had to be careful and bide his time. A few months later, Hitler spotted his opportunity. Hearing rumours that Von Cramm was involved in a secret homosexual affair, Hitler set about publicly exposing the Baron for his illegal activities and made sure he had a very public outing across every possible medium available throughout the world. Once this was done, Hitler finally sent him to jail in disgrace.

This was one *out* call that even Hawkeye couldn't dispute. In retrospect though, I'm not sure that locking the aesthete Baron into a building with several hundred other men and forcing him to shower naked with them was ever going to be quite the horrific punishment that Hitler had intended it to be!

TENNIS INVENTS X-RATED LOVE GAME

It's not unusual to hear the sound of women grunting loudly on a tennis court these days, Maria Sharapova has been recorded with a scream of 105 decibels. Some players find it intrusive and claim it's gamesmanship, whilst many of the protagonists claim that they're totally unaware that they're even doing it. But it's rare when the screaming becomes so loud that it stops play. But there is one case where it really did hold up a tennis match and, what is more, it wasn't even any of the players on court that were doing the grunting.

In 2017, a clay court match between Frances Tiafoe and Mitchell Krueger at the Sarasota Open in Florida was interrupted by the sound of a couple having extremely noisy sex in an apartment opposite the court. It was so loud that it filled the entire stadium. The players, the crowd, the TV commentators, and even the viewers watching at home, were privy to the passionate cries of the couple. At one stage it was so intense that a protective mother was seen covering the ears of her young son.

The players themselves tried to dampen the couple's enthusiasm by hitting tennis balls towards the block of flats and shouting at them to quieten down. But it was all to no avail. As the woman's ecstatic moans grew louder and louder, Tiafoe became so distracted from his serve that he stopped midway through his serve. Exasperated, he shouted across to them *"It can't be that good!"*, much to the amusement of the crowd.

The TV commentator didn't help proceedings, getting the giggles themselves when they realised that their own commentary on the game could be misinterpreted, with comments like, *"Was that in?"* *"I thought that was out."* *"There's nothing between these two now"*. And *"Yes, it's very tight"*.

The match itself though never reached the same heights of ecstatic climax as its off-court rival. Frances Tiafoe eventually won 6–3, 6–2, but the incident did prompt a stream of puns on social media, the best of which were:

"Tiafoe may have 'won to love', it's just that that wasn't the score line – that was the setting."
"The sound of tennis kinda lingers!"
"The Joy of Sets."
"Courtus Interruptus."
"Fifty Shades of Clay."

But my favourite comment was:

"Not bad, this girl wasn't even playing in the championships but still got the best seeding of the tournament."

TENNIS INVENTS OJ SIMPSON-STYLE MURDER TRIAL

The Wimbledon Tennis Championships had only been running a few years when, in 1879, they spewed forth one of the most gruesome murder mysteries of the era.

The Irish Open Tennis Champion was called Vere St Leger Goold, who was as wild and unpredictable in his tennis play as he was as a person. Goold's success in the Emerald Isle prompted him to sail o'er the ocean and try his luck in this Sceptred Isle to enter Wimbledon.

Sure enough, his fierce and bludgeoning style stunned many of the favoured players and the youngster had a truly spectacular run, causing a mini sensation as his thunderous forehand took him all the way to the Wimbledon finals.

Unfortunately for Goold, he didn't win, and although that was the last time Goold ever appeared at a tennis championship, it would not be the last time his bludgeoning forehand would make headlines. His next appearance would be even more spectacular and went on to shock not just tennis but the entire world. Only this time he wasn't on his tactics *on* court that attracted attention but *in* court.

We don't hear much of Goold again until he shows up many years later in France. By this time, Goold had run up huge debts, rumoured to have been caused by his love of gambling and women, although not necessarily in that order. Pastimes that neither his debtors nor his young wife took kindly to.

Whilst staying at a hotel in France, Goold quite unexpectedly decides to send a large trunk back to England and orders it to be sent by sea freight. The hotel porter who was instructed to take the trunk felt Goold's behaviour was rather odd. The porter noticed that the trunk was not just exceptionally heavy for something that was only supposed to contain clothes but his suspicions were further aroused by the fact that there was a most repugnant smell emanating from it.

The hotel alerted the police and when they prised open the trunk they found the dismembered body of Emma Liven, a wealthy widow, from whom Goold had borrowed a great deal of money.

Goold's court appearance was the OJ Simpson trial of its day, it was followed around the world by aghast fans and a horrified public as the gruesome facts slowly emerged day by day.

The murderous Wimbledon finalist never fully explained his actions, but it was generally thought to have been about the money that he owed to the widow, Liven, and was unable to repay.

Goold was unanimously convicted of murder and forced to serve out the rest of his days on Devils Island until his death in 1909.

But who knows, if only he'd hired an army of lawyers like OJ Simpson, then we may yet have had the name of a cold-blooded murderer engraved into the Wimbledon trophy. So thank heavens for that, the good name of tennis and Wimbledon remains untainted.

Wait! What? They've found a hundred-year-old absurdly ill-fitting glove in the evidence room? Oh no, surely not ...

TENNIS INVENTS MURDEROUS BAROQUE MASTERPIECE

Anyone who has ever played club tennis will have witnessed many a heated dispute over a line call or a scoring error. Tennis has that effect. It taps into our most primal instincts. But, while most disputes are settled with a begrudging *"Let's play a let"*, one such disagreement didn't end quite so magnanimously. It escalated into a brutal murder that took place on the court itself.

When good friends Ranuccio Tomassoni and Michel Amerighi set off for a friendly game of tennis in the spring of 1606, they could never have imagined the gruesome events that were to occur. Ranuccio could have guessed that it might not all be plain sailing since he knew his friend was a volatile character with a criminal record as long as his racket.

Amerighi had assaulted a colleague at work in 1600; was charged with grievous bodily harm against an armed soldier in 1601; held for possession in 1602 as well as a misuse of weapons charge in the same year; imprisoned in 1603 for multiple offences from drunk to disorderly; arrested in 1604 for hurling bricks at a Roman guard as well as being jailed in 1605 for wounding a man during a fight over his mistress. Although, by far my favourite was when he was imprisoned for attacking a useless waiter by using a bunch of artichokes.

But Ranuccio got a lot more than his recommended five-a-day when he agreed to play tennis with Amerighi. Needless to say, quite a large wager was placed on the game, so when a dispute about the scoring turned into a heated argument, it quickly became physical. As the brawl disintegrated further, it soon turned ugly and escalated into a violent fight.

Out of nowhere, Amerighi drew a knife and the next thing you know, Ranuccio was lying in a pool of his own blood. He died right there on the tennis court.

Realising the horror of what he'd done, Amerighi panicked and fled to Rome. As the authorities closed in on him in Rome, he went on the run, ending up in Naples only to get into another fight and was himself left for dead at the side of the road. Incredibly, he survived the injuries and continued to live a life on the run. Fleeing on from Naples, he absconded first to Malta, where he narrowly escaped arrest, before bolting to Sicily.

After four years as a fugitive, Amerighi was tired and longed for his old life back, one where he had mixed in the higher echelons of society, enjoyed royal patronage and his only worries were which choice of vegetable to use for brawling with inefficient restaurant waiting staff.

In the end, Amerighi tried to draw on his old society contacts and wrote to the Pope begging him for forgiveness and requesting a Papal Pardon but, after many months, he had received no word, so decided to risk it all and head back to Rome to seek a pardon from his friend the Pope face to face.

Amerighi got as far as Tuscany when he caught malaria, survived the fever but died shortly afterwards from the ensuing pneumonia. A few days later, a letter arrived for him. It was a Papal Pardon.

It is a tale of deadly irony all round. Perhaps if our fugitive had eaten more vitamin rich, leguminous vegetables instead of using them as weaponry, Amerighi might have survived the pneumonia. If so, the world would definitely have been a richer and better place, yes, a few more sloppy waiters may have had to endure being assaulted with an hors d'oeuvres, but on balance I think it would have been a price worth paying.

Because, believe it or not, Michel Amerighi was perhaps better known as the great Italian painter Caravaggio, often cited as the father of the Baroque and a genius of such talent that Rubens, Bernini and Rembrandt all openly credited him with influencing them.

He was only 37 years old, quite young for an artist who would probably have matured to even greater heights, and so died without producing more of what would have undoubtedly been some of the great masterpieces of the period.

So remember this cautionary tale the next time you find yourself in a dispute over a line call. And, if things ever get really out of hand, then you know what to do.

What? No, not a let! Playing the point again is for wusses. Gentlemen settle arguments the old-fashioned way – artichokes at dawn!

TENNIS INVENTS CLUEDO

Playing Cluedo as a kid, the killer always seemed to be Colonel Mustard, with the Candlestick, in the Library. And it was always poor old Mrs Peacock who ended up being murdered, although I always thought that the Reverend Mr Green was the one who looked the most suspicious.

I was also convinced that Professor Plum and Miss Scarlett were having a secret affair as they invariably ended up in the Billiard Room with the coquettish Miss Scarlett left holding the salaciously symbolic Lead Pipe as Professor Plum did his best to look all innocent whilst secretly contemplating whether to pot the pink or the brown.

But, let me take you away from the playing board and slip you back into the horrors of reality, and replace the board game's pretend Mansion House with a genuine Vicarage; Colonel Mustard takes on the real life guise of Captain Vere; and the Candlestick, well, you guessed it, is now a Tennis Racket.

It's the glorious summer of 1883. Victorian England was an idyll of blossoming romance across many a sun-kissed tennis court. None more so than for the most splendidly named Captain Hubert Wigram Vesey De Vere, a dashing young blade who enjoyed many a game of mixed doubles with a deliciously demure young woman with an equally evocative name, Miss Eleanor Eveleen McKay.

Captain Vere had become quite smitten with Miss McKay ever since her recent arrival in the parish, and the Vicarage tennis lawns proved a fruitful way to court her whilst being suitably chaperoned by various watchful parishioners to keep everything proper and correct.

Unfortunate timing meant that De Vere was suddenly posted out to Egypt, tearing him asunder from his sweet. Over the next few months, as he fought in the dry desert sands and bullets whistled past his head, he couldn't help wishing himself back on the lush green grass of home, sipping on an ice cool Pimm's and exchanging furtive rallies and clandestine glances with the luscious Miss Eleanor Eveleen McKay.

Upon his return, he sought her out immediately to regale her with tales of his military heroism and formidable bravery across the desert sands, only to find that some slippery solicitor with a feathery forehand had slithered his way into becoming her mixed doubles partner and won her affections.

Taking it as a slur against the good name of Captain Hubert Wigram Vesey De Vere, he hurried away heartbroken, his tail between his legs. This is not what he had risked his life for while he'd been away fighting for Queen and country, and that night he was wracked with sinful thoughts of revenge. After a sleepless night full of torturous imaginings, he could take it no more. The next day he grabbed his army pistol, stormed onto court, shooting wildly at both the deliciously duplicitous Miss McKay and the shady solicitor before turning the gun on himself.

But it seems that the old adage of *"the devil has powerful friends"* is true, as only the solicitor survived.

So, in the final reveal, at the last throw of the dice, as the concluding card was drawn, it seems no further clues would be needed in our imaginary game of Victorian Cluedo. It was definitely Captain Vere, with the Pistol, on the Vicarage Tennis Court.

TENNIS INVENTS GRUESOME BLOOD STAINED MURDER SCENES

Now, if you're a budding detective on the hunt for a psychopathic serial killer and you have about you your standard issue ultra-violet torch that can highlight even the tiniest of blood stains, and you happen to wander into an old rackets court, don't get too excited when the entire court lights up like a giant disco to reveal a wall-to-wall slaughter house across the court.

Try to remain calm, you haven't just stumbled into one of the most savage blood-soaked murder scenes in criminal history. It is merely that when they built the old Rackets courts, they used to paint the plaster of the walls with the blood of an ox.

Sounds a bit gruesome I know, but it was very practical on several levels. First and foremost was because when the blood dried it contracted, bonding the plaster really tightly, hardening it up, to give it the super strength it needed to sustain the constant battering of a rackets ball. Secondly, as it dried and coagulated with the plaster, it also turned an extremely dark black colour making the white ball much easier to see. That is why the walls of Rackets courts throughout the world are still painted black to this day.

According to Heiner Gillmeister's book, *Tennis: A Cultural History*, the exact ingredients were recorded by Francois Alexandre de Garsault in an old recipe dating back to 1767. It was a formula that had been handed down to him from several previous generations, so it was even older than the records suggest. The main ingredients were listed as *"half an ox's head of blood, fourteen bushels of lamp black and a bucket of urine"*, or what they call breakfast in China.

TENNIS INVENTS HIP-HOP GANGSTA RAP

The US Open holds the dubious distinction of being the only Grand Slam to have play suspended by a genuine gangster style shoot-out. John McEnroe was playing his fellow countryman Eddie Dibbs in a third-round match at Forest Hills in 1977 when play was suddenly halted by a commotion in the crowd.

Word quickly spread throughout the spectators that someone had been shot, but the chair umpire dismissed it as ridiculous and assured the players that was not the case and ordered them to carry on.

But after a while the commotion started to grow and they realised that a spectator in the crowd was down on the ground, wounded and bleeding badly. (A strange expression that, you never hear of anyone bleeding well. *"It's OK, don't bother with the ambulance, he'll be fine, he's bleeding fantastically well, the blood is gushing absolutely everywhere, he's bleeding brilliantly, best I've ever seen!"* But I digress, let's get back to the tennis match.)

Officials were called and a man was taken away to be treated and play was eventually resumed. McEnroe went on to win the match but it later emerged that 33-year-old spectator James Reilly had indeed been shot in the leg. An investigation was launched and it transpired that he had been hit by a stray bullet from a New York gang shoot-out from the surrounding streets of Queens.

Luckily Wimbledon Centre Court has no history of anyone ever being shot during a match, although official records show that Cliff Richard did murder several songs there during a rain break in 1996.

SECTION 6

THE REALM OF PSYCHOLOGY

The world is full of brilliant tennis players who, at some point in their career, have beaten just about every top player in the world, but never seem to quite make it to the top or win a Grand Slam.

In terms of true talent and ability there is generally very little difference between most of the world's top stars. The only thing that really differentiates them from the rest is their mental capabilities, their self-belief, their ability to deal with stress and the strength of their psychological ability.

And tennis is the perfect showcase ...

TENNIS INVENTS GAMESMANSHIP

The art of Gamesmanship is defined as the use of dubious methods to gain a serious advantage in a game but without technically breaking the rules. A ploy that has undoubtedly been going on since games were first invented, but it is tennis that can legitimately claim to have invented the actual word, if not the art.

The term originates from Stephen Potter's 1947 book, *The Theory and Practice of Gamesmanship, or the Art of Winning Games without Actually Cheating*. In the book, Potter confirms that the phrase stems from a match he played at Birkbeck College in 1931. He and his doubles partner, the philosopher Cyril Joad, were playing doubles against two vastly superior, younger, more agile and more talented opponents.

Potter and Joad were being completely swept aside when suddenly Joad made a light-hearted joke that not only changed the flow of the match, but also the world of psychology and with it the course of Potter's entire life.

His opponent had just served a sequence of aces that neither he nor his partner could even lay a racket on, yet alone return. For the next serve, Joad tried to guess where his opponent might serve and moved early and took a wild and rather hopeful swing at it. Quite fortuitously, he guessed correctly and found that he had managed to hit the ball in the centre of his racket, right in the sweet spot. Unfortunately, though, he was totally unable to control it and his return was nowhere near being in play.

In fact, it fizzed back at such tremendous speed that it flew past his opponents and was travelling at such pace that when it hit the top of the back fence on the other side of the court, it was still on an upward trajectory.

Having won the point, the server moved across the baseline to position himself ready to serve the next point, and this was when Joad made a purposefully glib remark, facetiously asking his opponents to *"Kindly state clearly whether the ball was in or out, please"*.

Now remember, this was the 1930s, and the young college students were terribly distressed to think that they had broken court etiquette and had offended their senior and therefore supposedly more respected opposition. So much so, in fact, that they even offered to play the point again in the hope of erasing their error.

Joad and Potter said it wasn't necessary but the two youngsters were so upset by the prospect of having affronted their respected hosts that their focus was shattered and their game totally collapsed. Potter and Joad went on to win the match over their younger and more talented opposition.

After the game, Potter and Joad discussed all the possible implications of this unlikely outcome at great length, culminating in Potter drafting his theory into a paper which he later expanded into *The Theory and Practice of Gamesmanship*. The book attracted great critical acclaim, defying its humorous origins, and has gone on to become a highly regarded source of reference that is still much cited in psychology studies today.

With that in mind, would the Pulitzer Prize judging panel *"Kindly state clearly whether this book will be nominated for their top literary prize or not, please"*.

TENNIS IS STILL INVENTING GAMESMANSHIP TODAY

As you've probably guessed, the art of gamesmanship didn't end with Potter's book. The dubious practice of grunting has once again been hitting the headlines with news that the loudest grunt has been set by Victoria Azarenka reaching a world record of 106 decibels, breaking Maria Sharapova's effort of 105 decibels in the 2009 Wimbledon Championships, a noise level said to be the equivalent of a jet plane landing.

But, just as we always suspected, players do gain a double advantage from all that shrieking. Firstly, by boosting their own efforts as sports psychologist Dr Thompson explained: *"If there is a forceful exhalation of air at the same time that the core abdominal muscles engage it may give more power."*

Secondly, it can be very distracting for their opponents, as a recent study published in the 2016 science journal *Plos One* disclosed. Students were asked to watch videos of tennis players hitting a ball. They then paused the tape and asked the students to indicate which part of the court they thought the ball would land. Some shots were accompanied with a loud grunt while others were performed in silence.

According to the study, *"The results were unequivocal: The presence of an extraneous sound interfered with the participants' ability to predict the performance, making their responses both slower and less accurate"*. So there you have it, and you can't argue with science, but if you do, make sure that you do it with a really loud grunt, then you might just get away with it.

TENNIS INVENTS SUPERSTITION

We all have a few foibles, good luck charms, quirky mannerisms or set routines that we like to adhere to when we play games and tennis has thrown up some real corkers. Even the pros are not immune to it. Look at the way Rafael Nadal will carefully position his water bottles and meticulously align his towels, or how Djokovic will bounce the ball a certain amount of times before serving. Murray often asks for a certain ball back because he deems it lucky.

But one man took all this to such an extreme that he became more famous for his mannerisms than his tennis titles. American player Art Larsen is remembered as one of the greats of tennis but not so much because of his Grand Slam title win at the 1950 US Open, which was impressive enough, it was more for how he did it.

Larsen, who had all sorts of unusual idiosyncrasies, was better known by his nickname of "Tappy" due to his infamous repetitive tapping of things. Larsen would tap anything he could get near; he would tap his racket, the court, the net, his shoes, the stands, a chair, often some unsuspecting fellow in the crowd, which would bring huge cheers. Sometimes he even tapped the umpire, which probably wouldn't be allowed these days. Occasionally, he was even known to tap his opponents during the change of ends. Such was his propensity for tapping things that in South America they gave Tappy another nickname, they called him *El Pajaro Loco*, the Crazy Woodpecker.

But his odd mannerisms didn't end there. Oh, no! Tappy would frequently talk to himself as well, or regale the crowds with stories during play. He was also renowned for alerting his opponent as to what shot he was about to play and where he was going to play it. He would then duly play it!

At one point, Larsen even claimed that he had an imaginary eagle perched on his left shoulder and would then proceed to chat away to that as well.

Some of his opponents took advantage of this and tried to out-psyche him before the game, calling him crazy and dismissing him as nuts, a fruitcake and a total weirdo. I'm sure today he would probably be diagnosed with some sort of pervasive disorder but in those days most of the players just accepted him as a bit of an eccentric character with some strange superstitions and a few quirky mannerisms.

Yet, rather like Dustin Hoffman's autistically savant character in *Rain Man*, Tappy also had an uncanny feel for the game. He knew instinctively how the rallies would flow and precisely where his racket should be. It was like he was at one with the flight and movement of the ball. He also had a sixth sense as to where his opponent was going to move to and to where they were going to hit the ball.

Larsen's spiritual instinct for the game, coupled with his natural grace and style, gave an almost poetic flow to his movement that was said to be quite entrancing to watch. Such was his elegance and poise that contemporary commentators described going to see Larsen play as less like watching a tennis match, but more akin to going to the ballet.

The Nutcracker perhaps?

TENNIS INVENTS A NEW TYPE OF PSYCHOLOGY

In the early 1970s, a former schoolteacher was on a sabbatical in California, earning a bit of extra cash by doing some tennis coaching. He was asking his student to try some adjustments that he thought might improve their game, but he noticed the amount of instruction given didn't correspond to the amount of improvement.

Perplexed, the coach stopped and asked the student what he was thinking and to talk through the thought process going on in their head. As the student relayed his train of thoughts, the coach realised that the more information he gave the student the more it blocked out his connection with the game itself.

The coach was Tim Gallwey and it was this simple question that led him to many years of research that culminated in his revolutionary book, *The Inner Game of Tennis*, first published in 1974. Gallwey's book explores ways to focus the mind of the player directly towards the observation of ball, body, and racket, and, just as importantly, to do this in a way that was totally non-judgmental in order to heighten learning, performance, and enjoyment of the process.

Gallwey's studies concluded that in every human endeavour there are two arenas of engagement: the outer game and the inner game. The outer game is played on an external plane to overcome external obstacles to achieve external goals. The inner game takes place within the mind, playing against obstacles of their own construction, like fear, self-doubt, lapses in focus, self-limiting concepts and pre-supposed assumptions. Gallwey's book explores ways in which to overcome those self-imposed obstacles in order to access your full potential. The book was so successful that it was turned into a six-part TV series, called *Inner Tennis*.

The TV shows were so successful that he was asked to do a follow-up series. Before long, Gallwey was being asked to apply his methodology to other areas, spawning a whole series of books. At first it was a simple transference to other sports like golf and skiing, but they were so popular that he was soon branching out into areas like yoga and music. More followed and it wasn't long before the corporate world moved in as well. These days, Gallwey's clients range from AT&T to Coca-Cola, as well as two leviathans of the computer world IBM and Apple.

The Inner Game has now evolved into a global academy with offices in the US, Spain, Italy, the Czech Republic and Brazil. They advise the corporate world on how to apply *The Inner Game*'s training methods to all sorts of practical business applications from management, achieving excellence in performance, adapting to changing strategies, and how to overcome obstacles like fear and stress.

It was clear from the beginning that *The Inner Game of Tennis* was not just going to end up being a guide for sportsmen, or a handy tool for business, it was an entire philosophy for life.

My own endeavours at philosophy were about as successful as my dreams of winning Wimbledon, and my attempted membership of the Royal Institute of Philosophy was dismissed outright, despite what I thought was my brilliant thesis on neo-post modernist ideology, entitled *"I selfie, therefore I am"*.

Oh well, when does Wimbledon qualifying start …

SECTION 7

THE WORLD OF PHILOSOPHY

Until the mid-1800s, psychology was classified as a branch of philosophy and the two often get confused. While there is still a certain amount of overlap, the two sciences have since developed into two very independent disciplines. To put it simply, psychology endeavours to understand human behaviour, whereas philosophy attempts to comprehend the existence of human life.

Over the centuries, tennis has provided us with many delightful insights into both ...

TENNIS INVENTS EXISTENTIAL SURREALISM

I'm sure you are questioning how tennis could have possibly inspired the likes of Kierkegaard, Jean-Paul Sartre, André Breton, Salvador Dali, Max Ernst, Franz Kafka, Joseph Heller, Nietzsche and Dostoyevsky into creating two such powerful philosophies as existentialism and surrealism, but, if you indulge me a while, I will demonstrate just how our humble sport has influenced such grandees of the philosophical world.

You may recall an earlier chapter in which the monk Caesarius wrote about the dim young clerk, who envisaged a malevolent band of demons playing tennis where they used him as the ball and his soul was the prize. That was a story that dates back to about 1150, so you could argue that this tennis fable was an early influencer on both existentialism and surrealism. And, if you're prepared to overlook some minor doctrinal differences, it predates all those named above by almost eight centuries.

But, I'm a generous fellow, I will let that small discrepancy pass and allow the illustrious dignitaries to keep their tenuous association as the founding fathers of their respective philosophies and, instead, propose that tennis not only sowed the seeds of these doctrines but also helped popularise their resurgence when they were waning.

With the arrival of the Swinging Sixties came a new force, a retrospective rebirth of the existentialist and surrealist movements. It was thought to have evolved to try and counterbalance the self-indulgent affluence that actually underpinned the *"Peace, Love and Understanding"* mind-set that was inveigling itself into the intelligentsia at the time. The example I am using here is considered to be one of the very finest.

Often cited as one of the greatest examples of this new movement was Antonioni Michelangelo's 1966 film, *Blow Up*. Antonioni's enigmatic masterpiece regularly appears in many critics' list of favourite films, and this particular scene is said to hold the key to unravelling the elusive themes of the entire movie. It goes without saying that the pivotal scene in question centres itself on non-other than a very surreal game of tennis.

For those unfamiliar with the film, the star of the story is an ethereal photographer played by David Hemmings who lives next door to an abstract expressionist painter. The theme of the movie is flagged up by the painter who admits he has no idea what he's painting when he first starts and the meaning only becomes clear later when it's finished.

When we first meet the photographer, his world seems very glamorous, full of fine cars and beautiful women but there's an emptiness in his soul signified by an ugly underbelly pervading the otherwise sumptuous look of the film. The photographer himself appears aloof, detached, languid, self-indulgent and uncaring. All this is juxtaposed against a stirring musical jazz score, which serves to emphasise his vacuous life while promoting the film's central theme of nihilism.

Coincidentally, Antonioni's nihilism is not to be mistaken for the type of nihilism that is the score line whenever I play tennis. But that's just my realism, let's return to the surrealism of Antonioni's mysterious movie …

The plot turns when the protagonist is developing some photographs of a girl in the park with whom he had been talking to earlier; she's played by Vanessa Redgrave. In one of the pictures, he notices that her expression looks like she has just seen something awful.

This arouses his curiosity, and so he tries to follow her line of sight by piecing together the other photos that he's taken around the park, and it leads him to what looks like an anomaly in one of the photographs. When he blows it up to enlarge the area in question, in a twist worthy of Hitchcock himself, it reveals what looks like a dead body in the bushes.

His suspicions of foul play are later confirmed when the girl from the park tracks him down and seduces him, but we realise she was not there for him at all because, as she leaves, she steals the incriminating film roll. Luckily, the photographer was on to her and had swapped the film roll. This delicious cameo, played by Vanessa Redgrave as the oh-so-remote seductress willing to reveal so much of herself in the flesh yet so little of herself in character, is said to be another insight into the theme of the film.

When the photographer returns to the park, he sees that he was right and that there really is a body in the bushes and he rushes back for his camera. Of course, when he comes back the body has gone. He looks around but all he can see are four people playing tennis in the park.

But this is no ordinary game. Not only are all the players incredibly beautiful but they are playing a game without a ball. The match seems to grow in intensity as the players rally fiercely. So much so, that the photographer finds himself strangely drawn into the fictitious game and moves closer to watch.

At this point, the players hit the imaginary ball off court and their gaze follows it to exactly where he is standing. They gesture for him to pick up the non-existent ball. He hesitates for a moment, but then goes along with the façade, picks up the imaginary ball and actually throws it back so they can continue playing their illusory tennis match.

This single act is said to be the defining moment of the film as it doubly commits both the photographer and the audience to the whole surrealist nature of the film. Much like the photographer, the audience itself only ever gets glimpses of what may be happening, or what may have happened. As each different scene gives us varying perspectives of events, leaving us uncertain as to what, if anything, was real, the murder, the tennis game, or even the film.

The reviews of the time credited Antonioni as claiming that his film is like life, in that much of how we interpret things depends on our viewpoint and that all is in the eye of the beholder. Reality is merely what we choose to focus on, or *blow up* and develop in the case of the film, with only our minds to imbue our own chosen significance onto events. The film, and the tennis scene in particular, are often cited as one of the great artistic interpretations of these two great philosophical disciplines.

Most critics agree that this imaginary tennis game holds the whole key to unravelling Antonioni's cryptic masterpiece. They suggest it makes us question our fickle, beauty-fixated, jazzed-up, celebrity-obsessed, media-orientated world. A world that bombards us with so many artificial stimulations that our natural feelings are numbed into an overwhelming sense of emptiness, destroying any sense of personal involvement or emotional connection to a world laden with such superficial vacuity that it makes us question our whole nihilistic presence in order to be able to define what is reality and what is not.

Which, coincidentally, is exactly the same argument I use when my opponent tries to call my serve out when it was really in.

Just make sure that you are well versed in the style of philosophical examination before committing to this particular line of defence though, because using existentialist surrealism to prove that the ball wasn't actually out takes a bit of practice.

I usually go with the concept that the ball wasn't actually out; it just preceded the existence of the court's own essence as defined by the reality of the lines themselves.

TENNIS INVENTS MORE SURREALISM – QUEEN'S CLUB STYLE

While we're on the topic of surrealism, it would be remiss of me not to tell you one of the all-time great stories ever to have come out of The Queen's Club. The incident is completely true and, even if it has been embroidered slightly through the years, it still remains one of my favourites. But before I regale you with the fully quilted and cross-stitched version of this yarn, let me first explain why it particularly resonates with me.

Having just written several chapters on philosophy, existentialism and surrealism, it riles me a little to have to confess that, as a youngster, I never fully appreciated the finer points of these disciplines, and it's a common human trait that we mock what we cannot understand. To prove the point, I used to make fun of it myself and my favourite joke was:

> Q: "How many surrealists does it take to change a light bulb?"
> A: "A Fish."

OK, so now you know why I got beaten up so much as a kid. In reality, growing up as child in the back streets of Horsham, the chances of exchanging any laddish banter on the finer points of existentialism whilst downing pints of snake-bite with the local skinheads down The King's Head, were few and far between.

But, by the time I became a teenager, my tastes in jokes had become a little more sophisticated and so a newer more erudite surrealist joke was required.

In retrospect, using words like "erudite" was probably one of the reasons the skinheads used to beat the crap out of me.

So anyway, eventually I managed to find an updated joke. It was one I stole from the droll stand-up comic Steve Wright, who used to open his gigs with: *"I just got back from a Round the World Trip. It's a nice enough place, but I wouldn't want to live there."*

He'd usually get a gentle laugh before continuing.

"I went on one of those all-in package deal holidays, only this one was a holiday for surrealists. Everything was free – so long as you could prove you weren't actually there."

Steve would get a few more laughs here and continue.

"The surrealist holiday I took was great. It was an all-in deal where you got fourteen days – but only three nights."

I've moved on a bit now, of course, and my favourite surrealist joke is not a joke at all, it's The Queen's Club story that I foreshadowed earlier. It was originally told to me by two former Queen's Club employees, Patrick, who was the Bar Manager, and Steve, who was the Events Manager.

Steve starts off the story about how a Member's guest once brought in a pet monkey to the Club. Now, I know what you're thinking, this can't be true, Health & Safety wouldn't allow such a thing, but this was long before anyone had even thought of Health & Safety Officers or even invented anoraks for them to wear.

Now while I am not going to say that the guest who had brought in the monkey was tipsy, let the record show that The Queen's Club's extensive range of refreshments was a lot less extensive by the time they left than it was upon their arrival.

Of course, it is possible that the guest in question was just suffering from what celebrity agents often call *"incorrect medication"*, but for all the guests to be have been incorrectly dosed that day seems to be bordering on medical malpractice on a grand scale. So perhaps, let's be honest here, these guys weren't just suffering from a slight chemical imbalance in their bloodstream, they were all half-cut, in fact half-cut would be an understatement, they were a cut of the fullest order. In fact, they were all completely cucumbered, three sheets to the wind, lamp-faced. Anyway, somewhere in the middle of all the chemically induced high-jinx and generally hilarious tomfoolery, the monkey escaped.

Now, I'm sure you are familiar with the old adage *"like a bull in a china shop"*, but let me assure you that the expression is a shallow void of metaphoric illustration compared to the damage done by a wild ape in a tennis club.

That said, The Queen's Club members are a pretty resilient lot, nothing much fazes them. They have survived the Blitz, famines, rationing and several global pandemics like the Corona virus; they've stood firm through the Great Depression, bankruptcy, scandals, takeovers and clubhouse fires. They've been bombed, blasted and shot at through two world wars – a marauding monkey running wild around the clubhouse wasn't going to stop them enjoying their libations, or let it take the fizz out of their tonic.

At first, some of the less steely Members may have responded with a slight raising of an eyebrow at the sight of a screaming simian swinging from the crystal chandeliers and defecating into the *moules marinière*, but as the novelty wore off and what was initially perceived as pandemonium was soon accepted as the norm, they just tried to get on with things as only the British can. They would simply manufacture a quick stiffening of the upper lip area and then it was back to business as usual.

Sure enough, it wasn't long before Members began to grow accustomed to the gallivanting gibbon fleeing across the dining room table, scampering through the vichyssoise, leaping back out into the Members' Bar, all the while accompanied by primal screaming of such visceral power and intensity that some of the more aged

113

crystal champagne flutes decided to give up on the idea of ever having to hold any more vintage Pol Roger and elected to shatter instead.

Eventually, those first few heady minutes of savage destruction slowly turned into hours, until this chaotic state of beastly bedlam assumed a sort of weird normality, as this usually sedate cathedral of tennis gradually got used to its boorish invader and returned to its customary occupational commerce.

Obviously though, at a prestigious old club like Queen's, there are certain rules and regulations, guidelines on behaviour that had been drawn up over the centuries, rules of politeness to adhere to, small points of etiquette that had been passed down through the generations, all intended to aid the smooth running of the aforementioned establishment in order to maximise its enjoyment for the Members.

Although there were no specific regulations on the matter, it was generally thought that feral primates rampaging a path of violent destruction throughout the facility was probably not what the founding fathers would have wanted when they set out its constitution. Something drastic had to be done. And done it was. Something that Members only do in times of dire crisis and as a last resort. They called for the Club Rule Book. A stalwart manuscript that had been the guiding light of civilised behaviour for centuries. Surely there was something in that ancient parchment that covered a situation such as this.

Eventually, a sharp-minded member of legal persuasion pointed out that the beast may well be in breach of Rule 42, Article 3, by *"being in the Members' Bar without a jacket and tie"*. Now a club like Queen's has certain standards to uphold and a breach of the Dress Code was considered a serious misdemeanour. And, although one sharp-witted fellow did offer up a spare jacket and tie, it was thought more judicious to capture the chimp rather than to try and alter its sartorial corsage. So it was all hands on deck to try and apprehend the wayward beast.

As you can imagine, there was total bedlam around the club as the guest, several of his friends and various staff members, all chased around the club trying catch this barbaric baboon. At one point the monkey even got into the kitchens and destroyed much of the food supply, including a giant vat of fresh cream that was now all over the kitchen floor. Make a mental note of the cream spillage here, as it becomes integral to the story later on.

Now, I don't know if you've ever tried to catch a wild monkey in full flight, but if you have you'll know that it's not an easy task at the best of times; but when *the chasers* are all completely pissed and *the chasee* has taken millions of years to evolve into a finely tuned athlete specifically designed to swing and leap from one place to another with millimetre precision in order to avoid being captured, then you'll know that the odds here are greatly stacked *against* the chasers and *with* the chasee.

If you add to that the encumbrance of a kitchen floor covered in full fat cream, with people slipping into each other left, right and centre, then that task becomes even less likely to end in success and more likely to end in the grand finale of a Laurel & Hardy movie. And if that wasn't ludicrous enough, things were about to take an even more surreal turn.

I'm pretty sure that if Lewis Carroll had witnessed this shambolic scene of absurdity before writing about Alice popping down the rabbit hole for a Mad Hatters Tea Party, he would surely have binned the idea for simply not being preposterous enough.

Throughout all this state of total baboonic bedlam though, Members and staff were trying to carry on as normal. One such Member was well known to Patrick. He was a professor of philosophy and a great admirer of Jean-Paul Sartre. He and Patrick had wiled away many an evening debating Sartre, surrealism and all the fineries therein. At the end of the night though, Patrick would always win the reality argument by presenting the esteemed prof with his bar bill.

However, on this occasion, the professor just wanted a quick caffeine hit and, with the marauding macaque temporarily out of the area, he seized the opportunity to approach the bar and asked Patrick if he could have a cup of coffee before adding *"Make it a black one with no cream"*.

In total contrast to the surrounding mayhem, a completely straight-faced Patrick coolly replied that the club was temporarily out of cream and asked if he could make it with no milk instead.

I am pretty confident that no matter how much older I get, this story will remain my all-time favourite surrealist story and my second favourite Queen's Club anecdote. Now, I know what you're thinking, but I can't tell you my favourite one for legal reasons, but see me in the bar afterwards and if you get me as squiffy as a zoologist who lets his pet monkey escape, then I may just spill the beans.

In conclusion then, the naughty wee monkey was eventually caught using the allure of bananas covered in suspiciously dirty looking cream and an improvised trap made, of course, out of several old tennis nets. Proving once again the superiority of tennis players' minds, even when they're completely mullered and likely to be driving home the porcelain bus all night.

I realise that the Health & Safety laws governing restaurant premises these days would prevent this from ever happening today, but I can't help thinking that the next generation of players are just not going to have the same calibre of stories to tell their grandchildren as we do.

Still, on the plus side, I guess they can sleep more soundly at night, knowing that their *moules marinière* will be free from simian effluence.

TENNIS INVENTS ANSWER TO THE UNIVERSE'S GREATEST MYSTERY

At last, tennis aficionados around the world will have the answer to one of the greatest mysteries of the universe. A conundrum so baffling that it has been puzzling philosophers and intellectuals for thousands of years.

I don't know about you, but I hate it when you ask somebody something that they obviously don't know the answer to but, instead of just admitting that they have no idea, the smarmy smart alec just shrugs and says, *"How long is a piece of string?"*

Well, now you can look them square in the eye and give them the definitive answer. It is, of course, 235 cm, which is the exact length of string it takes to string a tennis racket.

If you happen to be British and need a translation of this – that's nineteen and a half feet.

Or if you prefer it to be measured in tennis terms, that's just over two Ivo Karlovitchs, or almost four Lleyton Hewitts!

TENNIS INVENTS A PHILOSOPHY FOR LIFE

This is a story told to me by a tennis coach from Queen's about a wizened old tennis coach. He had asked his players all to come around to his house for a team talk before they set off to play another club.

As he greeted them each on arrival, the coach just showed them into the living room to let them chat amongst themselves before they sat down to the serious business of discussing tactics and team strategies. He'd brewed a large pot of coffee and told them all to help themselves to a cup.

The coach watched as the players settled in and the conversation turned to the theme of the day, the kit. The club they were about to play against had a really cool new kit with sponsors, club logo and all the trimmings, very smart and all paid for. They were complaining that the club gave them no such kit, didn't fund them, and they had to buy their own mishmash of a kit – and generally they were all grumbling and griping about the unfairness of the matter.

Knowing that the kit discrepancy was a long-standing problem, the coach had prepared for it and called for their attention. The coach told them:

> "You may have noticed that I had put out a large assortment of coffee cups for you all to choose from – delicate porcelain ones, cheap plastic ones, expensive crystal, ordinary glass, some plain looking and some exquisitely refined ones. Now you have also noticed that all the nice looking, expensive cups have been taken, whilst all the plain looking, cheaper ones have been left untouched. While it is, of course, normal for you to want only the best for yourselves, this can also be the source of much of your dissatisfaction, problems and stress, both on and off the court."

The team listened in intrigued as the coach continued.

"You chose those cups because you perceived them to be more expensive, of finer quality and therefore more special. What you failed to realise is that the cup itself neither adds to, nor distracts from, the quality of the coffee. What you all really wanted was to savour the experience of a good coffee, not the cup, but you unconsciously went for the best cups. I watched as some of you even vied to get the best cup first or began eyeing each other's cups to see if yours was as good as theirs.

"This is directly relevant to the complaints I've been getting about the kit situation and could also be indicative of any problems you might be having in life generally. You see, life is represented here by the coffee; whereas things like the kit, jobs, money, possessions and your position in society are all just the cups. They are just tools and structures that contain or hold together the current story of your life. You cannot allow such external entities to define your life, or change the quality of the life you want to live. Sometimes when we fall into the trap of concentrating only on the cup, we fail to fully enjoy the coffee. What I'm saying to you is, savour the coffee not the cups. What we all really want is to enjoy the flavour of the coffee as we sip it, just as what we all really want is to enjoy the flavour of life as we live it. The happiest people don't always have the best make of everything, but they always make the best of everything they have.

"It's exactly the same with your grumbles about the team kit. What you are wearing neither adds to, nor distracts from, the quality of your game. So today, here's what I want from you; let the opposition savour the experience of wearing a nice new bit of kit, but what I want from you all is to savour the experience of playing your best ever game of tennis."

I don't think I need to tell you that the crappy-kit guys won convincingly that day and celebrated with a lot of very fancy beers in very ordinary glasses!

SECTION 8

THE ANCIENT WORLD

While many of tennis's most coveted mysteries remain lost to history, some of the game's origins can be traced back to the ancient world by knitting together some of the faint threads that they left behind in an effort to establish the basic tapestry that forms the game we know and love today.

Here are a few that fit this category and maybe shine a light on some of the ambiguities of the game's beginnings, and where better to start than one of tennis's greatest and most enduring mysteries – the origin of the game's strange scoring system ...

TENNIS INVENTS PECULIAR SCORING SYSTEM

Fans of Monty Python's 1979 film *Life of Brian* may recall the infamous scene where John Cleese, who's playing Reg the Activist, is trying to bolster support against the Roman invaders with his rallying cry of *"What have the Romans ever done for us?"* And people from the crowd keep shouting back all the things that the Romans have actually given them, forcing Reg to constantly go back and revise his speech by adding new bits every time somebody shouts out something else that the Romans have given them. He gets more and more riled each time, until his speech gets longer and longer and poor old Reg becomes increasingly exasperated.

The theories on the origins of the tennis scoring system are a bit like that scene, just when you think you have heard the latest theory another one emerges. It's a mystery that historians have been arguing about for over six centuries and was long thought to have been lost into the sands of time. But I think I have found the definitive answer at last, and one which is correctly revealed here for the very first time.

So let's run through the most commonly proposed theories, as they were presented through the centuries, and then you can make up your own mind as to which one you wish to pin your flag to.

A good place to start is at the beginning, so let's zip back in time to 1520, when we find the tennis scoring system being questioned for the very first time by Jan van den Berghe in his tome *Das kaetspel ghemoraliseert*, when he writes: *"Earlier we explored the manner in which a game of tennis can be won ...What was not explained was how players can win fifteen points for a single stroke. Why is not one point given for one stroke?"*

Frustratingly for Berghe, almost half a century later, it seems that no one had been able to answer his question because in 1555 we find the eminent Italian doctor Antonio Scaino de Salo revisiting the conundrum in a treatise that he wrote on Ball Games called *Tratta del*

Giuoco della Palla. Only, this time, Scaino attempts to resolve the issue himself.

Scaino records that the argument of how the tennis scoring system came into being had already been raging for many centuries with no satisfactory result, so hopes of a resolution were slim, but he persisted anyway, even if, by his own admission, his theories on scoring are only conjecture.

Certainly, Scaino's treatise is fascinating because it offers us some of the earliest ever insights into the medieval game and how it was played, which in themselves prove to be truly enlightening.

Scaino notes that there were three types of tennis game played in those days, the Single, the Double and the Triple. All of them involved betting, of course, and the Single was won when you won 4 points and your opponent only won one point. The Double was when you won four points and your opponent won none. The Triple was when you won five clear points in a row, even if your opponent had won the first two.

Scaino argued that the Triple was the Holy Grail of tennis and represented the ultimate honour and reward, if you did this three times then that was like winning three sets of tennis and thus the game. The points of all these three sets added up to fifteen and therefore he suggested that this figure of fifteen was the highest symbol of tennis excellence that a player could possibly attain. The doctor felt that this might have been how the figure fifteen had become enshrined into the game of tennis and how it became synonymous with any point scored.

Whilst most of Scaino's musings were well received, and are still much lauded and revered today, his tennis scoring theory must have been considered tenuous even in 1555 as the debate has prevailed for a further six centuries, suggesting that the good doctor's assumptions about scoring gained little traction amongst tennis scholars.

The debate undoubtedly raged on, but it wasn't until about a quarter of a century later that anyone came forward with a credible alternative. It is a little-known book, and one that is even rarer and more sought after than Scaino's and written by a French nobleman called Jean Gosselin. Gosselin was a much-respected historian and held the prestigious royal post of Keeper of The King's Library at the Royal Court in Paris. In 1579 he published his prodigious research in a book entitled *La Declaration de deux doubtes qui se trouvent en comptant dans le jeu de paume*. Gosselin may not have had a natural flair for coming up with catchy book titles but his tennis scoring theories are worth a second look.

Gosselin speculated that the tennis scoring system was based on the physical sign of the circle, or a sextant, as used by astronomers, who broke down the circle into one sixth of a circle. Gosselin didn't really manage to back this up with anything other than it was a common measurement at the time and so a logical conclusion to make.

One of my favourite Groucho Marx quotes is when he is trying to defend a moral stance he has taken and declares haughtily, *"Those are my principles, sir, and if you don't like them, well, I have others"*. And just like Groucho's principles, Gosselin himself didn't seem to rate his sextant circle theory too highly either, because, just like Groucho's principles, he had others. The Frenchman's second theory was that if you didn't like his circle theory, then how about a square one?

Gosselin maintained that in Roman times, the Roman square was a common form of measurement, so just as we use square footage to mark out the size of a piece of land, so did the Romans, only they used to measure it in chunks of fifteen square feet at a time. This square theory showed much more promise than his circle theory but, just like his first theory, Gosselin never actually managed to make a direct connection to the game of tennis, and much like Groucho's principles, proved to lack any historical fortitude.

Another common theory, that you often hear bandied around

tennis clubs, is that the tennis scoring system is derived from horology, and is based on the time systems used by clocks. The theory dates back to a writer called Alfred Crawley, who wrote copiously upon the matter of tennis scoring.

Probably his most persuasive piece was posted in *The Observer* newspaper in 1920 where Crawley laid out his theory in full. He suggested that the division of the day into twelve hours goes back many centuries and once again relies on the sexagesimal system, which had become embedded into the medieval mind-set as the answer to everything. All the big inventions, like the clock and the sextant all conformed to the sexagesimal system, it explained time, aligned the stars, and gave them the celestial navigation system that allowed them to circumnavigate the Seven Seas and map the solar system. It is understandable how this system was revered, almost to the point of worship, as the magical answer to everything.

In those days it was natural to assume that the figure sixty was considered to be the whole, a complete figure in itself, as they had been making sense of the universe with that figure since Babylonian times, and had been dividing it into quarters for just as long, so it's understandable how the figure fifteen would have become almost as significant.

Crawley goes on to suggest that it could be this same logic that led them to believe that a tennis game could also be considered to be whole, and thus complete, when you reach the point of sixty.

To further back up his sexagesimal hypothesis, he points out that the figure sixty was so important that the French language didn't even bother with coming up with any new words for things like seventy and eighty, they just referred back to their Svengali-like sixty figure. So much so that any numbers after sixty were regarded almost as inferior and so the number seventy referred back to sixty and became known as *soixante-dix*, and, until recently, eighty used to be *soixante-vingt*.

Crawley wrote that the invention of the circular face on a sundial was an equally epoch-making turning point, not just for horology, but for tennis as well. With the invention of the mechanical clock, horologists could then further break down time into sixty-minute segments and each minute into another sixty seconds, further proving just how embedded the sixty figure had become into the culture. Crawley suggested that as the clocks chimed every quarter of an hour, signalling fifteen minutes, so each winning strike of the ball would signify a score of fifteen points.

Doubters used to debunk Crawley's theory saying that if this was true then we would call 45 after three points and not 40, but Crawley argued that this was simply human laziness and was just a verbal shorthand for calling out 45 and gives several examples where words have been similarly shortened over the years. This is one part of Crawley's argument that has now been generally accepted, in much the same way as many modern players sometimes shorten the 15 score line to a call of 5.

Although many historians like the idea of the sexagesimal clock theory, it was usually argued down by two very simple points. Firstly, there is just no historical evidence to back it up. Surely this would have been mentioned somewhere in text and, more importantly, if clocks were really so integral to the scoring, then certainly one or two of the early pictures would have depicted this crucial piece of equipment, but none do.

Secondly, and perhaps more importantly, there's the small matter of the fact that mechanical clocks hadn't been invented by the time that tennis had already been up and running for several centuries. And even if they had been, to have one on a tennis court would have proved to have been totally impractical, the balls were so hard that it would have been smashed to smithereens in seconds – or at least as soon as somebody had actually invented seconds.

Much like Gosselin and Groucho, Crawley also had a backup

theory in case you didn't like his horological one. Gosselin's second proposal claims to originate from the betting world. This is a much more promising start, as there is a medieval cartload of evidence showing that betting and tennis were forever entwined in each other's early history.

Crawley argues that the betting theory lies in the coin of choice in the 15th and 16th centuries. It was a French coin, used across Europe, called the Denier, which was worth fifteen pence, and that this was the source of the fifteen points per point scored. Crawley expands the theory by pointing out that there were also several other coins in circulation which if you put all four of them together added up to sixty. There was even another coin, called a Gros Denier Tournois, which was worth the full sixty pence. So maybe tennis players were playing for one Denier per point up to the maximum stake of sixty pence, or a Gross Denier for a game, which would have been sixty.

What is also intriguing about this theory is to know that at that time betting had gotten completely out of hand. So much so that it accounted for a large percentage of all bankruptcies and imprisonments. The authorities were under huge pressure to do something about it, so they passed a law forbidding gamblers to lay any bets in excess of sixty Deniers.

This certainly adds weight to the sexagesimal theory, as the coin can then be broken down by the quarterly division of sixty to give us our 15, 30, 45, all the way up to sixty, which would then represent the conclusion of the maximum allowed bet of sixty, and thus the game.

Crawley tries to lend extra authority to his theory by suggesting that this is exactly what Scaino was referring to in 1555 when he wrote about the Single, Double and Triple games, leading to a point of fifteen and concluding at sixty. Indeed, for many years, Crawley's answer was considered to be the most likely but, just like all the other theories, they all lacked any evidence that connected them to tennis. So, appetising as they all are, none of these theories have ever proved conclusive and that is probably why we are still arguing over the origins six centuries later.

Until, of course, today. Because I think that Gosselin was on to something with his Roman Square theory. I realise we largely dismissed the idea earlier in the chapter, but that was only because Gosselin didn't have enough facts on hand to lend it enough credence, coupled with the fact that he was unable to give it a convincing link to tennis. Today we have far more sophisticated archaeological tools at our disposal, and six hundred years' more research to work with. Although I don't subscribe to Gosselin's Roman Square theory any more than I do to his Sextant Circle theory, there is something to it that may have been overlooked at the time.

If you recall, Gosselin states that the Romans marked out areas of land in chunks of fifteen square foot at a time, which means that there is very definitely a way to link that to tennis – and here's how.

The Romans had an early variation of the game of tennis called *Harpastum*, which they inherited from the Greeks when they invaded Gaul about 2000 BC. The Greeks actually called their game *Phaininda* or *Phaeninde*, which was in turn a descendant of an even older game played by the Ancient Greeks called *Episkyros*. But, as we all know, history is written by the victors and the all-conquering Roman army weren't going to use a Greek word, they wanted their own name, one worthy of a victorious army, and so *Harpastum* was born.

Harpastum was a type of ball game that lies somewhere between *T'su-Chu*, the Chinese Emperor's game we talk about in more detail later, and the French game, *Longue paume*, sometimes referred to as *Field Tennis* in England, from which we get *Jeu de paume*, *Palla* and *Pelote*, all of which, historians agree, lead us eventually to the game of tennis.

Harpastum, *Phaeninde* and *Episkyros* were all similar sorts of games, using the same sort of rules and, more importantly, much the same scoring system. So what was it? Well, here is the crux of it. Soldiers, of course, win battles and wars by capturing territories, and thus it is that we get our first real clue to the origins of the tennis scoring system.

Just as in tennis today, all these ancient games begin when the server hits the ball into the opponent's side of the field, and each side plays a ball back and forth in a rally, but if the opponent fails to return it, then the winner of that point gains that piece of territory. We've already established that the Romans measured their land in chunks of 15 feet at a time, so if your team wins a point – you gain 15 feet of territory from the opposition.

If your team wins another point, you gain another 15 feet, giving you 30 feet of territory, making it progressively easier to return the ball as you get nearer the net. Hence, as you win three points you gain 45 feet of territory, which of course gives you a huge *"advantage"* over your opponent. We've also established that they use the sexagesimal system, which means that the court measured 60 feet each side. So once you won that fourth point you had won all 60 foot of your opponent's territory and thus won the game. Sounding familiar yet? Well, there's more …

What makes this territorial theory even more compelling for tennis historians is that each point would be physically marked with a peg or flag, to ensure there could be no cheating about the score, or who won which point, where and when. For instance, for the first point a marker would be placed at the 15-foot mark. If you then won the second point, you'd mark it out at the 30-foot point; 45 foot for the third point; and finally if you won the fourth point it meant that you had won all 60 foot of your opponent's territory, signifying that you had won that game.

A scoring system, I think you'll agree, that sounds almost identical to the scoring system we use in tennis today. The two scoring systems have other similarities as well. For instance, the first team to win the opponents' territories six times would be declared the winner. This is almost identical to how a set is won today, being the first to six.

What is more, the French word *chasse* literally means *to hunt* and this marking system is almost identical to the way Real Tennis is scored today, where they lay down a *chase* in their opponent's territory, only instead of placing physical markers on the court, they use markings on the side of the walls as a guide to where the ball landed and as to where the *chase* has to be played from.

What is even more convincing is that in some early 15th-century drawings of tennis, there is actually a marker peg that you can see on the court, signalling that, even then, they still used to actually physically mark the territory just like they used to in Roman times.

And it's not just the physicality of the evidence that links it to tennis, there's the linguistic connection as well. It is easy to see how the French and Roman words, *chasse* and *cache*, from our *chase* and *catch*, could well be the origins of the word *chase* used in Real Tennis today. It's even possible that these marker points could also explain why points are called points, because that is the exact point at which you would lay down the old markers. Hence the term point and hence why each point is counted in units of fifteen.

So, we have the theory, we have the written evidence and we have a historical lineage linking it directly to our modern game of tennis. I think this might be a good time to point this out to our old friend, Reg the Activist.

Over to you Reg ...

> *"Yeh, alright, alright, but apart from the tennis scoring system; proper law and order; sanitation; medicine; a good education system; crop irrigation; decent roads; nice wines; beautiful architecture; fresh drinking water; and world peace ... what have the Romans ever done for us, eh?"*

TENNIS INVENTS SEX

Not content with taking the credit for inventing the word *love* in tennis, there are some Dutch scholars who claim that their nation invented the word *sex* as well.

It's true that the Dutch are often overlooked when it comes to their historical impact on many games; their claim to being the inventors of golf is especially compelling and, it seems, we should perhaps tilt them a nod of appreciation for their influence on *sex* as well, albeit via the slightly circumnavigational route of tennis.

The previous chapter covered the origins of the tennis scoring system pretty extensively, but one possible theory that I omitted was the Dutch claim to the tennis scoring system. The theory goes that it was once again based on the all-conquering number of sixty. Only, it being Dutch, it is related to a much older game than the venerable game of tennis, in fact one that is often referred to as the oldest game of all – prostitution.

I know, I know! I sincerely expect this book to be found on a dusty bookshelf in years to come with this page splattered in coffee stains from where many an elder statesman has choked on their morning refresher having read that such bawdy insouciance be associated with our noble game. But, even today, this type of scoring system still exists on some streets of Amsterdam. Extraordinary as it sounds, the price of a call-girl goes up according to how beautiful she is. So, the lowest ranked escort would cost you 15 derniers; the next lady up would cost you 30 derniers; a more nubile *fille de joie* would set you back 45; but if you found one at 60 derniers then you could rest assured that she was the most beautiful courtesan on the street and you knew you had truly won the jackpot.

The idea that tennis borrowed its scoring system from the oldest profession further extends itself, if I may use such a phrase, to explain that this ancient Dutch sex-worker grading system could also be where the actual word *"sex"* comes from, it being a colloquial contraction of the word *Sexagesimal* itself.

I realise that this bawdy Paphian scoring system is not a widely accepted theory in the tennis world, but it's just such a salaciously wondrous concept that I felt it would have been thoughtless slapdashery of the highest order if I were not share it with you. Plus, it gives a whole new meaning to the phrase, the Wimbledon Seeding Committee! You can practically see the cream on their lusciously red and perfectly ripe strawberries curdling at the very thought.

It may just be coincidence, but the Dutch government also passed a law at that very same time that banned any citizen from gambling or frittering away any more than 60 derniers at a time, so maybe this is also where the phrase a *"Dutch Cap"* comes from as well?

"Oh, I say," as Dan Maskell used to declare at moments of heightened play.

TENNIS INVENTS A SCORING SYSTEM WHERE THE LOSER WINS

Whatever the truth of tennis's weird and wonderful scoring system, you can bet your bottom dollar that Stefan Edberg is not a big fan of it, and for good reason.

In 1991, the brilliant Swede was the defending Wimbledon champion, the tournament's number one seed, and ranked world number one. He had stormed through the tournament with a master class of serve and volley tactics and was all set to play a match against Michael Stich of Germany in the semi-finals.

If you just looked at the stats, you would conclude that the Swedish superstar had won the match comfortably; he never lost a single service game throughout the entire match. He won more points than his opponent, and yet he lost the match!

In fact Stefan had won all his service games quite comfortably and had won many more points against Stich's serve, but never quite managed to break it. Stich won very few points against Edberg's serve and, although he struggled to hold on to his own serve on many occasions, he just about managed to cling on and avoided being broken. So over the course of the match Edberg accrued many more points against the Stich serve, but never quite succeeded in breaking it.

So it all came down to three very close tie-breaks and Edberg was unlucky in a just a few points and lost all three of them. So he was knocked out of the tournament despite never losing his serve and having won more points than his opponent – such are the intricacies of the tennis scoring system.

As one wry commentator quipped at the time, *"It was a complete Stich up"*.

TENNIS INVENTS LOSER TAKES ALL

Tom Okker, a well-known player from the Netherlands, would probably not rail against the tennis scoring system quite as profusely as Edberg. But whatever Okker's thoughts are on tennis's crazy scoring methods, I'm guessing his thoughts on the system for allocating prize money is much more positive.

Okker remains the only man in tennis history to receive the full winner's amount of the tournament's first prize money allocation at the US Open despite the fact that he never won the tournament.

The talented Okker had just played the tournament of his life to battle his way through to the 1968 US Open final, but eventually lost to the late, great Arthur Ashe.

But although this upset Okker, it unsettled the tournament committee even more as it left them with a huge dilemma. Arthur Ashe had entered the tournament as an amateur, therefore he was not allowed to accept the prize money and so, after much um-ing and ah-ing, all prize money for winning the US Open was eventually awarded to the loser, Tom Okker.

Hmn …

> *"Dear National Lottery,*
> *I know I didn't actually win last week's lottery draw but, as the winner was not a professional gambler and, as such, can be regarded as an amateur, I was wondering whether you'd like to consider awarding the £60m jackpot to me instead …"*

TENNIS INVENTS ITS OWN IDENTITY CRISIS

The route to tennis finally being called tennis was, as Paul McCartney might have said, a long and winding road. If we go back several thousand years and include all the possible derivatives, from the early Mesoamerican games to Ancient Greek, Chinese and Japanese adaptations, then we have quite a roll call.

The Chinese had many ball games that had tennis-like qualities, some of the better known ones were called: *Cuju, Cnapan, Caid, Ba, Calcio, Chuiwan, T'su-Chu, Dakyu, Sepakraga* and *Iwandja*, with their Japanese counterparts preferring *Kamari, Hanetsuki, Oibane* and *Tzukibane*.

The Ancient Greeks, Romans and Italians shared many names for the game, including: *Caccia, Episkyros, Ephetinde, Follis, Folliculis, Harpastum, Jo de Paumo, La Corda, Paganica, Palla, Pallota, Pelota, Phaeninde, Pila, Tambourin, Tchigan, Teneyzen, Tenes, Aporrhaxis, Ourania, Trigonalis* and, of course, *Sphairomachia* or *Sphaeristeria*, that Major Wingfield appropriated to name his first incarnation of the game, *Sphairistikè*.

The French probably had the most diversity with names such as: *Chasse, Le Closhe, Le Tenesse, Tennois, Tainia, Tamis, Tenez, Jeu de dedans, Jeu de carré, Jeu de bonde, Jeu de lune, Longue paume, Pelote à main, Boundadou* and, of course, *Jeu de paume*. And the Spanish were not far behind with *Juego de la Chaza, Mano Desnuda, Bote Luzea, La Choa, Rebote, Pelotamano, Cuerdas, Chicun, Chicane, Chigan* and *Pelotamixteca*.

Tellingly, in terms of possible historical origins, the Dutch had almost as many names as the French, the favourites being: *Beugelen, Caetse, Caetsen, Cache, Caetsspel, Destuit, Kaatsen, Kache, Kaetspel, Ketsen, Kaetsere, Parkspel, Staitu, Steute* and *Stotu*.

Just behind them we have the Germans coming in with names like: *Katzenspil, Teneyzen, Tenni, Kas, Katt, Keats, Ballenspiel* and *Tenne*.

The Scottish had their own variants as well, including: *Cachpuyll, Cachepuyle, Caich* and *Caiche*.

In the Far East we have tennis-like ball games called *Savlajan, Chigan* and *Tchaugan*.

In England there is evidence that we used several of the French, German and Dutch names for many years, as well as creating a few of our own, such as: *Tenetz, Teneys, Tennesse, Tennikoits, Tens, Pawne, Paune, Tenese, Paulme, Palmplys, Lawn Tennis, Real Tennis, Court Tennis, Royal Tennis* and, of course, Major Wingfield's very own *Sphairistikè*.

The Mesoamericans had various ball games that date back not just several hundred years but several thousand years, including *Nahautl, Ulama, Xochpala*, and my favourite one of all *Pitz*.

This must have been what John McEnroe was alluding to when he shouted at the umpires, *"You guys are the absolute Pitz of the world!"* Maybe the umpires wouldn't have penalised Mac so severely, if only they'd realised that he wasn't insulting them at all, he was merely complimenting them by acknowledging their historical lineage to the ancient game!

John, I hope the cheque is in the post!

TENNIS INVENTS ITSELF – TWICE!

So, as you can see from the previous chapter, there have been many variations of the game with a plethora of different names. So how did we end up with the one we now use? As ever with tennis, there is no shortage of theories, so let's look at some of the top contenders.

The Arabic culture often claims the city Tinnis is the original source of the name, mainly because the name was sometimes spelt as Tennis. There are also some early images of ball games painted on the walls at several Egyptian sites, along with some rubber balls in a sarcophagus in a royal catacomb, but this remains the sole evidence for the claim, and few historians outside of Egypt credit Tinnis as the source of the name.

There is also a place in France called Tennois where tennis was avidly played and whose residents occasionally pop out from behind their baguettes to lay claim to being the originators. Locals from another French town, Tamis, also occasionally break from quaffing Beaujolais long enough to proclaim that their town may be the source. The claim is mainly based on phonetics, but Tamis actually has some added weight when you consider that the word also means *sieve*, which was what tennis players occasionally used in the Middle Ages to start the serve with if no roof was around to serve from. But again, few historians are prepared to nail their flags to the stick with either of these. Some historians are prepared to pin their pennant to the pole with claims that it derives simply from the word *ten*, as early forms of the game like *Longue paume* were often played in the street with ten players. And although the doubters point out that the French would have been unlikely to adopt an English word for their game, some still argue that the way language evolves would make it possible. But, much like a Norwegian tune at the Eurovision Song Contest, historians usually dismiss this with *nul points*.

Other equally learned academics have also presented a theory that the term tennis ironically comes from the game of Fives. And there is some corroborative evidence to substantiate this. Apart from the fact that Fives doesn't use a net to divide the territory, many of its earliest incarnations were almost exactly the same as tennis. For instance, it was often played with more than the standard two people we associate it with today. Usually it was played with five people on each team, giving a total of ten, so to distinguish this game from Fives it became known as Tens.

This "ten man game of Fives" theory for tennis is later supported in literature when, in 1591, Queen Elizabeth is recorded as being a guest of the Earl of Hertford at Elvetham Manor in Hampshire. Letters record her majesty being entertained by:

> *"after dinner, about three o'clock, ten of his lordship's servants, in a square greene court before her majesties windowe, did hang up lines, squaring out the forme of a tennis-court, and making a cross line in the middle; in this square they (being stript out of their dublets) played five to five with hand-ball at bord and cord as they tearme it, to the great liking of her highness."*

This is further borne out by the fact that in Tudor times the spelling of the word ten is recorded as having many variants including: *Tenes, Tennes, Teneis, Tenice, Tennice, Tenys, Tynes, Tenneis, Tenyse, Tenice, Tennies* or *Tennis*. All of these early spellings of ten exactly mirror the various spellings given to the word tennis at some point as well, so it is certainly a tempting theory.

The theory never gained any serious traction with scholars though, which is a shame because it would be nice to be able to mathematically prove, once and for all, what you and I already know, that Tennis is twice as good as Fives!

As we've seen, the most commonly accepted view amongst modern academia is that Lawn Tennis originates from the game of

Real Tennis via *Jeu de paume*, from France around the 11th or 12th century, whilst at the same time merging with a similarly styled ball game played by French monks in the enclosed courtyards of the monasteries.

The majority of historians today tend to favour the theory that tennis comes from the French word *"Tenez!"*, the imperative form of the verb *"tenir"*, meaning *"to hold, receive, take"*. It was thought that the monks would yell *"Tenez!"*, warning them to *"get ready"* or *"prepare for this"* just before they served the ball, in order to alert their opponent that the next point was about to begin.

Other translations have come to a similar conclusion but with a slight variation in that the monks called the word *"hold"* as they held up the ball in front of them, to show their opponents that they were about to serve and start the next point. This is an even more tantalising translation, as the word *"hold"* in Old French is *"Tenys"*, which was a name commonly associated with the early game in France.

Further credence can be added to this argument as the custom of calling out a warning just before serving is still exhibited today in Rackets and Real Tennis. During a match many players, and spectators alike, often yell out *"Serve up!"* at the start of a new point. Some of the more seasoned players prefer to tap their racket against the side wall to alert their opponent that they are about to serve and start the next point.

This theory gains even more momentum when you also consider that tennis was played mainly for money in those days, and so rakish shysters might attempt a sneaky serve while their opponent wasn't quite ready in order to win a quick point to try and secure the wager more easily.

To eliminate this fraudulent chicanery, players were instructed to call out *"tenez"* to signal to the opponent, and to the Marker, that the server was about to serve and that a new point was about to begin.

Indeed remnants of that tradition survive in today's modern

game. If you watch carefully in the professional game, every time new balls are allocated to the court, the player who is about to serve with them will alert his opponent by holding up the new balls and won't proceed to serve until their opponent has acknowledged it.

In fact it's a tradition that is still to be found in games all over the world, especially ones that owe their lineage to tennis, or have historically been played for money. In many of the French rackets games there is still a call of *"A vous, ball"*. Or *"Nous"*. In Italy, the cry of *"Eccola!"* is often called, or *"Juego"* in Spain. Other sports, like golf, still alert the players ahead with cries of *"Fore!"* and in archery *"Vite!"* to forewarn others of your impending shot. Even in the more sedentary game of chess it's not just polite, but essential, to alert your opponent that you are in a position to attack their king, with a call of *"Check"*.

All of these traditions are believed to have evolved because of betting and to prevent any dastardly charlatan type gyp artist from unfairly cheating you out of your hard-earned wager.

Lastly, and perhaps most conclusively, the oldest known appearance of the word tennis dates back to 1324, when it was mentioned by an Italian writer Donato Velluti. Velluti was writing about 500 French soldiers who had descended into Italy from north of the Alps and singles one of them out, saying: *"He played all day with them at ball, and this is the first time in these parts that anyone is playing at tenes."*

In England the first written mention of the actual word tennis dates back to 1399 in John Gower's ballad to King Henry IV, with his line, *"... of the tenetz to winne or lese a chace"*. *Tenetz* then is the earliest recorded form of spelling for the word tennis ever found in English literature, which seems to confirm the idea that *tenez* is indeed its likely origin.

TENNIS INVENTS MOSQUITO REPELLENT

The origins of the Japanese game *Hanetsuki* are as murky as those of tennis itself. Most historians concur that the game probably originated as a ceremonial ritual used as a visual enhancement in religious festivals. Archaeological evidence shows that the ball, or shuttlecock, they used was made to resemble the head of a brightly coloured dragonfly and would often have elaborate tails painted onto the shuttlecock. This would have the triple effect of stability, prolonging the flight and mimicking the dragonfly.

However, there is a train of thought that believes that the design and function of the shuttlecock was not entirely decorative and could have had a much more practical reason.

In Japan the dragonfly is a natural predator of the mosquito and is used as a deterrent, so when the shuttlecock was struck back and forth, it mimicked a dragonfly in flight, thus scaring off any pesky mozzies who fancied nipping a Nipponese dignitary. Therefore, the ritual served as being both ceremonial in its beauty and practical by providing a natural protection from mosquito bites to all the gathered luminaries.

A very clever, safe, natural and eco-friendly insect repellent! So next time you travel abroad, forget the Deet, just pack a small box set of *Hanetsuki*.

HOW TENNIS INVENTED FIREWORKS

Intriguingly around this same time period, there's also evidence of a similar game played by the Zuni tribes, who were part of the Puebloan people, an early Native American tribe that can be traced back at least 1,300 years, possibly more.

The Zuni game is called *Pokean* and used a ball similar to that of the modern-day shuttlecock, only it was made from corn husks and fitted with feathers to give it flight. The idea of *Pokean* was to hit the shuttlecock high into the air to keep it in flight for as long as possible.

The Zuni tribe is thought to be the ancient ancestors of the Anasazi, which means *Ancient Ones*. The Anasazi, one of the oldest Native American peoples who can be traced back 3,500 years, had a virtually identical game called *Kwaitusiwikut* that was also played with the hand and used a similarly styled shuttlecock to the Zuni tribe.

It's believed that *Kwaitusiwikut* was not just a recreational game. The shuttlecocks were decked out in brightly coloured feathers and reserved for special occasions. The shuttlecocks are thought to have served as a bright backdrop, thrown into the air by dancers as part of a ritual during celebratory feasts and religious festivals with great prestige bestowed on the most beautiful shuttlecock and cheers and honours to those who could throw the beautifully painted adornments the furthest and highest.

So they would have been decorative extravaganzas to light up the sky and fill it with vibrant colours to commemorate important occasions, in exactly the same way that we use fireworks today.

TENNIS INVENTS RUBBER

Although Charles Goodyear is often credited with inventing rubber in 1844, it was actually only the process of manufacturing vulcanised rubber that he perfected. In reality, the Ancient Mesoamericans were the first people to discover the merits of the rubber tree and put it to good use. When I say "put it to good use" I mean to play tennis with, naturally, and they did this about 3,500 years earlier than Mr Goodyear.

The Ancient Mesoamericans found many different uses for rubber. For example, they used it to create spectacular fireballs for sacrificial offerings, also to mould various figurines for significant burial ceremonies, to fashion face masks for religious rituals, but most importantly, of course, for ancient ball games in an early derivative of tennis.

The game was probably more like *Jeu de paume* or *Palla* in its execution, a version of which is still played in South America today called *Ulama*. Interestingly, this is thought to be the first tennis-like ball game that used a dividing line across the middle, which acted as a kind of early precursor to the net we use today.

One possible candidate for the birthplace of the *Ulama* ball game is in the lowlands of the Soconusco coast along the Pacific Ocean. It was here, at Paso de la Amada, that archaeologists have found what they believe to be the oldest ball court ever discovered, dating back nearly three and half thousand years to approximately 1400 BC. Since then many more such ball courts have been unearthed in South America, mostly from the Mayan and Aztec cultures.

The Ancient Mesoamericans used to create these rubber balls by mixing the sap from the rubber tree with *Ipomoea Alba*, a flower more colloquially known as *Morning Glory*.

Several thousand years later, it's good to know that little has changed with some of our modern ball games and that we are still using rubbers with our own form of morning glory.

Hey, if smutty puns were good enough for Shakespeare, then they're good enough for me!

TENNIS INVENTS ASTROLOGY

The reason so many rubber balls have been found in Mesoamerican funeral marshes is because to them the sphere was not just a ball for games like tennis, but actually an important religious symbol used in ceremonial rituals. To them the ball was an earthly representation of the sun, a solar globe that they worshipped and prayed to. It was an icon of all life, and signified new birth, spring, youth, love and beauty.

For this reason, during the funeral of an important person, they would throw a ball through the air and into the boggy marshland. The ball would be painted bright yellow, or sometimes even set alight, and propelled into the sky. Its trajectory figuratively re-enacting the rising and setting of the sun, as well as symbolically commemorating life's journey, the rise and fall of the deceased person they were honouring.

The blazing fireball represented the spirit of the dead person burning brightly like the sun before being extinguished as it sunk into the soggy marsh, and, just like the sun, their spirit was expected to rise again from the marshland and ascend into the next world. This mimicking of celestial star movements and relating this to their own fates on earth is thought to be one of the earliest known examples of a culture that attached human significance to astronomical events, and is considered to be one of the earliest forms of astrology.

Of course, if they'd truly mastered the art of astrology, then there would have been no need to have that commemorative funeral sphere thrown into the marsh, as the dead man wouldn't have been killed hunting that wild boar that day, because he would have known in advance that Taurus had a new moon in Jupiter and it was a bad day to go hunting but a good day to stay in and relax with family.

These days, of course, we all know that astrology is a vital guide to help us make life-changing decisions. For instance, today is a bad day to tell the boss to go and stuff it and that it's best to wait until the planets align more favorably with Jupiter next month. But, with affectionate Venus on the rise, then today is a good day for you to rush out and buy another copy of that brilliant book *How Tennis Invented Everything* to give as a gift to a friend, which in turn will make you much more attractive to the opposite sex and bring you greater wealth, happiness and prosperity!

SECTION 9

THE LITERARY WORLD

Considering it's just a sport, you might be surprised to discover that tennis also played an integral part in shaping our literary playground, from the early metaphysical poets all the way to modern best sellers like Stig Larson, with a small diversion on the way to invent the Mafia, whilst stopping off only briefly to invent Shakespeare himself.

What? You don't believe me? *Read on MacDuff ...*

TENNIS INVENTS FIRST FICTIONAL CHARACTER TO PLAY THE GAME

Many famous fictional characters have played tennis over the years: Mickey Mouse, Homer Simpson and Snoopy the dog, to name a few. But, long before they were even a twinkle in their animator's eye, another ancient character had already stepped out of the pages of literature and onto the tennis court. Incredibly, this took place more than a thousand years ago, and so holds the title of being the world's first fictional character ever to have played tennis.

In the 6th century, Latin scholars and philosophers wrote about a man called *Apollonius, the King of Tyre*, a story later translated into English and, incidentally, often regarded as the first ever English novel.

Like Hercules, Apollonius is set various tasks, and one of them involves him having to solve a thorny riddle in the form of a poem.

The person who sets the riddle is a beautiful young woman who, knowing that Apollonius loves tennis, conceives a puzzle that refers to as many aspects of the game as she can think of, even down to the hair they used to stuff the balls with. In the poem she alludes to rallies, chases, courts and dedans. Dedans, in this case, meaning both the spectators courtside viewing area at the service end and, more salaciously, also its literal meaning of *"within"*.

But as the beautiful young maiden sets the riddle in the first person, then there is also plenty of added spice and sexual ambiguity to keep the hapless Apollonius guessing as to whether she is referring to tennis or herself. The saucy little minx!

Here's a translation of the naughty riddle that set Apollonius's pulse racing all those years ago …

> *Of hair, have I plenty*
> *Such as a cow or horse*

But no one can see it, as it's all dedans.
I am struck into the air to chase
And from hand to hand I go
As swiftly as the wind I fly
And just as hard to court.

The original riddle is in French and, if you want, you can find it in the Arabian Classic *A Thousand and One Nights*. My translation is not a completely literal one, my French is of a fairly schoolboy level, but it is translated in a way as to keep all the tennis allegories and sexual innuendoes alive.

That said, it is still a lot more accurate than, say, the guy who did the sign language translations at Nelson Mandela's memorial.

TENNIS INVENTS THE MAFIA

The Mafia is widely considered to have started in Sicily in the early 1800s and flourished under *"the relaxed and flexible interpretations of the law"* by the local Italian police force. In America, the Mafia didn't really gain public prominence until Prohibition in the 1920s when a healthy Italian immigration flux into New York realised the full potential of *"alternative means of supply and demand"*.

Some of the earliest references to the Mafia appear to stem from the Italian region of Calabria, in southern Italy, where they used to be called the *Camorra*, a sort of secret society in the neighbourhoods around Calabria and Naples. The earliest written reference is in 1861 when a Calabrian policeman refers to having trouble with the local *Camarristi*. These local secret societies, or *Cosche* as they were known, often operated outside of the law and are thought to be the origins of what we now know as the Mafia.

The term Mafia can be applied to various groups of Camorra but in actual fact the biggest and most treacherous is the *Ndràngheta* who are thought to have formed around the same time. The *Ndràngheta* are regarded as being so large and dangerous now that even film makers are advised against committing any of their stories to celluloid, or even make mention of them for fear of retribution. Blimey! Might ask my publisher to edit this bit out!

Recent estimates put forward by the FBI suggest that the *Ndràngheta* accounts for about 3% of the entire GDP of Italy and, if combined with the rest of Italy's Mafia operations. it could easily top 5%, and that's just what is known about and recorded so, in reality, the figure could easily be two or three times that amount.

The literary world, however, suggests that the Mafiosi may well have been operating for several hundred years before that in the murky world of gambling where tennis truly thrived, and it's through this lens that we view some of the earliest evidence of the Cosa Nostra at its most diabolical.

In John Webster's play *The White Devil*, written in 1609, we find some of the first literary evidence of that burgeoning organisation *La Cosche*, who sometimes referred to themselves simply as *The Family*, but there is nothing avuncular about this clan. They exhibit an entirely different set of family values to those recommended by church and state.

In Webster's play, the four Mafiosi conspire to murder the young Duke of Florence because he has double-crossed the powerful Medici family. The hoodlums need to carry out the killing in such a way that the law can't possibly trace it to them, whilst, at the same time, leaving everyone in no doubt that it was the Mafia that killed him. That way they would set an example of him, so that nobody else would dare cross them.

So, like all good Mafiosi, they first get to know their potential target to establish his weaknesses and his habits in order to assess where and when he might be at his most vulnerable.

Their initial findings reveal that the Duke is a very religious man and a regular church goer, so plenty of potential there. They also establish that he likes riding and is a proficient horseman, another very promising area; maybe they could contrive a terribly unfortunate hunting accident. But then they strike gold. They discover that not only is he a very vain man but also that he is having an adulterous affair, and they realise that this could be a rich a vein to explore, as maybe they could catch him off-guard with his mistress.

But then the true genius of the Cosa Nostra's creative malevolence is revealed when they discover that the young Duke has a passion for tennis, and that he gambles profusely on the outcome and is so competitive that he cannot bear to lose. They also find that he swears and curses like a trooper when he is not winning, and it is this that inspires their master assassination plan, a plot so devilishly delicious, so fiendishly foul, so insidiously sinister, that even the secret love-child of Arthur Conan Doyle and Agatha Christie couldn't have made it up.

The Mafiosi plot to poison the handle of the Duke's tennis racket while he is playing against an opponent who is far better than he is. And that is the truly evil part, because by ensuring that he is playing a superior opponent, they know that he will not only be losing, but also that he will swear a lot in the process. And that's the significant part which shows just how deranged these malignant Mafiosi geniuses were, because not only will he die, but he will die whilst swearing. The reason that this is noteworthy is because it means that he will be blaspheming at the time of his death and thus when he goes to *swim with the fishes*, he will be consigned to the eternal torment of Beelzebub's satanic basement and reside in Hell's burning inferno forever.

Ouch! You wouldn't want to mess with these guys, they make the Corleone family look like the Vienna School Boys' Choir.

TENNIS INVENTS THE GIRL WITH THE DRAGON TATTOO

It's more than 35 years since the legendary champion Bjorn Borg retired, yet he remains a huge name in tennis with a string of titles and records behind him that still stand the test of time.

Yet few people outside the tennis world will have heard of the man behind the legend, the enigmatic Sven Lennart Bergelin, who travelled everywhere with Borg. Bergelin was not just his coach, friend and mentor, he acted as Borg's manager, his physical trainer, dietician, psychologist, PA, agent, masseur and even strung his rackets for him.

At the time, many players on the tour questioned their relationship, regarding it as too one-sided and that Borg treated Bergelin more like a slave than a coach, friend or mentor. One night as a joke, Vitas Gerulaitis bet Borg $1,000 that Bergelin would even agree to kill someone if Borg ordered it. A disdainful Borg initially dismissed this as ridiculous but the other payers goaded him so much that Borg said he'd prove them all wrong by playing along with the prank and instructed Bergelin to take out one of his main rivals. Bergelin just nodded calmly in passive agreement, got up and headed towards the exit to carry out the task. Borg froze in horror for a moment before quickly sprinting after him and ordered him to stop.

After Borg's retirement, Bergelin disappeared from the tennis circuit and withdrew into the Stockholm BDSM underground movement and is said to be the inspiration behind Stieg Larsson's book *The Girl with the Dragon Tattoo*.

Bergelin was no Lisbeth Salander, she murdered on command several times, but Borg was certainly playing with fire the night he kicked that particular hornet's nest.

TENNIS INVENTS ALLEGORICAL POETRY METAPHORS

Cor, blimey! What?

Yes, I've really pushed the literary boat out on this one. In fact it's not so much a boat, more a ship of Titanic proportions, indeed you may well want to conclude that this is a theory worthy of a fate similar to that of the infamous liner. But, before you call fault on my lofty rhetoric, give me time enough to explain the point further.

The Middle Ages loved its newly discovered art form, the allegory, and the popularity of tennis meant that it was often used as the metaphor to hang this new-found literary device upon. In Wilhelm Verlag's industrious tome, *The Cultural History of Tennis*, published almost 40 years ago, and lovingly translated by Heiner Gillmeister, he gives us numerous examples.

In 1439, Charles d'Orléans, infamous prisoner from the Battle of Agincourt and the last of the courtly poets, uses the fact that he's turning 45, also the crucial match point figure in tennis, as the focus of his mid-life crisis point in real life. He uses his poem to play a metaphorical doubles match pitching Hope and Fortune against Old Age and Worry, playing for a very high wager – life itself.

In 1539, Guillaume de la Perrière similarly berates tennis players who try to play it safe and let the balls bounce, and writes to suggest that there is greater reward for the player who takes risks and storms to the net for a volley. In modern terms, that philosophy has certainly survived through to today in the form of *"Fortune favours the brave"* and has inveigled itself into the tennis world, especially when playing doubles, as many tennis coaches like to promote this philosophy with the phrase *"First in, wins"*.

Guillaume de la Perrière obviously enjoyed the game as he uses another tennis allegory in a second poem to illustrate the dangers of mocking your opponent before your serve because it may come back at you twice as fast. In real life, this philosophy still survives today, with phrases like *"He can serve it up, but he can't take it"*. Or, more commonly, *"If you can't stand the heat, get out of the kitchen"*

The metaphors come thick and fast after that. Chabot in 1557, Beacham in 1612 and Withers in 1613, all using tennis as their preferred allegorical reference and all going for similar themes of playing against the gods and being *"forced fall"* and *"strucken to the ground … with might redoubled, mountes highest of all"*, and *"smite us to the ground … then up to heav'n we shall rebound"*.

Francis Quarles also employs tennis in his 1632 poem *"Divine Fancies"*, which, although it sounds like the kind of delectable cake you might be served at Fortnum & Mason with an aromatic cup of Earl Grey, it is actually a deliciously dark verse where God and Satan play a game of tennis where the winner gets his soul.

TENNIS INVENTS SHAKESPEARE

I'm sure you have heard many compelling arguments, from drunken bar flies to literary scholars who all have their own theories, to suggest that Shakespeare was not in fact the author of the great classics we know and love today.

Many of these scholars have put forward varying notions that support a multitude of candidates, ranging from Christopher Marlowe, Francis Bacon, Ben Jonson and Edmund Spenser through to Mary Queen of Scots, the Pope, Uncle Tom Cobley and all. There's probably even a large online contingent that voted in favour of naming the real author of all Shakespeare's plays as Beardy McBeardface.

But, amongst all the jetsam and flotsam, there is one candidate who is cited more often than anyone else as the true writer behind the works of Shakespeare, and he is Edward de Vere, the 17th Earl of Oxford.

There are several books on the matter, the most authoritative one is a book called *The Great Shakespeare Hoax* written by Randall Barron, who quotes extensively from another scholar, the rather unfortunately named John Thomas Looney, who, in turn, uses many arguments put forward in Frank Harris's book *The Man Shakespeare*. All of whom cite some compelling arguments that De Vere is by far the strongest candidate to have been the true author of Shakespeare's plays.

But the real clincher in this argument, the vital point that all the historians agree on, is an intriguing one, and one that really tips it in De Vere's favour. It is the one thing that even the most outlandish Shakespearean conspiracists can agree on and it is what has become known in academic circles as *The Tennis Court Incident*.

But before I go into the details of that particular incident, let me set the scene by presenting a few of the background facts that have led these intellectuals to believe that De Vere was the true author of the bard's plays.

The big question mark that has always hung over Shakespeare is how his father, an impoverished and several-times bankrupted glove maker, a man who slipped in and out prison frequently, could have afforded to educate his son to command the English language to a level of unparalleled beauty and heightened elegance that was unrivalled then and has remained so ever since. His works, they conclude, must have been written by a highly educated university graduate or at least someone with a collegiate level of English. Shakespeare had neither. De Vere had both.

The writing suggests that the author was certainly a man of worldly travel and one who obviously had good royal connections or, at the very least, extensive acquaintances at Queen Elizabeth's court and knowledge of the inner workings of Royal life. Shakespeare had neither. De Vere had both.

Any man who wrote with such astounding wit and genius would surely have been revered amongst his contemporaries and famed not just throughout London but the whole land, both during his lifetime and long after his death. Shakespeare was not celebrated at all in his lifetime and strangest of all there was no mention made of his death in any circles at all until several centuries afterwards. On the other hand, De Vere's writings were celebrated throughout his life and much commemorated at his death.

To compound the mystery further, there seem to be hardly any plays or poems that bear the De Vere name. This is doubly odd as he was much acclaimed as a writer, so where is all the material he wrote that would justify the praise accredited to him in his lifetime? Perhaps, if we dig a little deeper into the culture of the time, then there may well be a very logical explanation for this conundrum.

In Elizabethan times, a theatrical life was not considered a worthy profession of a well-to-do gentleman, and so playwrights of noble birth would often use a pseudonym to protect their aristocratic reputation. This is something that De Vere was renowned for doing and may well explain why so few works bear his actual name.

Barron's book proposes that the style of writing and tone displayed throughout the plays and poems suggest that the author must have been ambivalent about both women and Catholicism. Shakespeare had no reason to be either. De Vere had good reason to be both.

Literary critics of the period cited De Vere as one of the greatest Elizabethan poets and singled him out as being one the best playwrights for comedy in the entire land. If he did write so many comedies and great poems, what became of them? The answer, they conclude, was that De Vere's plays did survive, it's just that he used the name of Shakespeare as his nom de plume.

Several other circumstantial pieces of evidence also back this theory. They show that De Vere held shares and had financial interests linking him to many of the most popular theatres. On top of that, the theatres that he had direct monetary interests in, curiously seemed to favour plays written by a certain Mr Shakespeare over and above any other author.

Also, as the reigning Earl of Oxford, De Vere supported and sponsored a group of actors known as "Oxford's Men", for whom he was definitely known to have written plays with, and alongside whom he even occasionally acted, but again using yet more aliases to protect his nobleman status, proving once more that he was a man who had an enormous proclivity for writing, acting and using pseudonyms.

Another curiosity, and one that truly whets the appetite of the De Vere supporters, is a literary one with a much more high-toned academic leaning. *"Venus and Adonis"* was one of Shakespeare's most famous poems, but it was written in an extremely unusual way, using a rarely seen form of stanza – the six-lined iambic pentameter. A style so unique that only one other poet of his era was ever known to have used it – De Vere himself.

Adding further grist to the mill is the fact that there are also some references that may have been just coincidences, but were far more likely to have been in-jokes made by his close friends who were teasing De Vere and letting him know that they were in on his little secret. For instance, there is record of him being greeted in the Royal Court with unusual toasts, the most famous example being *"Thy countenance shakes a spear, sir"*. The naysayers claim that this could just have been a greeting admiring De Vere's jousting skills, but it certainly seems strange, especially as De Vere was not known to joust and the fact that such greetings were recorded on more than one occasion.

Other references were more bawdy and lewd, as was the fashion of the time, and revolved around various *double-entendres* alluding to willy jokes about the name that De Vere had chosen as his first name, William, and usually alluding to size. Some have dismissed these as just coincidence again, but as any good detective will tell you, they don't like coincidences, and they recurred rather too often.

So, if De Vere did use William Shakespeare as his pseudonym, are there any clues as to why he may have chosen that particular name? Well, yes, one very big one, if you'll excuse the continuation of the nob gag theme. One of the biggest clues could be on the Earl's family crest as it depicts a lion brandishing a spear. Or, to put it another way, a lion that *shakes a spear*.

What about his elected first name? Well, William could have just been a random choice but a closer inspection of the family lineage may reveal some clues there too. De Vere owed all of his inherited wealth to a distant relative they were linked with, one of the most famous names in all England, in fact one of the most revered names in British history, William the Conqueror. De Vere's ancestor Aubrey De Vere was William the Conqueror's Commander-in-Chief, and it was he who had planned the entire invasion of Britain that handed William the crown and made him king of all England. For that success, De Vere was richly rewarded and handed vast swathes of the country to which the De Vere's owe their fortune. It was a lineage that the family was extremely proud of, and one they often made reference to, even boasted of, some say, a little too often.

Which brings us to the final piece of the jigsaw, the real clincher, a scene stealer worthy of any Shakespeare finale, the infamous *Tennis Court Incident*. This refers to a particular game of tennis in 1579 where De Vere pulls rank on the lowly Philip Sydney and throws him off the tennis court in the middle of a game, just because he wants to get on and play.

This much referenced incident is of huge academic interest, not just because it's a rare, written reference to the game of tennis, but also because it positively links De Vere to the game, proving him to be a very keen player. So enthusiastic as to be darn right rude and offensive to his associates in order to get a game.

But the scholars also argue that there is another, more pertinent, reason as well. The significance being that Shakespeare makes six major references to the game of tennis in his works and makes several other metaphors that could also allude to the game. That is more than he gives any other sport or game in all his writings.

They are not just passing references either, they are all obviously written by someone with a deep knowledge of and affection for the game, suggesting that this person must have played it from a very young age. We know De Vere played a great deal, and there is even record of him being presented with a racket aged just two years old. So we have conclusive proof that he was an ardent player and we know he lived close to several courts.

Shakespeare, on the other hand, had no known connections to tennis, had no access to any courts growing up, didn't live close to any courts in later life, and there were no courts in Stratford either.

The best way to get access to a court was through a royal connection. Shakespeare was not born into any such connections. De Vere had all these connections throughout his life from the day he was born.

To counter this argument, some intellectuals claim that De Vere may have died before the last two Shakespeare plays were published, but the De Vere advocates dismiss these claims as completely invalid as a publishing date in those days was not a reliable date of authorship. For example, we know that several of Shakespeare's plays were performed many years before they were actually published.

As ever, the arguments rage on through the centuries, but *The Tennis Court Incident* is what sways it for many of the scholars who line up to support Edward De Vere, the 17th Earl of Oxford, as the real bard.

But then, maybe the great man left us a few clues, when he said, *"One man in his time plays many parts … conceal me what I am, and be my aid, for such disguise as haply shall become the form of my intent"*.

SECTION 10

FILM, TV AND THEATRE

There have been hundreds of films that feature tennis, too many to list but here is a quick snapshot of some of my favourite writers and directors who have shown their love for the game by paying homage to it through their work.

William Shakespeare, Walt Disney, Alfred Hitchcock, Woody Allen, Jaques Tati, George Cuckor, Joseph Losey, Powell and Pressburger, Chaucer and even The Simpsons, to name but a few, but let's start with that most quintessential of Englishman, the spy master general himself ...

TENNIS INVENTS JAMES BOND

Where better to kick off our film section than with one of the greatest screen heroes of all time. Now, I understand that Bond aficionados will be appalled by the suggestion that tennis invented James Bond and would shoot down the whole villainous idea with a volley of bloody bullets.

Tennis fans, on the other hand, might like to dream a little bigger, because as every film fan knows, shooting Bond isn't always enough to kill him off. So, although the concept is in trouble, strapped to a table with a death laser beam slowly approaching, as we all know, in Bond's world being left for dead is not the same as being dead.

Going back to that infamous laser scene from *Goldfinger*, Bond manages to bluff his way out of it by pretending to know all about Goldfinger's evil plan, when really all he knows is its code name that he just happened to overhear. And, deliciously for us, this leads us neatly into our first hint of a tennis reference because the code name used was *"Operation Grand Slam"*.

OK, so our theory has now escaped imminent death, so let's report back to HQ, flirt a bit with Moneypenny, have a quick chat with M, pick up a few gadgets from Q, fire up the Aston Martin and get back to our assignment – to search out just how big a part tennis may have played in the creation of the world's most famous spy.

So, after our near-death opening sequence, let's start in true Bond style with a sweeping landscape to set the scene before building to a thrilling showdown at the end. Most film fans know that Ian Fleming appropriated the name James Bond from an American ornithologist called James Bond, but what they might not know is that without tennis, England's premier spy might have been called something completely different.

You see, had it not been for tennis, Bond, the ornithologist, may never have written *A Field Guide to the Birds of the West Indies* at all.

The Philadelphia-born Bond moved to England as a boy and was sent to Harrow, an expensive private school in England, where he was said to have first played the noble game. He later studied at Cambridge University, where he was also recorded as being an enthusiastic exponent of the game. After graduating, he moved back to Philadelphia to work for a bank, but it was a job that he hated, so when a tennis playing friend offered him a place on a forthcoming expedition to the Amazon run by the Academy of Natural Sciences, Bond jumped at the chance. He did so well on the exhibition that the academy offered him a permanent job. He quickly became quite an authority and rose to become Curator of Ornithology, specialising in birds of the Caribbean, which culminated in the now legendary book *A Field Guide to the Birds of the West Indies* by James Bond.

Ian Fleming, who was living in Jamaica at the time, was a keen bird watcher and freely admits he stole the name of his lead character from the author. He later wrote to the ornithologist's wife, Mary Bond, apologising for his blatant act of embezzlement, and explained his reasons by saying,

> *"I wanted the simplest, dullest, plainest-sounding name I could find, and 'James Bond' was much better than something more interesting, like 'Peregrine Carruthers'. Exotic things would happen to and around Bond, but he would be a neutral figure — an anonymous, blunt instrument wielded by a government department."*

I'm sure Mary Bond felt much better after hearing Fleming's apology, what wife wouldn't be cheered up by hearing their husband described as a neutral, plain sounding, anonymous, simple, dull, blunt instrument! Like his infamous creation, empathy was obviously not one of Fleming's greatest traits.

And all brought together through a mutual love of tennis, so in that respect we must consider ourselves lucky that Fleming was a bird enthusiast rather than a science fiction fan, or England's most famous spymaster may well have been called Philip K. Dick.

"The name's Dick. Phil Dick."

Doesn't have quite the same ring to it.

Our second tennis connection to Bond is a little more tenuous, but may not be any less important to the genre. For instance, not many people realise that the name of Ian Fleming's first ever Bond girl, Vesper Lynd, from *Casino Royale*, was actually named after a cocktail he had been given in a Jamaican tennis club. In the novel, the character explains that she was born *"on a very stormy evening"*, and that her parents named her *"Vesper"*, which is Latin for *"evening"*.

In case you're curious, a Vesper Martini is a mix of iced rum, fruit and exotic local herbs, and shot to fame shortly after the novel's publication. Bond's usual cocktail of choice, a martini, containing both gin and vodka, with a little shot of Kina Lillet instead of dry vermouth, garnished with a common olive instead of the more traditional lemon peel.

The Vesper Martini is described in the book as *"extremely strong, very cold and incredibly well put together, although it leaves you with a slightly bitter aftertaste"*. A description often perceived by fans to be an insight into the character of Vesper Lynd herself.

It was the Vesper Martini that also gave rise to the famous *"shaken, not stirred"* catchphrase so immortalised by Sean Connery in the film *Goldfinger*.

Of course, true doyens of the martini will know that Connery changed the line. It was originally *"thrown, not stirred"*, but it was felt that movie-goers wouldn't understand the terminology used by professional mixologists and so the line was changed and a movie legend was born.

In 1993, journalist Don McCormick claimed that Fleming based his Vesper spy character on a real life Polish agent called Krystyna Skarbek, but this remains purely apocryphal as, so far, no one from the Polish Secret Service has confirmed the claim.

The tennis connection is further strengthened when you know that all the James Bond stories were written at Goldeneye, the house Fleming built on Jamaica's north coast and where he would spend several months each year writing. The house has its own tennis court on the grounds and who's to say that Fleming didn't come up with a few ace plots, sipping on an ice cool Vesper, watching the odd ball thunder around the tennis courts?

But Fleming often let slip his love of tennis through his writing. In *Diamonds Are Forever*, he uses a tennis analogy by coming up with one of his most murderous sporting metaphors. In the book, Bond was being hunted by six assassins. As Bond disposes of the last one, Fleming comes up with the dismissive phrase, *"Hmm, six corpses to love"*.

A more blatant tennis connection to Bond features in the 1983 film *Octopussy*, in which the Indian tennis player, Vijay Amritraj, plays an MI6 agent who goes undercover as a tennis player. This culminates in the infamous scene where Vijay famously swats away various villains with his racket during a car chase through a small street market. Vijay's forehand always was a lethal weapon.

Tennis also takes centre stage in a more recent Bond book, this one commissioned by the late Ian Fleming estate and written by Sebastian Faulks, incidentally a fine player himself. Entitled *Devil May Care*, Bond takes to the tennis court for his first meeting with the villainous Dr Julius Gorner, an evil pharmaceutical tycoon. Bond gambles about £15,000 worth of MI6 money on the outcome of the game.

Tch! What would Q say?!

Well, Q would probably say what he always says, *"Pay attention,*

007", because this is where it gets a bit complicated. It could be that Bond's most loyal and beloved sidekick, his Aston Martin, also owes its famous starring role to tennis.

Fans of Ian Fleming's original books would probably remember that in the first few books Bond actually drove a more sedate Bentley. But all that was about to change thanks to tennis.

While Fleming was staying at his house on the Kent coast, he spotted a rather sporty looking number parked in his neighbour's drive. It was the very latest addition to Aston Martin's family, the DB 2/4 Mk I Vantage, and Fleming couldn't resist moseying on down to take a peek.

Now, some say the owner of the car was a tennis friend of Fleming's neighbour, while others say he was the son of Fleming's former boss at MI6, who is also thought to have been the inspiration for M. Either way, the legendary British roadster parked tantalisingly outside belonged to the delightfully named Honorable Squadron Leader Phillip Ingram Cunliffe-Lister, a well-known rally driver of the time, who was only too delighted to show the young writer his latest set of wheels.

Lister had had several modifications made to the car. Apart from the beefed-up engine, there were several hidden features and plenty of juicy gadgets that must have caught the curious author's eye, some of which you may recognise.

For instance, Lister's Aston had extra thick, reinforced steel bumpers that jutted out more to protect its tyres from any rival cars, which in those days often bumped into each other in the rough and tumble of the race. But when Fleming saw the car's distinctive triple-spiked wheel hubs, he didn't just steal the idea, he took it one stage further, giving Bond's car the ability to extend the spikes to shred the tyres of any enemy agents who came too close.

Lister had also modified the interior adding several extra buttons and gizmos as navigational aids when he was rallying. For instance, one of the Aston's dials had been converted into a Halda Speedpilot Screen, which was an early computer used by rally drivers of the day. This was a trick later replicated by Fleming in his novels when he converted one of the dials in Bond's car into a radar-tracking computer screen.

Fleming also saw that the centre console of Lister's Aston opened up to reveal a concealed locker – the perfect size and place to hide a Walter PPK, the legendary spy's handgun of choice.

Lister then showed Fleming another little gem. Under the armrest was another hidden compartment with various other switches and buttons that Lister had installed to house other racing gizmos, which Fleming then repurposed to give Bond all his infamous contraptions such as the bullet-proof pop-up rear screen, the instant oil slick, hidden machine guns and the giant smoke screen.

Fleming must have been in Little Boy Heaven at this stage because Lister was practically writing his next book. Lister's Aston also had a specially converted overdrive button set under a flap on top of the gear stick which, by the time Fleming has finished with it, becomes perhaps the most notorious feature of them all, the infamous ejector seat button immortalised in both book and film.

This was all the convincing Fleming needed, Commander Bond's sedate Bentley was returned to Q and Bond was re-issued with an Aston Martin DB3 with all the aforementioned custom-made features finding their way into Fleming's next book, *Goldfinger*. Now, I know what you're thinking, it was a DB5, not a DB3 that is the iconic Bond car, and yes, you're right, but the difference in time from the book being written and the film coming out, meant that Bond could have the newer, faster, sexier DB5.

This is a partnership that has endured for over 60 years, making it one of the longest standing pieces of product placement in film history. And, to hit that home, the DB5 that Sean Connery drove in 1964's *Goldfinger* sold for £4.6 million in 2010 and was recently valued at nearly three times that, a second vehicle that was only used in the promotional campaign, sold in 2019 for £5.2 million.

But if Bond and Aston have a long and historic lineage, then Bond's tennis connections have a pretty thorough pedigree as well. For instance, James Bond even married a tennis star. George Lazenby, who played Bond in *On Her Majesty's Secret Service*, was once married to legendary tennis champion Pam Shriver, although the marriage did end rather acrimoniously and their divorce was said to have been a long and hard fought five setter and there was definitely no tie-break in the final set either.

Bond's tennis associations don't end there. Did you know that the king of tennis, Roger Federer, once played the spy? The record 20-times Grand Slam champion slipped into his best Bond tux and shot off an array of secret weapon tennis balls as he played 009 in a Jura coffee commercial. Tennis fans were in double-oh heaven as Fed swapped Bond's famous *"shaken not stirred"* tag-line to suit the ad. Whilst leaning suavely on the bar, Fed orders a coffee, then pauses sardonically before adding, *"ground, not capsuled"*.

Our penultimate link connecting Bond to tennis makes us wonder if Fleming was a sore loser on the tennis courts. *The New York Times* reported that a baker in Manhattan was having a little fun with the Bond brand name by substituting the famous two zeros of the 007 with a picture of two of his tasty bagels in front of the number seven, but this didn't go down well with the producers. Possibly it brought up some painful memories from his past, maybe some distant memory of being handed out a double bagel thrashing on court, and it was just too much for our spymaster to bear. Whatever it was, the producer's legal team were quickly dispatched on their own secret mission and crushed the poor baker with a volley of lawsuits, forcing him to withdraw all his Bond-themed bagel promotions.

But I have saved the best for last, because if all that wasn't enough to convince you of the importance of tennis in the creation of the world's most iconic spy, then I leave you with one last solitary fact which may just persuade you. It's a fact so juicy that it could moisten the driest martini, because one of the earliest known names ever given to the game of tennis was in fact, *Jeu de bonde*.

All together now, in your best Connery impersonation …

"The game's Bonde, … Jeu de bonde."

I can practically hear the medieval lutes twanging out the stirring theme music before each game:

"Dundedun dun dun dun, dundedun dun dun dun: Dundedun dun dun dun, dundedun dun dun dun: De DON Do do do; Badap ba daa ba da, daa ba daa da deda daa; Badap ba daa ba da daa ba daa da deda daa."

All we need now is some villainous medieval tennis umpire who bears an uncanny resemblance to Donald Pleasence, stroking a fluffy white Persian cat as he sits by the side of the tennis court, greeting the players upon arrival in a strange Russian accent: *"Ah, Jeu de Bonde players, vee haf bin exschpecting you …!"*

Now, if all that hasn't left you feeling a little shaken, if not stirred, then perhaps this will. I lied. That wasn't the last piece of evidence at all. I double-crossed you. But in my defence, that's what any good agent would do. Besides, like any half-decent spy story, there's always one final twist, a tiny last morsel of evidence that I have saved until the very end. And to top it all, this is a fact that Ian Fleming also knew well and used to such brilliant effect that it has gone on to become part of espionage folklore.

You may recall in the chapter on *Tennis Invents the Secret Service* that I talked briefly about John Dee, one of Elizabeth I's favourite spies who masqueraded as a tennis player both here and abroad whilst secretly gathering information for her. What I omitted to tell you, was one very tantalising detail. In his letters to the Queen, Dee signed off with a secret insignia that only he and the Queen knew, so that when the Queen saw it, she would know that the letter was genuine and from him. Dee's secret moniker, the code that he used to sign off all his covert letters to Her Majesty Queen Elizabeth I way back in the 16th century, was *"007"*.

Cue the music …

TENNIS INVENTS THE WORLD'S MOST FAMOUS FILM QUOTE

Mae West is often credited with one of the most famous film quotes of all time when she purred: *"Is that a gun in your pocket or are you just pleased to see me."* She was rumoured to have originally said it in the 1933 film *She Done Him Wrong* but censors had it cut out of the final edit for being far too saucy.

West certainly used the line a great deal in her stage and personal appearances and versions of the quote have appeared in many films ever since. But actually Mae West can't take credit for its origins, because, you guessed it, tennis invented it way before her.

In Shakespeare's *Henry IV, Part 2*, Prince Henry berates Poins for his salaciously sagging, peach-coloured stockings and questions Poins about a suspiciously large bulge in his undergarments with the immortal words, *"Keepest thou a racquet there?"* Pausing in true Mae West style before questioning if maybe Poins is just *"pleased to see him"*.

TENNIS INVENTS THE SILENT 'K'

While we are on the subject of famous film quotes, it gives me a good excuse to mention one of my favourites. In 2017, a new tennis star burst onto the scene in the shape of Karen Khachanov from Russia. The name perplexed commentators and spectators alike who were surprised when they learned that Karen was actually a man. I can only assume that Karen's father was a country music fan and loved Johnny Cash's 1966 hit *"A Boy Named Sue"* where the father purposefully gives his son a girl's name knowing that he'd have to get tough or die.

If that was Khachanov senior's philosophy, then it seems to have worked, because just like Sue, Karen grew up fast and he grew up mean, his serve got hard and his wits got keen, and at six foot six this giant of a man, regularly serves over 130 mph and punches his forehand with equally destructive speeds. Good job, Pa!

That said, it actually wasn't his first name that used to cause the commentators the most problems when he first appeared on the tennis circuit. It was his surname that flummoxed them because the K is completely silent. So Khachanov is actually pronounced 'Hatchenoff', which is a peculiarly English thing to do. Think of Knight, Know, Knife, Knee, Knit, Knock, Knead, Knap, Knot, Knuckle, and various other Knick-Knacks where the K is silent.

The real reason for mentioning the silent K is that it allows me to segue into the quote I mentioned at the start. Accounts of the meeting offer no record of the exact location in which it took place, so let's just imagine it was at a tennis party, or near a tennis court, so that I can at least pretend to include it with some sort of integrity.

It is, of course, the classic encounter between Margot Asquith, the aristocratic Lady Oxford, the wife of Anthony Asquith. Margot didn't appreciate the way a certain young actress was flirting blatantly with her husband, who also happened to be a film producer. The actress in question was the Hollywood blonde bombshell Jean Harlow. So when Harlow repeatedly kept pronouncing the T at the end of Margot's first name, Margot couldn't resist correcting her with this now legendary retort, *"My dear, it's pronounced Mar-go, the T is silent, as in Harlow"*.

Ouch! Game, Set and Match to Margot.

TENNIS INVENTS SUPERMAN

One of the earliest depictions of the game of tennis, is an illustrated medieval manuscript from about 1450 by Hesdin and Gonesse which is held in The British Library. It shows the game being played in the courtyard of some monastic cloisters, which many historians claim is the origin of the roofed galleries still featured in the traditional Real Tennis courts of today.

The player depicted is Scaevola who, intriguingly, is portrayed as playing against himself. He is watched from the galleries by Scipio and Laelius. These characters were actually the superheroes of their day as depicted by Cicero, who embodies them with the ideal qualities that all humans should aspire to, all of whom go on to become mythical characters of fiction.

On closer inspection of this historic manuscript, it clearly shines a light, not just on the look and dimensions of these early courts but it also shows the players wearing their underpants on the outside of their tights. I can't say for sure whether DC Comics based their own superheroes on these tennis-playing medieval ones, but it can't be a coincidence that both sets of superheroes wear their underpants on the outside of their tights. Which means that the great illustrators at DC Comics decided, quite correctly, that tennis players must be men of such superhuman strength, agility and mental fortitude, that it would be completely appropriate to design Superman's costume around this earlier 15th-century concept.

Anyone who has ever attended Comic Con will know that one of the perennial debates that goes on each year is who would win in a fight between Batman and Superman, which naturally begs the question that we now want to know: Who would win a game of tennis between Batman and Superman? Answers on a postcard please.

TENNIS INVENTS THE X FACTOR

While the Western world is quick to proclaim themselves the originators of tennis, compelling evidence suggests its roots could lie much further afield in the Far East or Asia and could date back to a time far earlier than we originally thought.

Its heritage could be traced back to ancient China, to the legendary Emperor Huang-Di, a man who has been credited with being the father of many things from cartography to medicine. Maybe tennis too should be added to Huang-Di's impressive credentials.

About two and a half thousand years ago, during the rather feline sounding Miao Dynasty, Huang-Di led an army of warriors who were renowned as the greatest soldiers of their time. The reason they were regarded as the best was because Huang-Di trained them longer, harder and with more discipline than anyone had ever done previously.

Among the many rigorous training regimes that Huang-Di imposed on his troops was a discipline called T'su-Chu, which many believe was a precursor to the game of tennis. Using something that was a sort of cross between a shuttlecock and a tennis ball, the exercise would begin with his troops forming a circle. The ball was struck in the air from one side of the circle to the other with the rule that it was not allowed to touch the ground.

Players were allowed to use both their hands and feet to keep the ball airborne, resembling a group of doubles players all practising their volleys with each other, or maybe like a giant version of keepie-uppie in football. T'su-Chu was initially conceived as a way of keeping the Emperor's soldiers fit and to sharpening their reflexes, in the same way as Judo and Karate, which were also devised for soldiers to mimic the actions they would need to wield their weapons in battle.

The rules of T'su-Chu were very simple, whoever was responsible for letting the ball drop to the ground was eliminated from the playing circle until the last soldier left was the winner and thus declared the fittest and the best and so rewarded by the Emperor.

But the exercise proved so popular that the soldiers were said to play it for fun, even when they were off duty and not officially training. When there were just a few players left, those on one side would tend to gang up on those on the other side and by the time you got down to four players it would look uncannily like a game of doubles today. Similarly, when there were just two left, it would bear a striking resemblance to a game of singles.

As other versions of the game began to evolve, the soldiers would form teams and play it over an obstacle, an early form of our modern net, and using rules probably similar to today's volleyball.

So, as tough as it may be for us westerners to swallow, Emperor Huang-Di may have laid down the foundations for just about every sport you can think of, from football to tennis with this single discipline. What is more, if there was a dispute as to who was responsible for the ball touching the ground then the players who had already been knocked out would vote on it, giving us another familiar format which is almost identical to just about every TV game show you can think of from *The X Factor*, through *Strictly Come Dancing*, to *The Great British Bake Off*, as in, the last person standing is the winner. Who wants to be the person who tells Simon Cowell that he stole all his game show formats from the game of tennis?

It's a *"no"* from me.

TENNIS INVENTS THE ANTIQUES ROADSHOW

If you're not from the UK then you may not be familiar with a TV programme called *The Antiques Roadshow*, in which members of the public are invited to bring in antiques and collectibles to have them authenticated and valued by various experts.

It's hard not to feel moved when you watch the stalwart owners put on a brave face over the soured expressions of disappointment in their eyes when they realise that their treasured family possession that they thought was worth thousands of pounds isn't worth as much as the chewing gum stuck to the soles of their shoes.

Equally, I love the ones who pretend not to care what it's worth, they say it's a family heirloom and has far too much sentimental value for them to sell, but when they hear it's worth £50,000 you can practically see the dribble running down the side of their chin and the pound signs whizzing round in their eyes like a cartoon slot machine as they envisage themselves on a sunny beach in the Maldives sipping cocktails from a freshly-hewn coconut.

So, imagine taking along an old can of tennis balls and being told they were worth about £100,000. That was the value of five such rubber balls that archaeologists uncovered from one of the sites known to have been occupied by the Ancient Mesoamericans, dating back to at least 1700 BC that are thought to have been used in ceremonial rituals and in ball games similar to tennis. The balls were found in a marshland at El Manati, along Mexico's Gulf Coast. The conditions in the marsh perfectly preserved the rubber balls, which are now kept in the Peabody Museum of Archaeology at Harvard University along with several other ancient figurines which were also found with them.

Now, I don't know about you, but I always feel a bit peeved having to shell out £7 for a new can of tennis balls that only ever last for a few hours. So paying £100,000 for a can of balls may initially seem a bit steep, but when you consider that they last for 3,500 years then the economics aren't as bad as you might think.

In fact, if I continued to play two or three times a week for the next 3,500 years, then that works out at only a few pennies for a can of balls for each match played. A real bargain compared with almost £4 million pounds I'd have to spend if I continue to pay £7 a can for the next 3,500 years.

Now, I know what you're thinking, there's a gaping flaw in my thought process here – that in 3,500 years' time I might not be playing quite as often as I did when I was three and half thousand years younger. Of course, I'm not an idiot, I've factored that into the equation by taking account of the fact that I'll be a little older and maybe not playing quite as often, but even so, when you counter that against inflation, then it works out that I'd still be saving several million quid.

TENNIS INVENTS THE THEATRE

Theatrical plays have almost certainly been around long before any official written evidence of tennis, so it is probably difficult to claim that tennis invented theatre. But you could argue that it did at least play a significant part in its development.

In the 1600s, Lisle's Tennis Court was a well-known venue for players to gather and play tennis. It was located just off Portugal Street by Lincoln's Inn in central London, and it was often transformed into a pop-up theatre or playhouse.

In those days, Real Tennis courts were ideal venues for visiting theatre troupes to stage their plays. The buildings themselves were long, with exceptionally high ceilings which were able to conceal scenery and props, and the courts would be surrounded with large viewing galleries and dedans with plenty of seating for spectators, making them absolutely ideal theatres.

The visiting troupe would only have to make a few minor adjustments to accommodate a play. The main one being the scenery, and so it was that the Lisle Tennis Court Theatre in London became the first public playhouse to solve this problem of how to change the scenery. Instead of curtains and unfolding backdrops they simply mounted it all on wheels, enabling it all to be easily moved around the court. This simple innovation proved so useful that it was quickly adopted on other courts as the troupe toured around the country. The concept proved so expedient to stage production that it became a standard feature of even purpose-built theatres from that day to this.

In purely tennis terms, and what other terms are there, it's interesting to note that back then actors were not called actors at all but players. Some would argue that quite a lot of acting continues to permeate the tennis court today, especially when players are on a losing streak. So, an unscrupulous player might try to buy time by pretending to need a bathroom break, or by feigning an injury in order to get the doctor out, all of which can take away the momentum from an opponent and change the course of a match back in their favour.

But I certainly wouldn't want to name names as to the kind of players who would use such dubious tactics. Suffice it say that the Joker was a popular character in the theatre in those days and the Djoker is still a very popular player today.

Alas, Lisle Theatre holds court to neither types of player today, the *"full of sound and fury"* of their life now but a walking shadow that struts and frets their hour upon the stage no more.

Ah, actually, I think I shall cease plagiarising that particular Shakespeare quote right there before it goes into the bit about this being a tale told by an idiot, signifying nothing. Damn cheek!

SECTION 11

THE MUSICAL CONNECTION

Now obviously, to the untrained eye, it would be difficult to spot any connection linking the music world to the game of tennis, unless you count my student days when I used my tennis racket to play air guitar to Lynyrd Skynyrd's *"Free Bird"*.

But, as you will be well aware by now, I have scraped more obscure barrels than that in the name of tennis archaeology, and so, as ever, I have managed to pluck a few tales from the musical spectrum of tennis for your delectation. And just as I began the Film Section with the world's greatest spy, it seems only right we honour the Music Section with the world's greatest band ...

TENNIS INVENTS THE BEATLES

When it comes to popular music, one has to start with the Beatles. But how on earth can tennis lay claim to inventing the Fab Four? Absurd as it sounds, tennis actually really did help launch the Beatles into the stratosphere of pop celebrity, the likes of which has never been seen before or since.

It was 1964 when the Beatles first landed in America, it's easy to forget that they were not the phenomenon that everyone thinks that they were. Sure, there were hundreds of screaming teenage girls waiting for them wherever they went, but there were dozens of singers and bands who had far bigger followings than this cute little mop-haired rock quartet from Liverpool. In fact, most of America had never heard of them and, bizarrely, the most famous Beatle, the one that the Americans most wanted to see, was Ringo. But all that was about to change, big time.

There was only one thing bigger than the Beatles; only one thing capable of changing them from cool British pop band to international singing sensations; only one thing with the power to turn four dudes with pudding bowl haircuts into modern media marvels around the globe – tennis.

When the Beatles' manager Brian Epstein first thought about looking for a venue for them to play in, the American management team suggested an unusual venue, Forest Hills, America's first tennis stadium and the birthplace of the US Tennis Open. Epstein initially rejected it. The idea of the Beatles performing in a tennis stadium was just too far-fetched, but he was soon convinced when he saw the kind of profits made from previous shows there, from various artists ranging from Barbara Streisand to Harry Belafonte and even Woody Allen. He signed them up.

The Beatles playing at Forest Hills is still regarded as one of the most memorable concerts in the stadium's history. Yes, Shea Stadium

189

was bigger in terms of numbers, and yes, the Ed Sullivan Show gave them wider exposure, but it was here in the citadel of tennis that proved to be a turning point.

Several incidents took place at Forest Hills that would change the Beatles forever – not just in terms of popularity, but also for their finances and for something quite unexpected, but crucial to their legacy, because Forest Hills proved a turning point for their style of music as well, both spiritually and soulfully.

Let me elaborate on each of those points. First of all, let's look at how it changed their finances. It was at Forest Hills that Brian Epstein first realised the full potential of the Beatles' merchandising power. It was while Epstein was sneaking around undercover, conducting covert meetings with his secret gay lover, that Epstein witnessed the true scale of all the illicit Beatles merchandising going on illegally around the tennis stadium and the surrounding streets. When he saw how the American fans were buying up everything and anything with a Beatles-related theme on it, he realised that he needed to take a stronger hold of this lucrative area of the business.

But it was also at this very same tennis stadium that is said to have transformed, not just their finances and their popularity, but also their music tastes and their recreational proclivities. For it is here that they were first introduced to pot by the freewheeling counter culturist himself – Bob Dylan.

This meeting with Dylan opened the Beatles' eyes to a whole new world and is credited with transforming them from a simple feel-good pop band to being far more complex and abstract lyricists.

In short, it turned them from naïve innocents into dope-smoking potheads expanding their minds and consciences to explore more socio-political themes and tap into deeper cultural subject matter, giving their work a far darker edge than anything they had previously written. A road which eventually led them to the Dalai Lama who encouraged them to explore their spirituality even further.

So now you know why Lucy was in the sky with diamonds; what made Lennon think he was a walrus; the reason Ringo was a day tripper on a yellow submarine; exactly where Paul's magical mystery tour took him; and why George's guitar gently weeps in strawberry fields forever. It was all because of that one innocent tennis gig where the Beatles discovered for themselves exactly what it was that Bob Dylan was blowing in the wind.

Suffice it to say that it was completely different to what Epstein was blowing in the back corridors of Forest Hills.

TENNIS INVENTS THE TAMBOURINE

Another curious missing link in the chains of tennis history may well be filled by the discovery of yet another early incarnation of tennis, a game called *Tambourin*.

Tambour was the name given to a frame made of two hoops with tightly woven strings, originally used for tapestries and embroidery. However, industrious tennis peeps found that the cross-stringing system used in these tapestry frames made a very useful racket, and one very similar to the rackets still used in the *Tambourin* game today.

Curiously, the term still lingers in today's Real Tennis courts where the rear wall is called the *Tambour*. A word that is likely to have stemmed from the Roman term *Tambour*, meaning *"fortification"*, normally for defensive purposes often to secure roads, gateways or other entrances.

This makes sense in terms of Real Tennis as the *Tambour* is something you have to defend vigorously. This also gains further traction when you consider that the old game is thought to have been played in monastic courtyards where you would also have had to defend the arches, gates or *Tambours* at each end.

Of course, if you add a leather hide to the strings of your *Tambour*, then it doesn't take much of a leap of the imagination to take us neatly to the musical instrument, the *tambourine*, and suddenly a whole new style of '60s hippy rock music that tennis can also lay claim to.

Groovy man.

TENNIS INVENTS CATGUT

Although it's rare for the average club player to string their rackets with catgut these days, many of the pros still use it because of the more natural feel and control it gives. And, over the years, a question you often hear asked is why the normally demure and feline loving tennis player chooses to ruthlessly mutilate cute little moggies just so that they can use their innards as strings for their rackets. Now seems like as good a moment as any to broach this delicate and somewhat disturbing subject.

So, is there some sort of cat stalking Jack the Ripper prowling around dark alleys and slaughtering unsuspecting kittens, gutting stray grimalkins and twisting their intestines into fine threads, just so we tennis players can tonk a ball about? Or is there a dark and seedy factory hidden in some remote outpost that is specifically breeding cute little kitty cats for some sort of furtive feline slaughter house?

Well, I am happy to report that neither gruesome scenario is true. None of our lovely, fluffy, furry friends are being, or ever have been, sacrificed for the pleasure of tennis. Catgut is not made from the gut of cats. The best catgut is usually made from the gut of a sheep, although gut from cows, goats, mules, horses, asses, donkeys, and even whales, have been tried at some stage. And, although this may explain why I play like a donkey's ass sometimes, it doesn't clarify the conundrum of why it's called catgut.

The riddle was thoroughly investigated by Malcolm Whitman in his book *Tennis Origins and Mysteries*, and yet Whitman could find no clues in the tennis world as to where the term came from. His enquiries eventually gave him a promising lead that took him to the medical world, where catgut was used extensively as surgical thread to sew up wounds.

But Whitman found that here too, although it was still colloquially called catgut, it was also made mainly from sheep. Once again

Whitman found himself in another dead-end as to how our mouse-munching moggies got caught up in such a seedy business.

There is, however, one other profession that has used our elusive catgut throughout the ages and where it is still common practice to do so – and long before tennis or the medical world. In fact, it is one of the oldest professions around; no, no, no, get your mind out of the gutter, not that profession – I'm talking about the musical profession. Although, apparently, Casanova did use the intestines of a various animals as a crude form of prophylactic, but I digress.

Back on the catgut trail, Whitman found several written references to musical instruments using catgut dating back three thousand years ago, and sure enough, it is here that he suspects the term originates.

Even then, catgut was made from the intestines of cows not cats though, and the term was originally called *Kitgut*, not because it used baby kittens, simply because it was first used to string a now obsolete instrument called a *Kit*, which was like a small violin.

Thus, the name *kitgut* became synonymous with stringing the *kit*, and as the popularity and versatility of kit gut caught on, various other stringed instruments started to see the benefits as well, and eventually the term *kitgut* just came to be applied to the gut strings of all instruments, which eventually spilled over into medicine and then tennis.

Whitman suggests that through the ages the name got distorted to become *catgut* in English. He adds that in England at that time there was also a popular pie, usually made with lamb, which also went by the name of *kitgut*, which may have hastened the distortion from *kitgut* to *catgut*, to help distinguish the two and avoid confusion.

I can't help wondering though, just how many times Mozart's Violin Concertos were ruined by having his prized Stradivarius accidentally re-strung with a meat pie before this had to be clarified.

Still, it may help explain just why Beethoven's *"Late String Quartets"* got so delayed.

SECTION 12

WIMBLEDON

It would be remiss of anyone to write a tennis book and not include a section on the home of Lawn Tennis, a quiet little croquet club on the outskirts of London that went on to host the oldest and greatest Lawn Tennis tournament in the world.

So here are a few old favourites alongside some spanking brand new stories as well, including a world first, our very own real life fairy tale.

AN OLD GRASS ROLLER INVENTS WIMBLEDON

Most tennis fans know that the very first documented tennis championship took place in 1877 at a private croquet club in Worple Road, Wimbledon; which we now know as the All England Lawn Tennis and Croquet Club, colloquially referred to the All England or as just Wimbledon. However, few of us know how or why a small croquet club in a tiny village outside London suddenly decided to put on a Lawn Tennis Tournament in the first place.

At the time, the All England Croquet Club was just that, a croquet club, who found themselves a bit short of cash and in need of money to repair a huge cast-iron roller that was essential for rolling their immaculate grass lawns to keep them so flat and true. So the club decided to hold a fundraising event. Because there was no money in croquet, the members were forced to think laterally.

A 46-year-old member called Henry Cavendish Jones proposed that the club host a tournament featuring this new-fangled sport that was inexplicably growing in popularity, Lawn Tennis. Of course, some of the more mature members baulked at the feisty young upstart's suggestion, the very idea of turning over their cherished croquet lawns to these racket wielding hooligans was unthinkable and the idea was quickly quashed.

But Jones didn't give up and approached the editor of *The Field Magazine* about the concept. In those days, *The Field Magazine* was the biggest thing in sport, it was probably the equivalent of today's Sky Sports, so when the editor offered to sponsor the event, throw in some prize money and even put up a cup, the members were forced to think again. Eventually Jones's dynamism paid off, and the members grudgingly agreed, within days *The Field Magazine* was running full page ads to promote the forthcoming tournament.

Several of the club's less treasured croquet lawns at the back of the grounds were converted into tennis courts in order to accommodate the invading tennis ruffians. The club drew up a set of rules in conjunction with Marylebone Cricket Club, the MCC being the ruling body at the time, and the All England Members braced themselves to receive the tennis hoodlums onto their hallowed turf. Any players who wanted to play had to pay one guinea to enter the tournament, and the club then charged spectators a penny to get in to watch the early rounds. The price of entry rose as the tournament progressed, culminating in one shilling to watch the final, which was attended by a healthy crowd of several hundred.

The tournament not only made enough money for the club to buy a new roller, but was such a resounding success that members agreed to hold it again the following year and even decided to turn some of their sacred croquet lawns into Lawn Tennis courts on a more regular basis.

By 1882, the game was becoming so popular that The All England Croquet Club was forced to bow to the changing times and admit that the brutes of Lawn Tennis weren't so bad after all and embraced them fully by changing its name to the one we all know and love today, The All England Lawn Tennis & Croquet Club.

And the rest, as they say, is history.

TENNIS INVENTS THE BYE

It was actually on 9 June 1877, that *The Field Magazine* placed the aforementioned advert announcing that the very first Wimbledon Lawn Tennis Championships were to be held exactly one month later. A few private invitations also went out to prospective challengers and eventually 22 players entered the tournament.

According to Gillmeister's book, *Tennis: A Cultural History*, among the 22 who accepted the invitation, registered his name and paid his one guinea entry fee, was an amateur gentleman by the name of Mr Bye.

Meanwhile, on the other side of the draw, a certain Mr Gore was making all the headlines with his unusual pattern of play, where he would storm to the net and tuck away a volley. It was a style that completely baffled the majority of the entrants who more regularly played the old form of the game, Real Tennis, where such rashness was considered almost ungentlemanly. As the championships progressed, commentators and spectators alike noticed that despite Mr Gore's magnificent run, nobody seemed to have seen a single match played by the elusive Mr Bye, despite the fact that he was progressing equally well through the tournament.

The reason for this soon became apparent when embarrassed officials had to admit that Mr Bye had not actually turned up to play in the tournament at all. This meant that one side of the draw was always a player short so there was always one player who didn't actually have anyone to play against, and so Mr Bye's name was written in on the Draw Sheets so that it all looked even. This all worked fine until the semi-finals when there were only three people to contest the two matches that day, giving Marshall a walkover against Bye and free passage straight into the Wimbledon final.

Gillmeister's book records this unfortunate sequence of events and claims that this was the origin of the expression *"to get a bye into the next round"* and the term stuck. So now, whenever a player gets a free pass through to the next round of a tournament without having to play a match, it is called a bye after the infamous Mr Bye who never showed up.

As charming and delightful as this anecdote is, it may not be quite as accurate as it first appears. Although Marshall and Bye do both appear on the original score sheets of the 1877 semi-final, we now know that there was no Mr Bye registered. Bye only shows up in rounds four and five. Closer inspection reveals that it was a certain Captain Buxton who had failed to turn up in the first round giving his opponent a bye into the second round. Some of the later score sheets left over from the original tournament do have the word *BYE* written into the Draw and Result sheets, hence the confusion, with many historians mistakenly concluding that Bye was a Mr Bye and that this was the origin of the word *bye*.

It would have been lovely if this was the case, but it appears that the word *bye* as a sporting term was already in common use. So in order to accurately pinpoint its origins, we may have to dig a little deeper.

What we do know is that the MCC were acting as the official rule maker for the tournament, as they did for many unregulated sports, so they would have issued the *bye* in the first place and it meant exactly as it does today, indicating a walkover into the next round.

Historians are split as to the origin of the term, obviously it is still used in cricket for when the batting team is awarded runs for when the ball whizzes past by the batsmen and all the fielders as well and goes straight to the boundary. It is recorded as four *byes*, not four runs, because the batsman didn't touch it with his bat.

Tempting as it is to assume the term came from cricket, there is no recorded legacy of this kind of *bye* being the kind of *bye* we are looking at in tennis. It also has a slightly different meaning and so warrants further investigation.

The oldest reference to a *bye* dates back to the 16th century, and appears in both dog racing and cockerel fighting. In both these cases the dogs or cockerels were awarded a *bye* through to the next round in the absence of a competing opponent, or when there was an uneven number of participants.

In the case of dog racing, this concession required that the dog run a solitary lap around the track so that it would not have an unfair advantage and would be just as exhausted as its fellow competitors in the next round. This was known as a *"run by"*.

In cockerel fighting, a bird could be awarded a bye in to the next round but only if the owner paid money to get into the next round, so literally had to *buy* their way in by putting up the stake they would have had to pay if they had been in the previous round.

So, although some competitors deemed this unfair as the cockerel hadn't had to fight its way through, and so would be fresher and stronger, the majority of competitors usually allowed it because it increased the size of the purse for the next round.

So, we have three different theories – the *bye*; the *by*; and the *buy*. It seems that all three versions have survived and merged to form the type of bye we use in tennis today.

Thank heavens nobody had invented our more modern use of the term *bi* in those days or, who knows, we could also be arguing that the term was coined by a 15th-century bi-sexual cricketer who liked dogging and bought his way into the next round of a tennis tournament with his fighting cock.

And on that note, I think it's time I exercised the other version of the word and said bye-bye.

TENNIS INVENTS MAGIC

All the best magicians have the power to make things vanish into thin air. But imagine making the finals of a Grand Slam tennis tournament completely vanish into the ether. Sound crazy? Well, read on.

Scrolling down the list of Wimbledon winners, you will see an entry dated 1931 that shows Sidney Wood as one of the youngest ever winners of the Wimbledon tennis championships, aged just 19. But here's the spooky part. The match never took place.

Like all good magicians, when you make something disappear from view, you always have to make it materialise somewhere else. To really impress, you should bring it back a few moments later in place close to where it disappeared and to the same audience, so this particular trick may have been a bit of a cheat, because it actually reappeared seven miles away and three years later!

Now, no good magician ever reveals how a trick is done, luckily, as a magician, I am no good, so I can reveal exactly how it was done with a clear conscience and without having to worry about losing my membership to The Magic Circle.

Let's rewind to 1931. The American Sidney Wood battled his way through to the Wimbledon final and was all set to face his long-standing friend and compatriot, Frank Shields. The trouble was that Shields had strained his knee slightly in his semi-final match the day before, so he was ordered by the United States Tennis Association to withdraw from the final to rest his injury in preparation for their vital Davis Cup match against Britain the following week.

This way, Shields' injury would not be agitated further and he'd have time to recover. This would also give Wood, his Davis Cup doubles partner, more time to rest before the big match as well.

Today, a move like this would be totally unthinkable because the Grand Slam events are considered more important than the Davis Cup, but in the 1930s it was the Davis Cup that was considered far more important. Internationally, the prestige of winning the Davis Cup was more akin to the Football World Cup of today.

Wood and Shields made a pact between themselves that the next time they met in a professional tournament, they would play for the 1931 Wimbledon title. They almost met several times over the next few years, but it wasn't until three years later in 1934 that they met again.

Fittingly, it was in London and in another final and, very appropriately, it was also on grass. They had both been drawn in separate halves of the draw at The Queen's Club Championships and so, at last, they could play their missing Wimbledon final.

Luckily, it was Sidney Wood who comfortably won the match, and the Wimbledon final that had vanished in 1931 had at last reappeared three years later, leaving no doubt that the name that was engraved on the All England Cup was the correct one.

TENNIS INVENTS THE SEVEN-YEAR ITCH

In 1910, the All England Lawn Tennis & Croquet Club had one of their worst ideas ever. They decided to add a new title to be contested during the famous Wimbledon fortnight – The Married Couples Championship.

Funnily enough, the idea was proposed by the six times Wimbledon Ladies Champion, who just happened to be married to George Hillyard, also a Wimbledon Champion himself. No fool, this Mrs Hillyard! They had obviously just moved to a larger house and had a few empty slots on their mantelpiece that were in need of filling. Indeed, the couple went on to win the title for the first three years, entitling them to keep the trophy.

But the idea was not a success. The title was never heavily contested and struggled to ever attain more than four or five entries, and at times couples were awarded byes straight into the finals. So while the Hillyard mantelpiece filled out, the event itself grew slimmer.

Eventually, after being married to the idea for seven tournaments, The All England Club decided it wanted to divorce itself from the title. The Committee agreed to an uncontested annulment, presumably citing irreconcilable differences, and the title was abandoned with the contestants free to go back onto the Singles market.

The deadly seven-year itch had struck again.

TENNIS INVENTS AMBIDEXTROUS RULE

Almost exactly a hundred years ago, there was a player called Giorgio de Stefani who was so adept at playing with either hand that he would swap the racket between shots and only ever hit forehands from both sides of the court.

Occasionally, he would even come on court with two rackets, one in each hand, and crunch forehand winners all over the court. His opponents claimed it was unfair and against the rules, but actually, as Stefani pointed out, there was no rule governing the amount of rackets a player could bring on court, and so he continued with his duplicitous double-dealing chicanery.

It wasn't until several years later that the authorities got wind of his skulduggery and Stefani's dubious tactics brought about a rule change, so from 1931 players were only permitted to play with *one racket at a time*.

If only they'd said *"one wooden racket at a time"*, then a young Jimmy Connors would never have had the audacity to walk on court with that dreadful aluminium monstrosity and change the nature of tennis forever.

TENNIS INVENTS AVIAN JUSTIN BIEBER

If you're thinking, *"Sorry. Wait A Minute. What Do You Mean? No Sense, Baby"*. Then you're obviously a big Bieber fan, but, as improbable as it sounds, tennis has produced an unlikely social media hero, almost rivaling his fellow songbird Justin Bieber in popularity. Although he has some way to go in terms of chart hits, he does have a similarly commanding presence in a stadium and an almost as impressive number of Twitter followers. Especially when you consider that he's only a bird.

Rufus, one of Wimbledon's most famous employees, is a Harris Hawk whose job is to keep the famous Centre Court and surrounding skies clear of pigeons and other annoying pests, during play. As such, he is one of the world's best-known birds, especially during Wimbledon fortnight, with almost 10,000 followers on his Twitter account, where he regularly, wait for it ... tweets. What else?!

As well as scouring the grounds of The All England Club, Rufus also prowls the skies around a number of Britain's most famous landmarks including the Tower of London, Westminster Abbey and the Houses of Parliament.

In fact, when Rufus was stolen from the back of his owner's car in 2012, it caused a massive outcry across social media and TV networks around the globe. The perpetrator couldn't be found, the police were baffled, maybe they should've gone to the Flying Squad! The disappearance was a mystery worthy of an Agatha Christie flewdunnit. The media pressure was so intense that apparently his captor chickened out and, in a panic, just released him back into the wild. Rufus was found a few days later, back dutifully patrolling his most prized territory – Wimbledon. What a trooper. Sir Rufus, perhaps? An OBE, at least?

TENNIS INVENTS BALL STATS

Wimbledon uses almost 55,000 balls every year during the tournament, with each ball lasting for between seven to nine games before being replaced. Every ball has to conform to a strict set of rules laid down by the International Tennis Federation. Although different balls are produced for different surfaces, they must all remain within certain guidelines. For instance, each ball must measure between 6.54 cm and 6.86 cm in diameter, and weigh between 56 g and 59.4 g, and must bounce between 135 cm and 147 cm after being dropped on to solid concrete from a height of exactly 254 cm.

The Wimbledon balls travel nearly 7,000 miles from their factory in the Philippines, before being tonked around for the equivalent of several hundred more by the players on court. And that is before you even take into account all the individual ingredients that go into producing a tennis ball, which have had to be shipped in from 11 different countries and four separate continents. Ouch, don't tell Greta Thumberg!

There's clay from South Carolina, silica from Greece, magnesium carbonate from Japan, zinc oxide from Thailand, sulphur from South Korea, rubber from Malaysia, petroleum naphthalene from China, glue from the Philippines, and wool from New Zealand, which is first taken to Gloucestershire in England to be woven into felt, before returning to the Philippines again. Phew, I'm exhausted before play has even begun!

It's an extraordinarily complicated and highly involved process, especially when you consider that its competitive lifespan is only for a few minutes of professional play. Or about three months if you play for Tim Pike's Sunday tennis group.

In the case of The All England Club, the unused balls are then stored in the Ball Distribution Office under Centre Court and kept at a temperature of exactly 68 degrees Fahrenheit. According to the

Wimbledon website, they employ the tennis equivalent of a wine Sommelier, whose official title is *Connoisseurial Ball Distribution Manager*. The post is currently held by Brian Mardling, who claims that he can tell at a glance, and a quick squeeze, exactly how many games each ball has endured. Let's just hope he refrains from using this technique in his private life or else he could end up in all sorts of trouble.

Eventually, all the used balls are collected up at the end of the day and sold back to the public. Every year the proceeds from the sale of used Championships balls are donated to The Schools Tennis Programme, which raises tens of thousands of pounds for kids all over the world.

TENNIS INVENTS PARSIMONY

Even though tennis balls are sometimes the subject of much environmental debate, given that they need to be replaced so frequently, don't throw them away. Manufacturers are trying to address this and now all the balls are all fully recyclable, along with the tins they're supplied in.

In actual fact, a tennis ball will keep its pressure inside an unopened can for many years and, even when opened, will only lose pressure at a very slow rate. This is known as the *rebound rate*. Once a can is opened, the rebound rate will only decrease at roughly .035 inches per day.

So, if you are a little parsimonious and want to do your bit for the environment, then instead of replacing the balls every time you play, just lower the net by .035 inches each day!

There! Job done! I'm expecting my Nobel Peace Prize nomination for *"Contributions to the Environment"* to arrive at any moment.

TENNIS INVENTS TENNIS-BALL INVENTIONS

If all that isn't enough for the Nobel Prize Committee to be FedExing me over my nomination, then here are the top ten recycling tips that I have stumbled across whilst chasing those allusive yellow spheres around the court all these years ...

Bottle Top Opener
Another great trick is to use a ball as a bottle top opener. Simply cut a tennis ball in half, then cover the lid top that you need to open with the rubbery inside half of the tennis ball and twist it off without a problem. I have even been able to use this method on pull-off bottle caps as well, although they are less common these days.

Curvy Sander
Rounded edges and curvy pieces of wooden furniture can be very awkward to sand down. Try using a tennis ball wrapped with sandpaper and you'll find the job a lot easier.

Hammer Muffler
Hammer muffling is probably not an expression you would want your kids to Google, but this is a useful tip when you haven't got a wooden mallet. Make a slit in your old tennis ball and place over the head of your hammer. The hammer will now work as a substitute mallet, or you can also use this method for nudging woodwork into place without damaging the wood.

Parking Assistant
If you don't have, or don't trust, your rear parking sensors, then the tennis ball parking method is said to be one of the most common uses for old balls. Simply hang a tennis ball on a string from the ceiling of the garage so that it hits the center of your windshield when you are

parked in the correct spot. This can be on the front or rear windscreen depending on which way you park. You can even hang an extra one on the wall just in case you overshoot, so that the ball takes the impact and not the bumpers!

Anti-Snoring Device

People who snore tend to do so more often when they sleep on their backs. If this is the case with you or your partner, you can prevent this by simply putting a tennis ball into an old sock and sewing the sock on to the back of a person's pyjama top. When the snorer turns onto their back, the tennis ball will prevent them from getting comfortable and they'll return to their side, reducing the snore factor considerably.

Bike Stand

Often your metal bike stand can use a little assistance, especially in mud, soft grass, wet soil or sandy areas like a beach. By cutting a slit in the ball and slipping it over the end of the bike's kickstand, it will stand firm and not sink into any of the aforementioned quagmires.

Super Fluffer-Upper

The next time you want to spin-dry any feathery items like down-filled pillows, baby comforters, quilts or puffa-jackets, simply throw a couple of tennis balls into the dryer to accompany them. They will fluff up again as good as new.

Darn It

It's probably been a while since you saw where your grandma hid her darning mushroom but, instead of throwing away your favourite pair of socks just because your big toe decided to jailbreak its woolly den and tear a hole in the end, you can easily fix it using a tennis ball.

Place the ball in the toe to stretch out the surface of the sock so that sewing it back up is a doddle.

Childproofing System

Another common use for old tennis balls, especially if you have young kids running around the house, is to attach them onto the corners of any furniture that sticks out, this can be a real life saver.

Making New Tennis Courts

And finally, a recycling scheme that started on the tiny island of Maui in 2019 is starting to gain traction around the world. The local club collects around 10,000 balls every year and sends them to be recycled as rubber crumbs which are then used in the construction of, wait for it, you're going to like this, new tennis courts.

Yes, ok, I know, I lied, that was twelve top tips! But *The Top Twelve Tips* just doesn't have the same ring to it, so I thought I'd blatantly fib and just hope that no one notices.

Well, it worked for Donald Trump.

TENNIS INVENTS ROLAND GARROS

All tennis fans will be familiar with the Roland Garros stadium, home of the French Open but, even in France, very few people know why the venue bears that name. Many just assume that the Roland Garros stadium was named after a past champion but few people know the true story behind it.

In reality, Eugène Adrien Roland Georges Garros was actually a well-known rugby player who represented his country for many years in the Five Nations tournament and who ironically never even played tennis. What?! *Sacré bleu!* This can't be true! Well, yes, but bear with me. Garros was a brilliant and daring aviator, probably best known as a First World War fighter pilot, but he also broke various altitude records, and is known for helping his country develop the forward firing machine gun. But, I hear you ask, how on earth does that explain how his name came to be emblazoned across one of the most famous Grand Slam tennis tournaments in the world?

Well, in 1928, more than a decade after Garros died when his aircraft was shot down near Ardennes, France was all set to host the final of the Davis Cup but they were in desperate need of a new stadium to hold it in.

The stadium construction contract was awarded to a certain Emile Lesieur, who happened to be a close friend of Roland Garros. The two had grown up together, had been in the same school and the same classes, they played as teammates in the Five Nations Rugby and they even fought alongside each other as pilots during the war. When Lesieur was awarded the construction contract he agreed only on the condition that the new stadium be named in memory of one of France's great war heroes. The authorities agreed to the idea in principle and that's when Lesieur suggested the name of his much missed friend, Roland Garros.

TENNIS INVENTS IMPOSSIBLE CONUNDRUM

Another good piece of pub quiz trivia took place at Wimbledon in 1984. John McEnroe won the Men's Singles, Martina Navratilova won the Ladies; McEnroe and Fleming won the Men's Doubles; Navratilova and Shriver won the Ladies Doubles; and they all had one thing in common. But what was the one thing that they all had in common?

The question usually draws many innovative guesses, like they were all left handers, or they all had the same coach, they were all sponsored by the same company, or they were all using the same type of racket, etc. But no one has ever got the right answer, so I usually give them a clue.

The trouble with the clue is that it really doesn't help and confuses them even more. The clue is:

> *"That although they all had one thing in common and this one thing had never happened before in the history of Wimbledon, this was actually the second time that this one-off thing had happened!"*

When I say this, this really upsets the applecart, with everyone shouting and yelling at me demanding to know how on earth can something have never happened before, if it's the second time that it's happened?! And they get all very huffity and uppity, as my grandmother used to say.

Well, the answer is devilishly simple; they had all won the exact same titles in 1984 that they had had all won the year before, thus allowing the normally impossible conundrum of a repeat that's also unique.

TENNIS INVENTS A FAIRYTALE

Once upon a time, long, long ago in an ancient old hamlet in Barrow, there lived a lovable Cuddly Bear. But he was no ordinary bear. This bear dreamed of being the bravest knight in the kingdom. He wanted to be a great gladiator of the arenas, fighting giants and winning courtly battles for his king and country so that he could win the heart of the fair maiden princess and live happily ever after.

But, although Cuddly Bear was kind, friendly and everybody loved him, he had one major flaw, he was a hungry munchkin and could resist everything but temptation. So much so that Cuddly Bear had to give up on his dream of being a brave knight because he had been tempted one time too many and had now put on so much weight that Cuddly Bear had completely lost his mojo. He no longer whistled while he worked and the twinkle had gone out of his little star.

One day, as he surveyed all of his 18-stone wobbliness, he asked, *"Mirror, mirror on the wall, who's the bravest knight of all?"* The Magic Mirror replied, *"Cuddly Bear, for 25 years we knew you had it in you to be the bravest in the land, but today we must reflect back to you the truth, 'tis King Fed who is the bravest knight of all."*

Cuddly Bear sighed. His head hung low. He felt grumpy. He knew that the Magic Mirror was right, he had squandered his talents having too much fun and had let his hair down far too frequently. He had become bewitched by the mystical allure of sugary cola elixirs. On too many occasions he had been enticed by the siren call of the Spice Apothecaries for his double order Friday night curries and distracted from his mid-week training by the tasty appeal of the super smooth Italian take-way pizzas with their exotic pork and pineapple combos.

And most of all, he had been all too easily led astray by the evil caskets of free-flowing golden ales and amber nectars with his mates. His tennis talent was his Golden Goose but he'd just eaten the bird long before it had a chance to lay any golden eggs or perform its magic.

All of these terrible habits had taken their toll on our Cuddly Bear. He was overweight, broke and living at home with Mummy Bear and Daddy Bear. He was in debt to Mr Bigbad Banks, and had maxed out all his evil credit cards to Mr Plastic Fantastic, and was even refused a loan by the Wicked Witch of the Nat West.

It seemed to be a never-ending story, Cuddly Bear accepted his fate, realising that it was probably too late now. Surely he could never find his way back home to full fitness, even if he followed the massive trail of his own food crumbs.

Anyway, it didn't matter. He had an offer of a 9 to 5 job in a land far, far away in Deepest Darkest Peru that would keep him supplied in sugary elixirs, golden ales and vindaloos from the Spice Apothecary for the rest of his days. He would be okay.

But then, out of the blue, just as he was about to set sail to a land far, far away in Deepest Darkest Peru, he didst espy a maiden that was the fairest maiden that he hadst ever espied. She stood at the end of a yellow brick road and had the most flowing of golden locks he had ever seen. Dressed in her little red riding hoodie, she was like the princess that he used to dream of, and Cuddly Bear's heart was ignited like a tinderbox.

He may have been a fella enchanted but her character was of such snow white purity, and her skin was as smooth as silk, that surely she could never love an ugly duckling like him, with his old rumpled stilt skin. He couldn't imagine a beauty such as her could be attracted to a beast such as he.

But the maiden looked past Cuddly Bear's fears and saw the brave knight that lay within his cuddlesome exterior façade. She pleaded with him not to run away to a land far, far away in Deepest Darkest Peru, but to stay and fight for her love like the true brave knight that she knew he was. She confided her belief in him and begged him to fight like a man of steel, lest the world saw him as a man of tin with no heart. She told him that he had to sacrifice what he is, for what he could become. If he just believed it was possible then the streets would be paved with gold for them. She urged him not to hesitate and to grab her hand so that together they could journey into never land.

Cuddly Bear sensed that he was at a crossroads in his life, a fork in the road and suddenly the mists cleared and he could see exactly what he had to do, causing a little smile to slowly creep across his face like a big Cheshire cat. It was as if the princess had kissed the frog and, flash bam alakazam, it transformed him, he was suddenly inspired and agreed that he would not leave for a land far, far away in Deepest Darkest Peru but stay and do it. The maiden leapt into his arms with joy. He was determined to show this leaping beauty that he was no puss in boots but a wolf in sheep's clothing, and didst resolve to enter one last fight to qualify for the biggest tournament in the land. A tournament so huge that multitudes gathered very year to applaud the brave deeds of the greatest knights, not just from all of England, but from all the kingdoms, in all of the world. 'Twas the greatest tournament of all, where a thousand and one knights would all gather, it was the legend of the Wonderful Wizard of Wimbledon.

This tournament was on such a grand scale, so magnificent that if Cuddly Bear could just get there to fight one round, he knew that he would be so rich and famous that not only would he win a treasure chest full of gold for his efforts but, best of all, win the love of his fair maiden forever.

Cuddly Bear gave up all the evil temptations that had been leading him astray and stayed focused on his training to get fit for the battle. For months, he trained hard and each day he lost a little more weight and gained a little more strength until he was trim and fit once more.

But to even get through the qualifying event was going to be fraught with danger at every perilous turn. He had to win six treacherous matches and fight off six deadly foes from all four corners of the globe, all of them as hungry as wolves to get in to the great tournament themselves. The first three lupine challengers huffed and puffed but they could not blow him away as he fought his way to three successive victories.

But Cuddly Bear knew that the next two challengers would be much tougher affairs. Sure enough they fought like brothers, grim with determination. They were as fierce as two dragons spitting flames of determination at him with every breath. But Cuddly Bear was a lad in a hurry and determined to slay the fiery dragons. He proved he was no cowardly lion and, before you could say Bibbidy Bobbidy Boo, he had defeated them both.

Now, there was only one last contender left, a tough, gruff, ruffian with a big beard, a crueler devil of an opponent you could not wish for. But he knew that if he could just beat Beard Bloke, then he would gain entrance to the Wonderful Wizard of Wimbledon. It was a long, tough match but eventually he blew Beard away. He'd done it! He was through all of the deadly qualifying rounds unscathed – he was going to the Ball – the Wonderful Wizard of Wimbledon.

Alas, when Cuddly Bear arrived in the grassy lowlands of Wimbledon, nobody knew who he was. He felt so small and lost in amongst all these famous gladiators and brave knights. His first match was against a fearsome monster from Lithuania called Beastly Berankis who was a real thumper of the ball, one bam be all it took for him to serve an ace. The Beast was favoured by the Cruellerist Queen of the Evil Ranking Seeds, whose curse ranked the Lithuanian Beast 750 times better than him. Cuddly Bear didn't stand a chance. He'd gotten to the Wonderful Wizard of Wimbledon only to be used as a sacrificial lamb to the slaughter.

The match was scheduled to be played in the furthest regions of the grassy lowlands of Wimbledon on the far recesses of Court 17, almost a land as far, far away as Deepest Darkest Peru. As he was led out to the slaughter, he saw his fair maiden, a few of his old college chums, and a barmy army of football mates who had gathered to cheer him on. The sight of them all lifted his spirits, but as the battle commenced, the steepness of the task in hand was immense. It was tough work and he seemed to be frozen with nerves and was struggling to keep up with the brave Lithuanian Beast. Cuddly Bear's normally flowing game was all tangled in knots, he could not slay the ugly demons of his nerves and it looked as if his Centre Court hopes were burnt to cinders in a goblet of fire.

But the Wonderful Wizard of Wimbledon held a secret. It had a magic mountain called Henman Hill. Legend had it that when all the Hill People gather there and all wish the same wish then magical things can happen. Sure enough, as if on cue, the Hill people started to cheer and sing to try and encourage him. Some of the Hill People even took off their shoes to wave in the air to show just how much they loved and supported him. The magic mountain seemed to be working because, sure enough, as if stardust had been sprinkled over him, Cuddly Bear was suddenly inspired. He fought a little tougher and began playing better and better.

Just as the clock struck one, the whole nation started to tune in to watch his antics. When he played, children followed him, even a previously occupied piper stopped work to watch him, as did a potter called Harold, a boxer named Pandora, and a little boy called Tom gave him a thumbs up. Cuddly Bear started to play like the true lion which had always been in his wardrobe, so much so, that he went on to beat the odds and win the match in straight sets. But the best was yet to come.

News quickly spread throughout the Land, that there was an all-new British hero, a Cuddly Bear that had been transformed into a gallant knight. The nation held its breath to see who Cuddly Bear would do battle with in the next round.

And as fate would have it, it came to pass that Cuddly Bear was to play the match of his dreams against his hero, the greatest and bravest knight of all, the all-conquering, King Fed. And, to top it all, not only were they going to play in the grandest tournament in all of the big wide world, but they were going to play it on the greatest stage of all – Centre Court, the biggest and most famous court in all the land.

If I were to tell you that Cuddly Bear managed to pull a genie out of the bottle and slay King Fed in straight sets and stole his champion's crown, then I fear my nose would grow to the size of a giant bean stalk, as, alas, it would not be true. King Fed smelled the blood of an Englishman. Cuddly Bear did fight valiantly, but he fee, fi, fo, fumbled at the final hurdle.

Not even the magic mountain could help him, because the Hill People loved King Fed almost as much as their new found hero. To the Hill People, King Fed was a big friendly giant. But that's not to say that our hero didn't play the greatest match of his life, because he did.

His gallant efforts gave the crowds a thrilling ride, frequently lobbing and passing the great champion. Cuddly Bear played brilliantly and hardly hit any bad shots and only a couple of fey balls but that was enough for King Fed to swoop – he sops fey balls up like a man possessed. Cuddly Bear couldn't quite lift his game enough to conquer the labyrinth of talent that was King Fed who went on to win the match.

But, let me stop the story there, because this was no children's fairy tale. This was real life.

In case you had forgotten, let me remind you how all this actually happened. The *Once Upon A Time* was actually in July 2016. The *Wonderful Wizard of Wimbledon* was, of course, the beautifully manicured lawns of the All England Lawn Tennis & Croquet Club, Wimbledon, London SW19.

Our big *Cuddly Bear* was, in fact, plucky Brit player, Marcus Willis, a total unknown tennis pro who was on the verge of giving up playing on the circuit to move abroad to work as a coach, when he met the girl of his dreams who persuaded him to give Wimbledon qualifying one last go. The *Fair Maiden* in question was really, Jenny Bate, a golden-haired beauty queen, who worked as a dental nurse, who persuaded Marcus not to take the job abroad *in a land far, far away in Deepest Darkest Peru*, which was actually Vancouver. *King Fed* was, of course, our real life king of the courts, tennis royalty himself, Roger Federer.

But the fairytale didn't end there. There was to be a real-life Cinderella ending after all. True love's first kiss had worked its magic once again, as Marcus not only won the heart of his practically perfect fair maiden, he also won the hearts of an entire nation.

In doing so, Marcus disney have to worry about money ever again and would no longer have to rely on the simple bare necessities of life as he'd secured the largest purse of his career, worth many thousands of golden coins to fill even the biggest treasure chest, enabling him to marry his princess bride, Jenny. They bought a home to make into their castle and together they have started to make little cuddly baby bear cubs of their very own.

And, of course, do I really have to say it? Oh, alright then, yes, they all lived happily ever after.

The End.

SECTION 13

MAJOR WINGFIELD

If it's difficult to write a tennis book without mentioning Wimbledon, then it's impossible to mention either without paying homage to the man who made all of this possible, Major Wingfield himself.

TENNIS INVENTS PATRIOTISM

Major Walter Clopton Wingfield is generally credited as being the creator of the modern game of Lawn Tennis. He's the man who first popularised it as a game and first laid down a proper set of patented rules in 1874.

Wingfield sold the game in boxes and called it *Sphairistikè*, a corruption of the name of the Ancient Greeks' ball game, *Sphaeristichea*, which was not unlike *Jeu de paume*. *Sphaira* was the Greek word for *"ball"*, and is where we get the word *sphere* from.

The good Major claims that he first took the ancient game of Real Tennis and played it on grass in 1869. Others say that Harry Gem and Augurio Perrera were playing a similar Lawn Tennis game in Leamington Spa at the same time, but until historians turn up some long lost photographs or some official rules that pre-date Wingfield's, then the Welsh-born Major will hold on to his claim to fame in the history books.

It seems cruel that a game that has brought so much pleasure to millions of people, and made huge fortunes for so many players, coaches, pundits, TV channels, media moguls and sports companies, brought little monetary reward to its inventor at all. In fact, Wingfield seemed to have lived a fairly poor and wretched life. All three of his sons died very early, each in pretty tragic circumstances, and even his wife was declared mad and spent the end of her miserable life in an asylum.

Some recompense was made to him in the form of royal recognition on 22 November 1902, when King Edward VII made Wingfield a Member of the Royal Victorian Order (MVO) for *"extraordinary, important and personal services to the Sovereign and the Royal family and for 32 years of faithful service to King and Country"*.

But by the time he died in 1912, Wingfield was such a forgotten pauper that his grave was completely lost for more than half a century, until its discovery by his dedicated biographer George E. Alexander in the 1970s.

Even then, it took many years before a group of Americans, calling themselves the Major Wingfield Club, fully restored it to a state befitting a man of such historical significance in 1980. Thankfully, now, The All England Club in Wimbledon have stepped up to the service line and undertaken to maintain it in perpetuity.

The Club has made further amends by casting his image in a grand bronze bust and dedicating a special section in their museum to him, as well as naming one of their biggest restaurants after him, The Wingfield Restaurant, which stands at the Main Entrance and is one of the first sights that greet you upon entering the Club. British Heritage have also honoured Wingfield by mounting one of their Commemorative Blue Plaques at his former home in Pimlico, and finally, in 1997, the Major was duly inducted into the International Tennis Hall of Fame for his outstanding contribution to the game.

I still think it was a pretty sorry state of affairs that this country had let things slip so much, but thank heavens the Americans recognised his contribution, stepped in and saved things. It seems to be a pretty regular failing of the British in being slow to recognise and honour their own heroes and it reminds me that it took another American to build a statue to honour R. J. Mitchell, who designed the Spitfire, often cited as the greatest plane ever built, and singled out by both Hitler and Churchill as the most significant asset in winning the Battle of Britain.

It was an American again, Sam Wanamaker, who was behind the project to recreate Shakespeare's Globe Theatre. It was Americans again who were the first to properly honour Frank Whittle as the inventor of the jet engine.

And it was Americans who were the first to fully acclaim Sir Tim Berners-Lee as the creator of the World Wide Web and set him up with his own charitable foundation.

I would like to add at this juncture that nobody in Britain has fully recognised my contribution to the literary world of tennis publishing yet either, so, you know, if you happen to be a philanthropic American billionaire, and if you have a major city square with a big void in it, that, I dunno, say maybe needs a tasteful statue …

MAJOR WINGFIELD DIDN'T INVENT TENNIS – IT WAS LORD WINGFIELD!

There is another fascinating footnote to the Wingfield tennis legacy that suggests that the accredited inventor of tennis, may not have been the first member of his family to have fallen in love with the great game.

Shockingly, about 400 years earlier, there's record of one of his ancestors, Lord Wingfield, being an even more avid player than the good Major himself.

In 1415, following the Battle of Agincourt, the Duke of Orléans was imprisoned for two decades in England, and it was during this captivity in Norfolk that the Duke introduced the game of Real Tennis to Lord Wingfield. History states that Lord Wingfield was so taken with the game that he played it almost daily. Considering the Duke was imprisoned for 20 years, one can only assume he must have been pretty good at it by the end!

It's tempting to imagine that Lord Wingfield may well have played outside at least a few times in those twenty years. I wonder if tales of his ancestor's fondness of the game didn't inspire the young Walter, four centuries later, to adapt the game formerly to grass.

If only the Wingfield family had got their act together and invented Lawn Tennis four centuries earlier, just think, that would've given us an extra 400 years to find at least one more British champion, hell, maybe two!

TENNIS INVENTS CORDON BLEU COOKING

Because his Lawn Tennis game never actually made Major Wingfield much money, he later abandoned his invention to turn his hand to other projects, including inventing a new type of bicycle called the *Butterfly*. As innovative as it may have been, the bicycle market was pretty saturated and fiercely competitive. There were bikes being made with all sorts of weird and wonderful names, among them were the *Touren Leipzig*, the *Humber Tandem*, the *Otto*, the *Invincible*, the *Personeu Verwandelbar*, the *Dreirad Gepack* and the *Renn Tricycle*.

There was also one called the *Velocipede*, which sounds more like a dinosaur. The *Saal* which I'm sure I've had as a side dish in a curry house. Then there was the *Manuped*, who sounds like a bloke you've just paid money to, but my favourite bike name was the *Sicherheits*, which sounds like a vomiting mountaineer.

On top of that, of course, what made it particularly difficult for the Major to peddle his cycle wares was that he had to compete with the most bafflingly successful bike of all, the Penny Farthing. With so many competitors all nabbing a big slice of the bicycle pie, it's hardly surprising that his *Butterfly* bike didn't do much to swell the Wingfield coffers either. The Major had to hang up his bicycle clips and was forced to look elsewhere for an income.

Wingfield was a keen smoker, so he thought he might try and make a living out of the hobby he enjoys. Thus, the Wingfield Tobacco Mixture was launched in 1886 by Robert Lewis, the world's first cigar store which opened in 1787. Wingfield blended mature Virginia leaf with a small portion of stronger sun dried leaves, creating the illusion of the more commonly used Latakia leaf when smoked.

The blend is renowned for burning well, rarely needing to be re-lit and is said to give off a light fruity undertone. The blend is still sold today and from the original Robert Lewis shop but, alas, it was never going to make the Major any money because, once again,

Wingfield's financial acumen let him down. Instead of taking a cut of the royalties, he opted to get a free supply of baccie each month.

As he watched another promising business idea go up in flames, it seemed to light another fire inside him. Walter next turned his hand to setting up a culinary master class for budding chefs to improve their cooking skills. Now this seemed to be an enterprise that had much more commercial potential. The only other real competition in the culinary world at the time was an aging Mrs Beeton. The way looked clear then for the Major to step up to the plate, sweep into the culinary world and feast himself on the profits.

Although in principle the idea was sound, there was one aspect that let the Major down a bit. For just as his *Sphairistikè* name for Lawn Tennis didn't catch on, so it was that his brand-naming skills let him down once again. When he finally settled upon a name for his cooking course he came up with *Cordon Rouge*.

Tch! I feel he was really close with this one. If he'd just stuck with it, maybe leaning towards something a little more cerulean in colour, something a little more azure, perhaps leaning towards indigo, then one can't help wondering whether the Wingfield name might well have claimed a second significant legacy to dine out on. But, no, the Major bleu it again.

Still, I'm sure he's looking down on The Wingfield Restaurant now, from his tennis court in heaven, where you never get any bad line calls, with a big warm, if slightly ironic, smile on his angelic face.

TENNIS INVENTS MORE WINGFIELDS

Digging deep into the family archives, it seems that the Wingfields have influenced more than just tennis through the ages. The earliest record of the Wingfield name dates back to the Norman Invasion and is thought to have its origins in a Saxon Thane called Robert de Campo Venti, which translates as *"Robert of the field of the wind"*. The name underwent several revisions through the centuries, going from de Fieltewind, de Wynkfeilde, to de Wingfield, before eventually settling on just Wingfield.

The first printed appearance of the name is in 1087. Robert de Campo Venti being one of the Thanes who bid farewell to Harold at Harleston when the Saxon King was on his way to fight the Normans in the Battle of Hastings. King Harold used a giant stone to step onto to help mount his horse, and thereafter the townsfolk named it Harold's Stone. The name stuck, but over the centuries, became shortened to Harleston, which survives to this day.

The Wingfield family seems to have inveigled its way into several tiers of English history, having originally found favour with William the Conqueror who granted them many lands, and from there the family kept close to that all-important royal patronage as they remained in favour to a succession of English kings. The Wingfield name being approvingly referenced in court records during the reigns of King Stephen, Henry II, King John, Henry III and Henry VIII as well.

Later records show that there was a Sir John Wingfield who fought at the Battle of Poitiers with the Black Prince, and a Sir Roger Wingfield who fought with the Knights Templars. Further delving reveals that the Wingfields continued their influence in high office being directly connected by marriage to both Thomas Cromwell and Oliver Cromwell.

Then there was a Robert Wingfield who bore witness to and made record of the execution of Mary Queen of Scots. The Wingfield name also has a direct blood link to English royalty, through the marriage of Henry III's daughters to Lady Jane Grey who was later crowned Queen of England, if only for a fleetingly brief nine days. Her reign as Queen of England may have been brief, but her Lady Grey name lives on in another established Wimbledon tradition, as an aromatic tea of choice, offered as a discerning alternative to the better known Earl Grey Tea.

But the munificent Wingfields didn't just confine their history-making loins to little old England, they generously spread their pioneering DNA sequence throughout the entire world.

Most notably, Edward Wingfield is credited as being the true founder of Jamestown, Virginia, the first successful English colony to settle in America in 1607, the story of which was made into a TV series in 2017. Not content with that, various descendants of Edward then migrated deeper into the Americas and various segments of his genetic material ended up in Nevada.

One such segment morphed into George Wingfield who is perhaps one of the great, unsung heroes of the American tourist industry, as it was he who first legalised gambling in Nevada. George Wingfield became so powerful in those early days of the wild west that he was known as the *King of Nevada*. It's undoubtedly the Wingfield legacy that forged the state into becoming the single most significant gambling force in the world today. I'm not normally a gambling man, but I'm willing to bet big that you didn't know that. There is a particularly beautiful irony here, as gambling is where tennis also has its roots and to which it owes much of its early popularity.

It's probably best that we don't mention the Honourable Lewis Wingfield, who although at first glance seems to have been an admirable man, being as he was a soldier, actor, artist, author and world traveller. On the surface then, a most honourable fellow, but Lewis had a very strange hobby.

Lewis liked to study all forms of executioner's tools and collected as much of their macabre equipment as he could find. He especially had a morbid fascination with all things connected to hanging and public executions. Collecting ropes from famous executions and swords from professional Japanese executioners as well. But it gets worse as Lewis had an even darker side to him because his absolute favourite pastime of all was extreme torture.

So I suspect that young Lewis would be absolutely delighted to know that his namesake's game of tennis has managed to torment and torture the English for the best part of two centuries as we watch the trials and tribulations of various Brits performing at Wimbledon every year.

TENNIS INVENTS IMPEACHING THE AMERICAN PRESIDENT

OK, I know this one sounds unlikely but there is one last descendant of the Wingfield tribe that I haven't yet mentioned. Strange as it may seem, but the origins of that very American act of impeachment can be traced back to the 14th century, to an English nobleman called Michael de la Pole.

For not only was de la Pole officially the very first Earl of Suffolk, he's also on record as being the very first man in history to be impeached. His crime? Well, it was an unusual one, he refused to pay the French government a ransom demand for the return of the town of Ghent. Now, please keep schtum about this, because I'm sure if the EU ever found out about this they would retrospectively add it to Britain's Brexit bill for leaving Europe.

De la Pole's impeachment is historically relevant to the American Constitution purely because the whole process of impeachment owes its origins to these very same ancient English laws. The reason for this is because the men who wrote the US Constitution all grew up under the thumb of English Law. They had studied it, knew how it worked, and were familiar with all its flaws and merits.

So when they drew up the American Constitution, they realised that having a mechanism to expel errant officials found guilty of any malfeasance, including elected presidents, would prove crucial in preventing the country from ever falling into the desperate hands of autocratic rulers or would-be tin-pot dictators. So they copied the impeachment clause from English Law, almost word for word. You can find it in Section 4; Article 2, which states:

"The President, Vice President and all civil Officers of the United States, shall be removed from office on Impeachment for

the Conviction of Treason, Bribery, or other High Crimes and Misdemeanours."

Only three presidents have ever been impeached, Andrew Johnson, Bill Clinton and Donald Trump. Several attempts were made on Barack Obama as well, but they all failed. Richard Nixon would undoubtedly have been impeached but he had the foresight to resign first.

The most likely route of all impeachments depends not so much on American law, but on how the American prosecutors successfully interpret that ancient phrase from medieval England, the purposefully vague legal term of *"High Crimes and Misdemeanours"*. The term *high* in those days meant *serious*.

So all impeachments owe their existence to the exact same phrase that stymied England's 14th-century nobleman Michael de la Pole. It's not known whether de la Pole was a keen tennis player or not, the only reference we have is that when he was in office he was confronted with a bill to outlaw tennis throughout the land. This was because tennis was blamed for much of the gambling that was consuming people's time and filling up the prisons with people who couldn't pay their debts. De la Pole, though, refused to blame tennis and the bill did not get passed. Hurrah! He sounds like a mighty fine man to me. He blocks laws prohibiting tennis and steals entire towns from the French. What more can you ask of an English politician than that?

Strangely, there are no records explaining why Michael de la Pole, who as Chancellor, didn't pay the ransom on the town of Ghent, maybe he was too busy playing tennis to be bothered to pay the French millions of pounds for a remote town in Belgium that in those days hadn't even bothered to get around to making decent chocolate yet. But, whatever the reason, by failing to pay it he was considered to have been guilty of a *"high crime"* against the king, and on

24 October 1385 he became the first person ever to be impeached and removed from office.

The fortunes of Michael de la Pole, and his son William, were incredibly turbulent. Their finances were closely linked to the royal family and the fact that they were constantly falling in and out of royal favour undoubtedly explains their yo-yoing fortunes.

But, ultimately, it was not the yo-yo that was used to metaphorically describe their vacillating destinies. Intriguingly, this leads us neatly to our penultimate record of anything that linked the de la Poles to the game of tennis, as a report in *The London Revue* went on to describe the fluctuating prospects of the de la Pole family as *"liken to the tennis ball of fortune"*.

But, by an astonishing coincidence, the tennis connection does not end there, because Michael de la Pole was actually married to a lovely woman called Katherine and not just any old Katherine this one. Oh no, she just happened to be Katherine Wingfield, an early ancestor of our very own Major Wingfield himself.

It is generally thought that that the two attempts to impeach President Trump were the main reasons why Trump lost the last election, so don't forget to send a small letter of thanks to the current Earl of Suffolk and the remaining Wingfield clan for all their help in restoring American politics back to some sort of normality again.

SECTION 14

WORDS DERIVED FROM TENNIS

The English language is one of the richest and most diverse languages in the world. It continues to evolve as new words become imbedded in our psyche in both written and spoken forms. Most of us use thousands of words a day without giving a second thought as to where they come from or how they came to mean what they do.

Some can be traced back to ancient cultures and other languages, whilst others can be directly ascribed to influential scribes like Chaucer and Shakespeare. But here are a few everyday words and phrases that owe their origins, or at least their popularity, directly to the world of tennis ...

TENNIS INVENTS LOVE

There's an old joke that says *"never marry a tennis player, because to them love means nothing"*. And although this is a good gag and sells well on a T-Shirt, I hope to demonstrate that the true origin of the word *love*, in tennis terms at least, will actually prove to mean the exact opposite.

Certainly, in terms of scoring a match, *love* in tennis does indeed mean *nil* or *zero*, and is used in exactly the same way in other sports as well. In fact, the term is so frequently used that it has graduated from just being a sporting term to our everyday vernacular. Which, at first, seems to only cement the notion of *"love means nothing"*, but if we just descend a little further back in time we find something very different indeed.

Originally it was thought that the word *love* had its origins in France from where early forms of tennis are thought to have derived. The most commonly held belief is that the term *love* stems from the French term *l'oeuf*, meaning *"the egg"*.

Many historians feel this is further substantiated by the fact that in the 16th century they specifically shaped their numerical zeroes in the shape of an egg to distinguish it from the perfectly circular letter 'O' in the written form. Indeed the egg symbol as a nought has also spilled over to many other sports. For example, when a batsman has been dismissed without scoring any runs in cricket, they describe it as *"being out for a duck"*, and, if they are out first ball, then it is known as a *"golden duck"*. All these terms were thought to stem from the abbreviated form of a *"duck's egg"* as it was originally called. In baseball, the term for a zero score is described similarly as a *"goose's egg"*, which all seems to lend weight to the love means nothing philosophy.

In more recent times, however, many respected scholars have been ruffling the feathers of history by putting this old egg theory out to roost and have plucked another hypothesis from the annals of time. Most now tend to crow about another possible alternative, one that dates back even further.

The more accepted hypothesis now is that the term *love* stems from the Dutch word *lof*, meaning *honour*. Although the Dutch are not widely credited with inventing tennis, there is some evidence to suggest that they were playing a form of the game, long before the English, and possibly even earlier than the French.

This theory is lent further weight by the fact that, in the 12th century, tennis was played for money. So, if a player was playing for nothing, in other words, not playing for money, then it was said that *"omme lof spleen"*, that they were *"playing for the honour"*. Thus, to play for the *honour* which was to play for no money or wagers of any sort. So you were playing for the love of the game, for *lof*, which shows how *lof*, or *love*, came to mean *nothing* in tennis.

As for the etymology of the word *love*, there are two main schools of thought. The first, and less commonly known one, is that it stems from about 3000 BC from the old Indian Sanskrit word *leubh*, meaning *desire*, which is thought to be directly linked with the English word *libido* and is the likely root and origin of our more amorous interpretation of the word, *love*.

The second theory in the evolution of the word *love* as a term of endearment is, once again, thought to derive from the Dutch word *lof*, often spelt, *lief*, meaning *"to have faith"* or *"honour"*, and which is a direct link to the English word *belief*, which is simply a contraction of the phrase *"being of faith"*.

This ties in with the historical lineage of the word *love*, as it first started appearing in written texts around the 13th century as *"one's beloved country"*. In other words, you would fight for the *faith*, or *belief*, or *love* of your country. And this term gradually spread via the royal courts to be used when doing something for the *faith*, *belief* or *love* of your king as well. And it wasn't until much later that the term

240

came to be applied to an individual and, even then, it was used more in the manner of *"a beloved person"*.

Thus. it has its origins closely interwoven with the previously mentioned Dutch word *lof*, meaning *"to trust in someone's honour"*. The two words are so closely linked that they were often interchangeable, especially around the time that the term entered into the English language, circa the 12th century.

In reality, it wasn't until about half a century later that phrases like *"love letter"* first started to make an appearance, and another half a century before the first *"love songs"* were sung. It seems there was a bit of a dearth on the love front after that, because it took a further century before the term *"falling in love"* was finally put to paper in the early part of the 15th century.

Fast forward another century and the term *"to make love"* starts to appear. Even then, though, it did not have any sexual connotations at all, it merely meant *to court* or *to woo* your intended. It wasn't actually until the early 18th century that *love* began to be associated with a partner that one was in a relationship with, and not until the 19th century that it began to take on all the connotations with which we associate it today.

From this it's easy to see how the term *love* came to be used as a modern term of endearment between partners. What could be a greater definition of a couple's love for one another than that they had total *faith* and absolute *trust* in one another, and that they *honoured* one another completely.

Therefore, contrary to popular thinking, *love* to a tennis player does not mean nothing, it actually means a great deal, something to be held in the highest *honour*, the utmost *belief*, in total *trust*, and of the strongest possible *affection* that is conceivable for one human being to give to another.

So, although this may be all very well in terms of historical detail, it makes for a lousy joke and just doesn't sell well on T-shirts.

TENNIS INVENTS THE ACE

The origin of the word *ace* proves almost as elusive for me to find in history as it is for me to execute on court. That said, many sports use the word, so let's see if we can try and narrow it down a bit by burrowing deep into the recesses of time.

Most dictionaries lean towards the word *ace* as coming from the Latin word for *one*, which was *as*, via the intermediary of Old French, which also used the same word, *as*.

In Latin, it's also said to have first referred to a kind of coin, called *as*. John Ayto's *Word Origins* suggests it may have been Estruscan in origin, and the *Oxford English Dictionary* states that it possibly stems from a Tarentine word, *as*, which, in turn, could be derived from the Greek word *eis*, or even from a Persian card game, *As*, similar to poker.

Following exactly how the word *ace* derived its tennis meaning proves to be an extremely circumambulatory one. The first recorded usage is in the 12th century in reference to the game of dice, where the side with only one dot was referred to as the *ace, ais, eis* or *as*.

In those days, an *ace* had the exact opposite association to that which we know it today, in that it was the lowest dice score you could get and simply meant just *one*, and therefore *ace* in those days meant something that was of little or no value. Indeed it remained that way for several hundred years until about the 15th century when cards started to value the *ace* as both the highest and lowest card so that it could be used in a run or a suit at either end of the pack. It is at this point in time when the term started to take on a new life.

Suddenly, the term *"an ace in the pack"* started to confer something good. When someone played an *ace* in a game of cards, it would trump any other card and mean that they would win the point with one single card. In other words, just like in tennis, an *ace* was an *"unreturnable play"*.

Incidentally, *ace* and the word *arse*, or *ass* as they say Stateside, share exactly the same etymology. The smutty, gambling, rowdy, medieval philistines of old obviously couldn't resist comparing the small single dot on the dice to the striking similarities it bore to, er, well, let's not go to the bottom of that particular rabbit hole.

Suffice it to say that over the centuries, not even tennis has managed to change the negative connotations associated with the word *arse*. So when a tennis player calls a line judge an *arse*, it doesn't infer that they think that the line judge is an absolutely ace guy or that all his calls are excellent and straight from the top of the deck; no, it's more akin the old-fashioned sense of the word.

Bummer.

TENNIS INVENTS DEUCE

Following neatly on from *ace* deriving from *one*, we have the word *deuce*, stemming from the French word for *two*. Originally it would have been called as *"a deux du jeu"*, which Literal means *"two points away from the game"*.

The lazy English shortened it first to *"a deus"*, but two syllables was obviously way too exhausting to keep uttering in the middle of a strenuous five setter, so it was further shortened to *deus*. It was then we started to pronounce it differently as well, but presumably that wasn't anything to do with phonology, we just wanted to annoy the French. And then, maybe as there hadn't been a war with France for a few years, we decided to further antagonise them by changing the spelling as well and, before you can shout *"Sacré bleu!"*, we had *"deuce"*.

Of course, language was pretty fluid in those days, even Shakespeare spelt his own name several different ways, so the upshot is that nobody really knows how it came to be shortened, but historically language has always found a way of contracting words and phrases. For instance, the 45 score line is perennially referred to as 40 these days, and, even in my lifetime, the call of *"Fifteen all"*, is often now called as just *"Five all"*.

I'm thinking that perhaps *"a deux"* sounded too much like a sneeze, and the constant retorts of *"Bless you"* reminded those hardened old medieval gamblers of just how far they had strayed from their religious paths.

Surely just being out on court, playing tennis, is blessings enough for anyone.

TENNIS INVENTS SERVICE

The origin of the word *serve* in tennis is equally hard to nail down convincingly. The one most favoured by historians seems to be the most logical in that it came via the French verb *servir*, from the Latin *servius*, meaning *to administer unto*. Hence when you make a tennis *serve*, you are simply administering unto your opponent by *serving* them a tennis ball.

The other theory bandied around by tennis boffs is that, supposedly, the term came from the generously proportioned King Henry VIII. The great man, being of such rotundity that he was unable to make the strenuous service action himself, employed his servant to throw the first ball into play for him because he was simply too spherically challenged to do it himself. And, because it was the servant who delivered the first ball, so the term *"servants throw"* became *"serve"* and *"service"*.

Personally, if I had been a king of such enormous of girth that I could hardly muster enough guff to even mete out a decent serve, I think I would have opted to have served the first ball myself and then wobbled off to the side of the court for a brief snifter of mead, to let my servant play all the other far more strenuous points.

The trick being to hire a really good servant, like say, Sir Rafael N'adal de la Rolan Garreaux.

TENNIS INVENTS THE RACKET

The most adhered-to theory about the word racket is that it can be traced back to the Arabic word *rahat*, meaning *"palm of the hand"*. This then gave rise to the Middle English game *raket*, which was itself a kind of handball, as well as the Old French word *rachette*, meaning *"palm of the hand"* or *"racket"*. There is also the medieval Latin *raschete*, meaning *palm*.

This all fits neatly with the fact that nearly all early forms of the game of tennis stemmed from some form of the original *Jeu de paume* game, which translates as *"palm of the hand"* because, before rackets were used, players used their hands.

The earliest written reference found to a racket can be found in Chaucer's 1385 poem *Troillus and Criseyde*, where he poses the titillating question, *"But kanstow playen raket, to and fro?"* What's particularly intriguing about this quote is that it was posed several centuries before any other written or pictorial evidence of a tennis racket can be found.

It's certainly one of great mysteries of tennis chronology, and one that has divided historians for years. Some arguing that tennis had a plethora of variants not only in court size and balls but also player numbers, styles and rules, and that maybe there were some local *"house rules"* where a racket was allowed to be used.

Others argue that the *raket* referred to cannot be a racket and is more likely to be the name of the game they were playing. What makes the riddle even more tantalising is the phrase *"playen raket, to and fro?"* which sounds like they were having a rally of some sort, which certainly sounds like an early form of tennis.

Either way, without further written evidence, I suspect that this particular argument will *ragen to and fro* for many centuries to come.

The next recorded reference to a genuine cross-strung racket, or *reticulum*, comes in 1522 when Erasmus Colloquia Familiaria mocks his opponent's tennis skills saying that he'd be better off using his racket to go fishing with.

What's interesting about this damning insult is that it implies that it was strung like a net, long before we find any other written or pictorial references which would confirm this. The next citation we find is in 1539, when the Spanish author Vines also mentions a racket and writes, for the first time anywhere, that they use catgut to make the strings.

It's around this time that a few illustrations of early tennis rackets first start to appear. The Duke of Brunswick's *Stammbuch* folios in 1597, *Das Ballhaus* circa 1600, the *Collegium Illustre* in 1598, and Hulpeau's *Le Rev de le paume* in 1632, are perhaps the best known early depictions of a racket being used in tennis.

Wooden rackets continued to evolve slowly and peacefully, without incident for nearly five centuries, until a certain Mr Connors walked out with his metallic monstrosity, sending shock waves through the tennis establishment, paralysing the game's law-making authorities, and changing the very nature of the game forever.

I'm with McEnroe on this one, in that they should have followed cricket's example and outlawed it as soon as it happened, to keep the game consistent so that we could compare players more easily through the ages instead of comparing technologies. Now there's another argument that's also likely to be *ragen to and fro* for many centuries to come ...

TENNIS INVENTS THE LOB

When Spencer Gore won the inaugural Wimbledon Championship in 1877, he used a then-unknown tactic of storming to the net and smashing away the volley. It was such an unorthodox shot that none of the Rackets players or Real Tennis players, who made up most of the Wimbledon draw, had an answer to this strange new tactic.

But the following year, Frank Hadow, who had been watching Spencer Gore's volley tactics, came up with a possible solution. He would hit the ball high over Gore's head and land it at the back of the court forcing Gore to retreat and give up his advantage. Hadow stuck to his game plan and their match was closely contested throughout. In the end, the ploy paid off as Hadow won the match and the championship title.

Little did he know at the time, but he'd just invented a brand new shot, the lob. Back then, the lob was a much tougher shot to execute, as the rackets were not as sophisticated as they are now, the courts were a different size and the net was set at five foot high at the sides.

The origin of the word *lob* remains one of my favourites. The genesis of the word is as lovely and simple as it is graphic and disgusting. It stems from an old Dutch word *lobbe*, that later came to be used in England in the late 1600s. It was a highly descriptive word used by medieval meat merchants that meant *to hang up a lump of flesh*.

This was a practice commonly used by butchers when they wanted to sell a piece of meat quickly as it had been hanging in the open air too long. So they would drape it high in the window at a discounted price to get rid of it as soon as possible. Consequently, the tennis shot that *"hangs in the air too long"* came to be known as a *lob*.

Of course we all know what happens to meat if it is left hanging in the air too long – it is not a pretty sight and not pleasant on the olfactory system either, which probably also explains how the

German word *Lubbe* also came to mean *a coarse, smelly person*. They obviously smelled like an old piece of meat that had been *hanging in the air too long* and were starting to attract flies!

So, there we are, the next time some coarse player has the audacity to lob you at the net, just turn away snootily and perhaps leave something hanging in the air for them as well.

TENNIS INVENTS THE VOLLEY

The word volley is much easier to trace and far less disgusting than the lob. It comes from the Old French verb *voler*, and from the Latin verb *volare*, meaning to *fly*, as in a volley of arrows or cannonballs that soar through the air.

Think of an arc of arrows or a volley of gunfire that goes straight from one side to the other, often over an obstacle like a castle wall or a defensive barrage, without touching the ground but falls directly into enemy territory.

Exactly, then, as the ball does in a game of tennis today.

TENNIS INVENTS THE COURT

Court comes from the Greek word *chortos*, meaning an *enclosed space*. Usually this is a space enclosed by the wings of a building and it's this association between enclosed yards and their buildings that led to the word *court* being applied to prestigious houses and more especially royal residences and palaces.

Because royals surrounded themselves with so many people, there were always a plethora of individuals hanging around the royal court, and so the term *court* eventually extended to encompass the people there too, which gave rise to the term *courtiers*.

These *courtiers* had to behave in an appropriate manner that was respectful of the royal circles in which they moved, hence the term *courteous*. It was around the time of Shakespeare that the concept of gentlemen being polite to women in order to gain their favour, by being *courteous*, became known as *a-courting*, which has since been abbreviated to *courting*.

The sovereign and their inner circle sometimes had to get together and hash out disputes and dispense justice according to their laws. These gatherings naturally also became known as the *law of the courts*.

By the time the word *court* made its way to England, all these derivations were already in common use, so the Real Tennis court was literally a royal courtyard, or a cloistered courtyard, in which to play tennis. The term stuck and has remained with us to this day.

TENNIS INVENTS THE GRAND SLAM

The term *Grand Slam* really owes its origins more to cards than tennis. In the Middle Ages, cards, like tennis, was played for money, as was every other sport at the time. In cards, making 12 tricks was called a *small slam*, and the much rarer feat of making all 13 tricks was termed a *grand slam*.

Strictly speaking, the term *Grand Slam* in tennis used to mean that a player holds all four major titles in the same year, now known as a *Calendar Grand Slam*, but it is so rare, and so hard to do these days, that now each major title is regarded as a *Grand Slam*. A *Career Grand Slam* is to achieve a win of all four majors at some point in your career not just in the same year.

Even rarer is to hold all four majors as well as winning the prestigious World Tour Masters Championships finals that takes place at the end of the year, often colloquially referred to as the *Fifth Slam*, to take the end of year world number one ranking slot as well. This is called a *Super Slam*.

There is, though, an even rarer title, a mythical beast of even greater legend than a *Grand Slam* or the *Super Slam* and that is the *Golden Slam* – where a player not only holds all four major titles in the same year but also the Olympic Gold medal as well.

Only one person has ever achieved such an astonishing feat, and that was Steffi Graf in 1988, when she won all four Grand Slam titles, as well as the World Tour finals to end the year as world number one, whilst also having time to nip out and win the Olympic Gold Medal; thus creating yet another prestigious tier to hold, the first and only ever winner of a *Golden Super Slam* in tennis history.

TENNIS INVENTS SMASH

OK, not the instant mashed potato type of *smash*, with the advert full of Martians all laughing at how humans still mash their potatoes by hand, even I would be hard pushed to claim that tennis invented mashed potato.

But long before the wonderful world of TV advertising came along, way back in the 12th century, the term *smash* had only negative connotations. Something that had been *smashed* meant that it was *broken with intentional violence*, like glass. Gradually, the term *smash* came to be associated with the actual blow that caused the break itself. Hence phrases like *"The army smashed through the enemy ranks"*. And so the term started to move away from meaning just *broken*.

Over the centuries anything that was *broken* came be termed a *smash*, so a *smash hit* was something that *broke* box-office records. Gradually, the meaning evolved to imply something more up-beat, for example when something was a box office *smash*, a sensational *smash*, an explosive *smash*, it meant a good thing and now started to take on much more positive associations.

When you combine the original meaning of an intentionally violent blow with the newer more positive *smash*, then it is easy to see how it merged to become the perfect word for the tennis shot we now know as the *smash*.

The first written evidence I can find of the tennis *smash* in print was around the 1880, when the Renshaw brothers dominated the tennis world and the phrase *overhead smash* was used to describe their deadly blows. It was a new style of play that made them famous, and whenever they were on court huge crowds would flock to witness this sensational new shot.

Soon the shot became known as the *Renshaw Smash* and loud cheers would ring out from the grandstands every time they executed one of their famous *overhead smashes*.

Over the years, as the Renshaw brothers moved on, it reverted to being called the *overhead smash* again, then over the years it was shortened down to *smash*, although many pros and tennis pundits still use the term *overhead*.

Now, back to that idea about how tennis could have invented mash potato, hmm ... let's see, if you crushed the potatoes through a well strung racket ...

... Oh, come on now, we were all students once, we've all strained the spaghetti through a nearby tennis racket.

What? Really? Just me?

OK, I'm a slob but I saw Jack Lemmon doing it in an old black and white film called *The Apartment*, so I thought it was perfectly acceptable. Oh, well, I guess that's the last time I'll be able to serve a *spag bol* at one of my dinner parties and get away with it.

TENNIS INVENTS SUDDEN DEATH

The phrase *Sudden Death* is used in many sports to break the deadlock between two teams or players in order to decide an outright winner by the end of an allocated time or set piece.

The earliest references of it being in use is in a dice game in which the fates of prisoners or debtors was decided on the roll of a dice; whether they would be deported, be imprisoned and sometimes even if they were to literally live or die. Today we tend to use the phrase *Dicing with Death* rather benignly but back then it was a very gruesome reality.

Gamblers would often allow each other one final throw of the dice to end an evening's play, which became known as *Sudden Death* when the winner would take everything in the pot. How *Sudden Death* is played out today varies from sport to sport, for instance in football it means the next team to score a goal wins the match, in tennis the next point wins the game, etc.

We very rarely see a *Sudden Death* point being played in professional sport these days, most have adapted the concept to make it a bit fairer. Football would have the game decided on a series of 10 penalties, and tennis would extenuate it to become the tie-break, which takes us neatly to our next morsel of tennis intrigue ...

TENNIS INVENTS THE TIE-BREAK

In tennis the sudden-death system had long been abhorred by players and fans alike, and there was huge pressure for the regulators to come up with some sort of compromise in close matches.

They needed something that would fill the gap between a sudden death point and the alternative of continuing to play the set indefinitely until one player goes two games ahead, which often resulted in the players being wiped out on the first day of an important tournament.

The deadlock was eventually broken when James Van Alen, who founded the Tennis Hall of Fame in Rhode Island, put forward a possible solution in the early 1950s. Dubbed the VASS System, the Van Alen Streamlined Scoring System, he proposed a nine-point "Tiebreaker", which basically meant that once the set had reached 6–6, then the first player to reach five points would win the set.

Van Alen was also a great showman, so when his scoring system was first adopted he would sit courtside and, when the set reached 6 games all, he would raise a big red flag to signal the start of the tie-break, adding to the drama and tension to the showdown.

The trouble with this system was that, once the players both reached 4 points each, they were effectively still just playing a sudden death point, all they were really doing was extending the set by a couple of points. The crowd loved it as it produced many short moments of extreme excitement, but the players hated it.

Then in the early 1970s, the 13-point tie-break was introduced with one crucial amendment, that instead of the winner being the first player to get to seven points, it was the first player to seven points with a two point lead. This was much better as it meant that it was impossible to lose a set with just one mistake, and meant that you had a chance to come back.

In essence, this system emulated the ebb and flow of a full set but in miniature. It was an instant success, the crowds still loved it for all the added tension it brought to the game and the players came to begrudgingly accept it as a fairer substitute.

For quite some time, different versions of the system were used, with Wimbledon and the Davis Cup being the slowest adopters, making the players wait until the score was 8 games all before starting the tie-break. Even then, they still retained the idea that the final set should remain an advantage set, until eventually in 2019 even Wimbledon gave in and changed it as well, setting a tie-break in the final set only if the score should reach 12 games all.

This means that the infamous John Isner v Nicolas Mahut match, which took place in the first round of Wimbledon in 2010, will remain the all-time longest match in tennis history. It was played over several days and lasted 11 hours and 6 minutes. Isner went on to win the set, which ended up going to a staggering finale, quite literally they were both staggering by then, 70–68 in the final set. The final set alone was longer than the previous record for an entire match.

To put it into perspective, Isner and Mahut made about £15 per point in that match. Whereas, in the final that same year, Rafael Nadal made about £5,000 per point. The crowd got a much better deal, as it worked out as the best value match ever for spectators at just 20p a game!

To rub more salt into the wound, Mahut actually won 24 more points than Isner did, winning 502 points to Isner's 478. That 24-point difference is almost as many as it took Serena to win the entire final set of some of her matches that year!

A few other records of note for that match were:

The most games ever played: 183 games
Record amount of balls used: 130 balls
The longest fifth set ever: 8 hrs 11 mins
The most games ever played in a fifth set: 138 games
Most aces served in a match: 112 Isner, 103 Mahut

Record for holding their serve consecutively: 168 times
Most times anyone has ever served to stay in the match: 65 times
Most winners hit in a match: 490 total. Isner hit 246 and Mahut 244
Largest amount of unforced errors: Isner made 52 and Mahut 39
Most calories burned during a match: about 16,000 each
Most amount of Google hits for a 1st Round match: 2.7 million
A record amount of money was also bet: £15 million
With the favourite on who was going to win changing 1,285 times
Biggest crowd ever for Court 18: 5,125 in a 782 seat court!
The longest an umpire has gone without a rest break: 7 hrs 40 mins
Longest gap between first match point and second: 183 games
Players consumed a record of 9 bananas, 40 bottles of water and 24 energy bars

TENNIS INVENTS THE BAGEL

Tennis, like the English language, is constantly evolving and, more often than not, instead of the tennis world being the originator of a word, it simply purloins a word and gives it new meaning. For instance, one of the TV commentators recently described a serve as *"a real McDonalds serve"*. He was describing a serve that was hit with such fierce spin and kicked up so high that its trajectory resembled that of the burger chain's golden arched 'M' that is its trademark.

And so it is with our next tennis word, the *bagel*. Originally defined as a hard bread roll made of yeast dough twisted into a small circular shape like the letter "O". The other thing that makes the bagel unique is that it's the only bread product that is boiled first before it is baked, giving it its distinctive crust and characteristic shine.

The word *bagel* actually has a fascinating history all of its own, way before tennis hijacked it for its own nefarious purposes. It stems from the German and Dutch words *bougel*, *beugel* and *bugel*, that mean *ring*, *bracelet*, *bracket* or *stirrup*. And there's a lovely legend dating back to the 17th century that explains how it came to be the tasty yeast loop we all know and love today.

Folklore has it that a local Jewish baker in Vienna, Austria, wanted to thank the King of Poland for protecting his countrymen from the Turkish invaders in 1683. So he made a special bread roll in the shape of a riding stirrup, which is called a *Bugel* in German, to commemorate the King's favourite pastime of horse riding, and it was this that gave the *bagel* its distinctive 'O' shape. It took a couple of more centuries for the bagel to reach the world of tennis, but let's start with how it reached the western hemisphere.

When the Eastern European Jewish immigrants began arriving in North America at the turn of the last century, they brought their scrumptiously tasty stirrups of dough with them. By the early 1900s, *bagels* were firmly established as part of New York's burgeoning food culture scene.

It was here that the term *bagel* started to infiltrate the tennis world. The late Bud Collins, one the sport's great writers and commentators, is often credited with originating the term *bagel*, which means beating someone 6–0. While it was unquestionably Bud who popularised the term, he graciously credits Eddie Dibbs and Harold Solomon as the ones who first coined it.

Solomon and Dibbs were one of the best known doubles' pairings of the '60s and early '70s, and both were renowned for eating cream cheese *bagels* for breakfast, lunch and dinner. Because they both looked quite similar to each other and had an almost identical playing style, they were soon dubbed the Bagel Twins on the tennis circuit.

Anyone who got a heavy thrashing by the Bagel Twins were said to have been *bagel-ed*, and because the shape of the *bagel* looks like a zero then it started to take on extra significance, especially if they won a set to love, which was when Bud Collins started to use it as a commentator in the mid-1960s.

The metonym quickly caught on with commentators and players alike, and thus it was that a shiny crusted, pre-boiled, hollowed out lump of Austrio-Semitic stirrup shaped dough became part of our sporting narrative. The term *bagel* is now satisfyingly and permanently embedded into the vast and ever-expanding lexicon of tasty tennis patois.

Other flavoursome appetisers that I've heard over the years to denote tennis score lines include:

A Sausage:
A euphemism for thrashing someone 6–1.

Be careful with this one though because, although it may be perfectly acceptable to boast that you *bagel-ed* your opponent, you might want to be more cautious about rushing home to your wife and boasting that you just gave your opponent a good *sausage-ing*, or else you may find yourself in the spare room and getting frowned at by the in-laws.

A Twix:

This is when the sets concludes at 6–2.

Named after a certain chocolate and caramel biscuit bar, famous for having two fingers in a pack.

A Desmond:

This is when you beat someone 6–2, 6–2.

And is named after the South African cleric Desmond Tutu, best known for his anti-apartheid and human rights campaigning.

A Kit-Kat:

Denotes a score line of 6–4.

And refers to the yummy milk chocolate-covered wafer snack that has four deliciously scrumptious fingers to each bar. Other chocolate bars are available, but they are obviously inferior to this one, which is the original and still the best. Nestlé, my agent has my address.

Sometimes, if a player wins two sets to love, you might hear them bragging of a double bagel, but I have also heard it referred to as a *bicycle*, or I have even heard the phrase *spectacles* as well.

I've also heard some players refer to a triple bagel as a *Tic-Tac-Toe*, after the noughts and crosses game when you win by placing three noughts in a row.

In England, the term *bagel* is sometimes substituted for the word *doughnut* as well, and I have even heard yet a third variation used when some poor unfortunate was beaten 6–0, 6–0, 6–0 in three consecutive sets. The winner, not wanting to boast numerically, came up with this rather novel expression: *"I gave him a bagel in the first set, a doughnut in the second and a Polo mint in the third."*

This makes the victor sound much more like a generous benefactor who comes bearing gifts of sugary goodness and likening himself more akin to a sort of tennis Santa Claus, rather than the mean-spirited, heartless savage that he really was.

All I'm saying is, be merciful with your euphemisms, you don't want to make anyone feel so torturously bad about their play that they might be forced to toy with the idea of giving up the beautiful game they once loved to take up some other sport, perhaps something a little less savage, like bare knuckle fist fighting in the back alleys of Kosovo.

TENNIS INVENTS SEEDING

The word *seed* has its origins in the US and it's as American as apple pie. Although probably best not to tell the Yanks that the English invented apple pie at least two centuries earlier than them, but I let my stomach digress again – must be all that talk of bagels and chocolate in the previous section.

The tennis *seed* can be traced directly to its obvious farming origins where it relates to planting. A *"scattering of seeds"* in this sense first shows up in print very early on in the 12th century.

Farmers would scatter *seeds* so that they were not too close together in the field, so that when the *seeds* sprouted and grew, they wouldn't block each other's light or encroach on each other's soil, giving each plant the maximum light exposure with the best opportunity to flourish and blossom.

Exactly the same concept is applied when *seeding* tennis players today. The seeding system ensures that all your top *seeds* aren't too close together in the draw and won't knock each other out in the early stages of the tournament. In this way, your best players are able to shine through and blossom in the later stages of the tournament.

The earliest written reference appears in the *American Lawn Tennis Journal* in 1898, which stated simply: *"Several years ago, it was decided to 'seed' the best players through the championship draw in handicap tournaments so that the players in each class shall be separated as far as possible one from another."* The fact that the word *seed* was marked in inverted commas, indicates that it was still in an early adoption of the phrase.

TENNIS INVENTS THE TWEENIE

We've all tried it and we've all risked wrecking our matrimonial procreation gear in the process – the shot between the legs, the one that the pundits like to term the *"Tweenie"*, or as us amateurs call it, the *"Ouchie!"*.

Some punters also refer to it as the *Hot Dog*, as you split yourself down the middle just like a hot dog. The *Tweenie* was actually invented by our old friend the sexagenarian champion himself, Jacques Barre, who is the first player to have ever been recorded to perform the shot in 1829.

Barre was an old fashioned entertainer and this wasn't the end of his showmanship skills. Another of his favourite tricks was to hold the racket the wrong way round and hit the ball with the handle instead.

Well, I've done that and from now on I'm calling it a trick shot, so I don't want to hear any more rumblings about it being a jammy miss-hit off the frame.

TENNIS INVENTS ROUGH OR SMOOTH

The custom of calling *"rough or smooth"*, before spinning a racket to determine who should serve first at the start of a match, casts us back to the days when tennis rackets used to be strung with a few extra lines of red thread at the top and bottom of the strings. The thread was a trimming silk which helped to keep the main strings in place and the practice was called *Trebling*.

To do this, the racket was placed in a clamp and the stringer would loop the stringing silk around the racket strings but the side that they tied it off and cut would always be the *"rough"* edges side, leaving the other side as *"smooth"*. Although there is no *trebling* these days, there is still a rough and smooth side to the racket as the strings themselves are tied off in a similar fashion and then cut, leaving one side of the racket with four rough knots and the other side all smooth.

Although professional tournaments still spin a coin to decide the serve, not many players carry coins with them on court, so spinning of the racket remains the fairest way to call who serves as both players can see the knots. Just be wary of the player who uses the logo on the handle and calls, *"up or down?"* as this method is easy to manipulate as they turn the racket round to show you.

Luckily, tennis players are mostly a good, honest bunch and I've only ever come across one player who does this. Suffice it to say that when it comes to the line calls of such a character you will also have to take the rough with the smooth.

TENNIS INVENTS A WALTER

This is another lovely tennis expression that deserves mention both for its originality and the fact that I had never heard it before, until one particularly creative member of that fine sporting establishment, The Queen's Club, enlightened me further.

When I asked him if he had had a good game, he uttered something along the lines that it wasn't a particularly good match but that they'd had a few good *Walters*. Spotting the perplexed curl of my eyebrows, he went on to inform me that this was Cockney Rhyming slang, referencing Sir Walter Raleigh, so a few good *Walters* means that they'd had a few good rallies.

Much as I love the expression, I cast doubt about whether it was really the Cockneys from London's East End that came up with it, especially as I have failed to find any reference of it in any Cockney Rhyming slang dictionaries. Still, I'm delighted to include it here, simply because it's a bit of a Steffi.

For any non-Cockney speakers in the house, believe it or not Steffi Graf actually does make it into the modern lexicon of Cockney Rhyming slang, with Steffi Graf meaning *laugh*.

If I hadn't read it with my own eyes, I would never have Adam n Eve'd it either.

TENNIS INVENTS HAZARD

Hazard

/haz'ard/

noun: chance, random risk, danger, accident.

Is how the dictionary defines *hazard*, but did you know that the word also owes much of its common usage to tennis?

If you play Real Tennis, you will already be familiar with the term. The *Hazard* is a side wall with an angled buttress on it, close to the receiver's end of the court. Appropriately, if a ball hits the buttress, it will fly off at a random angle to its original trajectory, making it very difficult for the opponent to adjust their shot in enough time to make a return.

Most historians concur that the word has passed down into common usage via the tennis world, and yet closer scrutiny reveals that it might predate tennis. In the 13th century *Hazard* was the name of a popular dice game based more on luck than skill, and it's more likely that tennis inherited the word from the dice game than the other way around.

The etymology of *Hazard* is thought to derive from the Arabic word *az-zahr*, meaning *dice*. It was probably picked up during the Crusades in the Holy Land and later transferred to medieval Europe. In France and Spain, the words *Hazart*, *Azard* and *Azar* started to appear around this time too relating to the game of dice, and latterly the word was adapted into cards as well, all of which lends support to the above theory.

Due to the very nature of the dice game *Hazard*, the word quickly became associated with anything unpredictable or risky, as fortunes could be won or lost on a single throw of the dice. This explains how the word *Hazard* came to be applied to the buttress on the Real Tennis courts because, when the ball struck it, it introduced a similarly unpredictable element to the game.

While the *Hazard* dice game faded over the years, Real Tennis kept its *Hazard* wall and the word has drifted into common usage throughout world to be applied to anything that has a random element of risk to it.

TENNIS INVENTS BEING UNDERHAND

The summer of 1989 was an historically momentous year. There was the fall of the Berlin Wall, Solidarity in Poland, Stephen Hawking publishes *"A Brief History of Time"*, the Romanian dictator Ceaușescu was deposed, there were the pro-democracy protests in Tiananmen Square, the Dalai Lama won The Nobel Peace Prize, and Michael Chang served that now famous underhand serve against Ivan Lendl at The French Open.

At just 17 years old, Chang went into the record books as the youngest ever winner of a Grand Slam, but his extraordinary accomplishment was almost completely overshadowed by that one surprising moment in his fourth round match against the world number one, Ivan Lendl.

Few people gave the teenager much chance against the three-time French Open champion, and the odds lengthened still further when the Czech took a two sets to love lead. But Chang showed real character and fought back heroically, to take the third set. But Chang wasn't used to playing the long gruelling rallies that clay court tennis produces, and by the fourth set he started to cramp up and could hardly walk, let alone run around a court.

Chang was serving 3–4 down and 15–30 down and was cramping so severely that he knew that he had no other option but to retire, but just as he was thinking of striding up to the net to offer Lendl his hand, he looked up and he caught his father's eye looking down at him. Chang knew that retiring was not an option his father would accept. It would be considered a highly dishonourable thing to do and bring shame to his family and country. So, being unable to move much he decided to just limp around the court and smash clean winners as and when he could. Lendl found this most disturbing and the crowds were cheering and jeering in equal measure and nobody really knew what on earth was going on.

Chang found serving especially hard as he was unable to stand on his toes and so, without even thinking, just as a way to avoid further pain, he hit an underarm serve. The crowd gasped at the audacity of it. It completely surprised Lendl who lost the point and showed his disgust in no uncertain terms. The crowd went ballistic. A furious Lendl totally lost his concentration and, amidst all the drama, Chang somehow managed to steal the set, taking the match to a fifth set decider, propelling the crowd into a total frenzy.

As the match went on, Chang not only started to recover from his cramp, but the whole episode seemed to inspire him as he went on to win the set and the match, leaving a stunned Lendl totally bewildered. It caused outrage in the press and throughout the tennis world, setting alight a huge debate on the rights and wrongs of the underarm serve. The Chang incident is still furiously contested in tennis clubs around the word even to this day.

All of which leads us neatly to the word *underhand* and to look at how it came to mean, *"in a surreptitious manner, by secret means, clandestine, unsporting"*. The term itself is often thought to have come from the dubious tennis tactic of serving *underhand*. We can refute this outright, as the original way to serve in tennis was underhand. It wasn't until more recently that it became more common practice to serve overarm.

A more robust explanation is that the origin of the phrase *underhand* stems from card sharks, gamblers and fraudsters who would use *sleight of hand* to manipulate the cards in their favour by dealing from the bottom of the deck, and that this is where the term *underhand* first gained its unsportsmanlike reputation. So, phew, the noble game of tennis is not guilty of that one and we can finally lay that debate to rest. Well, until the next Nick Kyrgios match at least!

NOT BY A LONG CHALK

It is a shame that this charming old tennis term now has such negative connotations, because it began life in much more positive territory. These days the expression *"not by a long chalk"* implies that someone is not anywhere close to achieving what they set out to accomplish.

Contrary to popular belief, the expression has nothing to do with the length of a piece of chalk but refers instead to the length of the winning column or margin. This relates to the fact that many sports used to be recorded in chalk on a blackboard by the side of the court, indeed many old Rackets and Real Tennis clubs, still use this method for scoring matches, just as they still do in sports like darts and bowls.

At the end of a match, the number of points that the winner had chalked up against their name was always longer than the amount of points chalked up by the loser, hence the expression *"not by a long chalk"*.

PLAYING TO SCRATCH

In both Real Tennis and golf, a player who plays to *scratch* is a player who is so good that they have no handicap and are known as *scratch* players.

The term is also used in horse racing, to *scratch* a horse is when the horse's name is removed, or quite literally scratched, from the list of runners. In billiards it's used when a player hits the cue ball into a pocket by mistake, so then your score is returned to zero, or *scratched* off the scoreboard. But how did the term come to mean *nothing* in the first place?

Scratch derives from the Middle English word *scracchen*, thought to be a fusion of the words *scratten* and *cracchen*, meaning *to scratch*. Here again the Dutch seem to be in on the act before everyone else, as they have an even older word *cratsen*, which means something similar.

As is often the case, it appears the phrase has its roots in gambling, a *scratch* player is someone who is considered so good that they will receive no odds in a handicap match, hence *nothing* again.

We also use the word *scratch* in terms of making a mark on something, and when we have an itch that we *scratch* it, sometimes marking our own skin. Occasionally, we also use the expression *"not up to scratch"* to describe something that is not of the quality we had expected.

Another common phrase is *"starting from scratch"* when we try something but fail and have to go back and start all over again. Amazingly, all three versions owe their origins to the ancient Greeks and the Olympians, who used to hold sprint races along ordinary roads. They would mark the starting point by scratching a line in the dirt.

After a false start, or some foul play, the runners would be ordered to go back and start again from the *scratch* mark, giving rise to the phrase *"starting from scratch"*.

If a runner was unfit, or not considered good enough to compete in the race in the first place, he was said to be *"not up to scratch"*.

So when a tennis player, or sportsman or horse, withdraws from a competition, it is said that they have been *scratched*.

A HAT TRICK

If a player serves three consecutive aces in a match, you will often hear the commentators describe it as a *hat trick*. A *hat trick* is a commonly used term in many arenas, implying that somebody has achieved three consecutive successes in their field.

Many attribute the origins of *hat trick* to the world of magic, in that magicians famously pull things out of a hat as a trick. Admittedly, there is something almost magical about pulling off a trio of successes, and it is probably this rather charming concept that has kept the myth alive.

Essentially, though, the term comes from cricket and was originally applied to a bowler who takes three wickets in three consecutive balls. It's called a *hat trick* because, in the 19th century, it was customary that whenever a player pulled off this extraordinary feat, their Club would honour the achievement by presenting them with a hat or cap.

Traditionally, that hat or cap would bear that Club's insignia or colours, and hence the term *"colours"*, which is still used today to honour collegiate sporting successes as well.

PLAYING FAST AND LOOSE

In tennis parlance, playing *fast and loose* has come to mean someone who is playing recklessly but, when applied outside of sport, it implies that someone is not careful, not to be trusted, a bit of a fly-by-night character.

There is a line of thought that suggests the phrase owes its origins to a popular Victorian parlour game that was marketed under the name *Fast and Loose*, but the game was actually quite a sweet and genteel pastime that belies the dodgy connotations that haunt the phrase today and so is unlikely to be the source.

If we trace the game back a little further though, we find that *Fast and Loose* was originally a game found at travelling fairgrounds and its shady origins suddenly start to make sense. The game involved pinning a folded leather belt to a board by passing a skewer through the loop. If the belt held, you would win a prize, if the belt came loose, then you would lose the game.

As is usual in those days, the prize to be won and the stake to be lost was money, so yet again it was just another form of gambling. What the innocent player didn't know was that the unscrupulous stall holder had folded the belt in such a way that it was virtually impossible to make the belt hold fast and so it would almost always come loose.

Which is how the term *"playing fast and loose"* came to imply a certain amount of deviousness about someone's conduct.

TENNIS INVENTS PUTTING THE BALL IN YOUR COURT

The expression of *"putting the ball in your court"* is a well-known English term that means that the responsibility has passed to you, and that it's that up to you to make the next move.

The origin of the phrase is much debated but most authoritative sources agree that it owes its origins to tennis. When the ball is played into your side of the court during a game of tennis, it's up to you take action and hit it to keep the game going, if you don't, it all stops.

Although the phrase didn't come into popular usage until the middle of the 20th century, it's thought to date back to very early forms of the game, possibly even as far back as Real Tennis and *Jeu de paume*, when tennis was more of a hand-to-hand ball game. The original expression is thought to be a contraction of the original phrase, which was: *"It's out of my hands now, the ball is in your court"*. In fact, sometimes people just use the first half of the expression and say *"It's out of my hands"* instead, but both have exactly the same implications.

The expression would be defined as an idiom. In that it has a figurative meaning that is not easily deduced from its literal definition. Such descriptive imagery is often used in the English language in order to convey a concise idea in pictorial form. These types of expressions fall into popular usage because they illustrate a point far more efficiently, and often with greater depth of emotion than a literal expression, giving the phrase connotations that go way beyond the literal meaning of the words.

The idiom *"the ball's in your court now"* often carries with it a sense of exasperation from the person uttering it, as if they have been rallying back and forth a long time to no avail, and are at their wits end.

TENNIS INVENTS BEING ON THE BALL

The expression of being *"on the ball"* is another term that is often linked to tennis but the consensus these days is that it might not be as clear cut as we originally thought

Most authorities agree that *"on the ball"* originates in the sporting arena, but the glaring question is, which sport, as so many sports use a ball? So it might be surprising to learn that the two leading contenders have always been running and boxing. The theory being that to do well in both you always need to be *"on the balls"* of your feet, implying that you are eager and ready to go, a similar expression to saying *"keeping you on your toes"*. But historians aren't convinced, simply because there is very little historical evidence to support it.

A more commonly advocated source of *"on the ball"* comes from a rather sedate and unsporting domain – the Royal Observatory in Greenwich. The term relates to the Greenwich time-ball which was installed in 1833 to signal the accurate time to ships sailing past on their way out to sea. It was, and still is, raised just before 1.00 pm each day and falls exactly at 1.00 pm, to match the clock in the famous observatory clock tower.

As every Greenwich tour guide will tell you, the time-ball at Greenwich is the oldest surviving and best-known time-ball in the world. They will explain how the time-ball was especially important in the 19th century as captains needed to have their ships' chronometers set absolutely accurately in order to navigate correctly. The slightest error could send them miles off course and end in disaster. Thus, explaining the incredible importance of being *"on the ball"*.

In this fast moving digital world, the concept of the time-ball has become slightly overlooked, although it's still part of the American tradition at New Year's Eve when the New York time-ball falls in Time Square to officially announce midnight and signal the start of the festivities.

The Greenwich time-ball, then, is the true origin of the phrase, as the captains really needed to be *"on the ball"* as this was their last chance before embarking on a long journey and needed to be deadly accurate. This is by far my favourite anecdote on the origin of the expression and the one I want believe most. But, alas, life doesn't always play fair.

As is often the case in these matters, the phrase *"on the ball"* appears to come from a contraction of an earlier expression *"keep your eye on the ball"*, which leads us back to the sporting arena. It was sound sporting advice dished out in virtually every known ball game since time immemorial. As for its source, we need to look at all the early ball games, such as cricket, golf, football, croquet and rounders, as it seems to be chronicled in many such sports and not just tennis.

In America, they like to claim that baseball is the origin of the expression, but the earliest written record I can find comes from the English game of rounders, from which baseball is derived – sorry America! It comes from William Kingston's *Book for Boys* written in the mid-1800s. However, there are various allusions to the game of rounders being played many centuries before that as well.

As we've proved many times throughout this book, tennis is far older than rounders, so I'm going to stick my neck out and say that I'm sure the expression was used in the ancient game of tennis, even if it went undocumented. And if I'm proved wrong? Well, I can always go back to my day job as a tour guide at the Greenwich Observatory.

TENNIS INVENTS A COMPLETE SHAM

At first, the link between tennis and the word *sham* seems a little tenuous, but that has never stopped me before and, more importantly, the word *sham* came to play an extremely important part in the history of tennis, shaping it into the modern game we know today.

We regard a *sham* as something that appears ostensibly to be one thing, but is in fact a counterfeit or fraud. Most etymologists agree that it is derived from the word *ashamed*, later shortened to *shame*.

In the 17th century, it was already being widely used in the modern sense of the word, most notably in William Hicks's *Oxford Jests* in 1671, and in Thomas Shadwell's *The Virtuoso* in 1676.

Its meaning was further enhanced with the emergence of the Chamois leather, which was made from a rare antelope called Chamois, or *Rupicapra Rupicapra*, to be found in only a few remote mountains of Europe. But fraudsters would often try and pass off cheap, ordinary leathers as Chamois in order to charge a higher price, and so the term *sham* started to gain its now more dubious meaning.

The trick of passing off cheaper versions of Chamois leather is now so common place that it is just accepted and the shammy leather we see these days is rarely the genuine article.

But it was tennis that firmly put the word back on the colloquial map during the 1950s and '80s. These were dark times for the tennis world, so much so that it was impossible to tell who was the best player in the world. This was because only *amateurs* could enter the top tournaments and the *professionals* were left to contest their own matches and exhibitions.

Tennis became so lucrative though, that many of the so-called *amateurs* started to secretly take payments from their national associations so that they could continue to represent their country. Likewise, many of the major tournaments would quietly get around the rules by paying their star players ludicrously high *"attendance fees"* and rather generous *"expenses"* in a desperate bid to retain their amateur status.

The situation became so transparent that everyone knew perfectly well what was going on and the word *"Shamateurs"* was coined. In 1968 Wimbledon, fearing that they would not attract the best players, pledged to resolve the increasingly ridiculous situation by opening up its tournament to all comers, amateur or professional, and thus the Open Era of modern tennis was born.

The phrase *sham* though was resurgent and remains a crucial part of one of the most pivotal turning points in tennis history, when tennis became officially recognised as a professional sport.

TENNIS INVENTS THE BOYCOTT

The term *boycott* first came into being in the early part of the 19th century. It started out as a colloquial expression in Ireland where a ruthless English landlord was so cruel that eventually all the locals completely refused to have anything to do with him, or his properties. He was called Captain Charles Cunningham Boycott and his name quickly spread throughout the land as a landlord to avoid at all costs.

Boycott first found its way into tennis in 1973 when almost half of the seeded players boycotted Wimbledon in protest because the club had banned the young Yugoslavian player, Nikki Pilic, simply because he didn't want to play for his country in the Davis Cup.

Many high-profile events, like the Olympics, are used to stage *boycotts* to gain media coverage or political leverage and, because of its global profile, Wimbledon has seen more than its fair share. One of the most notable was when the former champion, Billie Jean King, called on all the female players to stage a *"girlcott"* at Wimbledon in order to secure equal prize money for women.

Although that particular term failed to gain any momentum, Billie Jean King's pioneering stance on gender equality did, and all the female players now enjoy total parity with the men. Today's players owe a huge debt of thanks to her indomitable spirit.

Although, in these politically correct times, we'd probably have to call it a *pansexual-transgendercott*.

TENNIS INVENTS THE STAG NIGHT

No matter how far back you go in history, which country, religion or culture you pick, they will all have some legendary tale, where a brave young suitor is forced to perform certain tasks and tests to prove he is worthy of the hand of a fair maiden.

These Herculean tasks vary according to your country, status and wealth. If, for instance, you were a nobleman, or of royal birth in medieval England, it was a tradition that at your wedding you would throw a tournament to celebrate the day. A popular choice at that time would be to hold a jousting tournament, where the young groom could prove his bravery and show off his physical prowess.

There was one slight technical hitch to these tournaments though, that the groom might end up being impaled or having his matrimonial tools rendered inoperative, or worse, he could end up dead and the guests have to do a quick clothes change to attend the funeral.

It may seem bizarre to us today, but getting wounded was an integral part of the whole idea. The wound was meant to serve as a lasting memory of the day, something to be cherished forever, the battle scars serving to reminding you of the youthful glories of the occasion.

Luckily, these days we can just buy a pair of cufflinks but, back then, you had to be a bit more creative in order to avoid your wedding tackle being forcibly removed by a mate's passing lance.

Some of the wiser and richer grooms would hire knights to joust for them and *"represent"* their bravery. Obviously, the richer you were, the better knight you could afford to hire, thus also showing your wealth and elevated status, which was also considered a good way to impress your bride.

As the prestige of jousting started to fade in the Middle Ages, presumably due to the lack of grooms living long enough to make it through to the nuptials, the nobles replaced jousting for something less fatal. One of the most common alternatives was to throw a hunting party so that the groom could prove his manliness by going off to hunt wild boar and stags.

This would serve as a double purpose; firstly it allowed them to bring back trophies symbolising their bravery; and, secondly, the stag was cooked as part of the wedding ceremony and feasted upon by all. So then, rather than looking at your jousting scars, you would instead hang the dead stag's head on the wall in memory of the day. A custom that is credited as being the origin of the term *"stag night"* that we still use today.

Less wealthy grooms, who couldn't afford to stage expensive jousting tournaments or hunting parties to impress their bride, would hold a smaller tournament like a horse race, a football match or tennis tournament to prove their prowess.

In fact, many historians propose that the popularity of ball games like tennis can be directly attributed to such matrimonial traditions, and even suggest that such sporting ceremonies go back thousands of years and tennis-like ball games may well have taken place at ancient fertility festivals as part of the celebrations.

The most notable books that endorse this idea are Harold Massingham's *The Heritage of Man*, and William Henderson's book *Ball, Bat and Bishop*, which makes sense to me. I have certainly been on many a stag night where balls, bats and bishops have all featured heavily, but that's another story completely, and nothing to do with the historical purity of the tennis narrative we are trying to procure here.

TENNIS INVENTS THE THREESOME

These days, if someone drops out of a doubles match the remaining three players will often play what has become known as American Doubles, where the two players play only into the singles court and the opposing singles player has the full doubles court at their disposal.

Rewind to the 15th century, though, and we'd find that it was not uncommon for three players to play on each side of the net, as recalled in Jan Van Den Berghe's tome *Dat kaetspel Ghemoralizeert*. There is also mention of such matches in the *Ystoire de Appollonius*, in poems by Charles d'Orléans along with several references in South America of players betting against pairings with one player less or an extra player on another side.

Henry VIII was often noted as recruiting an extra player to assist him in his wins. There's also a famous print of Jan Wouter at Beaumont Abbey playing three-a-side, and a number of accounts of the game in Frisian and Flemish records, where they reference four or even five a side.

All these variations can be traced to the French game of *Longue paume*, which was often played in the streets by teams of seven or more each side.

So remember, next time you're invited along to a threesome, take your tennis racket, just in case.

TENNIS INVENTS A SCRUMDIDDLYUMPTIOUS NEW ADJECTIVE

I was delighted to hear that, in order to celebrate Roald Dahl's 100th birthday in 2016, one of the words that was added to the *Oxford English Dictionary* was the lovely new adjective used in the headline above.

But writers have been making up words for thousands of years and one of my childhood favourites was a writer called P. G. Wodehouse. I can remember the very moment I stumbled across a paragraph in his book, *The Code of the Woosters*, where Bertie Wooster was looking at the indomitable Jeeves and trying to work out whether Jeeves was annoyed or not, and it went something like this:

> *"I could see that, if not actually disgruntled, Jeeves was far from being gruntled."*

I'm not sure if *gruntled* has entered the *OED* yet, but if not then it definitely should, because it made me giggle then and it still does today.

This got me a-thinking. So many nouns have their own adjectives to describe something that is either relating to them, or shows characteristics pertaining to them. For instance, cats have feline, dogs have canine, wolves have lupine, and it got me thinking that it's about time that we found one for tennis.

I'm going to throw it open to everyone, but here are a few that I'd like to lob into the pot and see if any of them stick. The obvious place to look would be at the sports history, so maybe: *Pallian* from the Italian game of Palla; *Katsian* from the Dutch Kaetsen; *Pelotian* from the Spanish game of Pelota; or maybe even *Harpastian* from the Roman game of Harpastum.

To me, none of these seem to jump off the page. They're a bit clunky. Maybe we should look to the Ancient Greeks for inspiration. We might opt for *Fenine* from their game of Phaeninde; or we could look to the word Sphairistikè, the name most notably highjacked by Major Wingfield for his very first version of the game, which might give us *Sphairian*.

Although some of these might work, I think there may be still one more contender to pop over the net and hit the sweetspot. When looking for a tennis adjective, you could do a lot worse than to look at probably the best known ancestor of the ancient game, the Godfather of them all, the early French incarnation of the game, *Jeu de paume*. And when it's recast into an English adjective, it looks pretty good too, *paumian*.

It's as crisp and punchy as a smartly struck volley and has the weight of historical lineage behind it, like a perfectly crunched forehand driven deep into the far corner. I look forward to hearing your proposals for a new tennis adjective but, until then, I'm going to try this one out for size and knock it around the courts a bit to see what it feels like.

Hopefully, before my 100th birthday, we might see an entry in the *Old English Dictionary* that reads something like this:

Paumian:
[paw-mee-un]
adjective
1. of or like the game of tennis; relating to or characteristic of tennis.
noun
2. *Jeu de paume*, ancient form of the game of tennis.
3. paumière, someone who makes their living from the tennis world, especially in the late 12th century. A paumière would play tennis, coach tennis, make tennis balls, carve rackets and even cobble tennis shoes.

From the old French name for tennis *Jeu de paume*, meaning, game of the hand.

If this scrumdiddlyumptious new word catches on, then you can bet your bottom dollar that I will be extremely gruntled.

SECTION 15

THE LEGAL WORLD

Every sport has its own regulatory body, official rules and regulations and anomalies peculiar to that particular discipline. But rather than delve into all the intricacies of tennis's long and complicated rule book, instead, I have dedicated this section to a few unofficial laws, more like myths and legends that have grown up around tennis.

Most of them have a direct link to what we in England call *Sod's Law*, which is also a close relative of our Irish cousin *Murphy's Law*, but all of them will be horribly familiar to anyone who plays, watches or talks about tennis.

TENNIS INVENTS ITS OWN LAWS

John McEnroe, former scourge of tennis umpires everywhere, turned media darling of the airwaves with his witty and incisive match commentaries, inadvertently came up with a law of his very own while commentating on a match at Wimbledon in 2003.

For the sake of politeness, I shall omit the name of the player he was talking about, but when McEnroe was asked if he agreed with all the reasons that this player had given for losing the match, McEnroe abruptly dismissed them, adding that the more you think and analyse your game, the more excuses you'll be able to find.

Mac advocated that you shouldn't give yourself the luxury of excuses, if you believe these excuses then you are giving yourself permission to lose and that's going to stop you believing in your own abilities.

To commemorate that idea, I have awarded Mac his own law.

> McEnroe's Law:
> *"The more excuses you fill your mind with, the less trophies you fill your mantelpiece with."*

Our second law derives from an elderly player at The Queen's Club who, in his youth, was renowned for the lightning speed of his serve. However, the older he got, the slower his serve became. He put forward the idea that when the speed of your serve drops lower than your age, then you should give the game up.

To honour this delightful premise, we have the Oldies Law.

> The Oldies Law:
> *"In tennis, the Oldies Law states that the combined speed of your serve in mph plus the age of the server in years shall remain constant."*

$$x \quad + \quad y \quad = \quad z$$
$$\text{(mph) \quad (years) \quad (constant)}$$

Our third law owes its origins to a game I was watching with another Queen's Club member in the winter of 2007. One of the players gave a particularly dubious line call that was so bad that I immediately looked up at the member next to me to see if he had seen the same offensive call.

He saw my shocked expression but wasn't fazed at all. He just nodded wisely and dismissed the call with the words, *"Bishop's Law"*.

I had never heard of this, and asked him to explain what that was, and he enlightened me thus:

> Bishop's Law:
> *"Bishop's Law decrees that the veracity of a player's line calls shall be inversely proportional to the moral integrity required by their profession."*

Suffice it say, the profession of the dubious caller was a well-respected solicitor, so I shall leave you to do the maths on the reliability of the call using the ecclesiastic law above!

For our fourth law, we go to Barnes, in south London, for a regular weekend fixture of mine known locally as Tim's Sunday Tennis. Many years ago a new player was inducted into the group and they turned up with an absolutely enormous, professionally sized tennis bag with double shoulder straps, quadruple zipped compartments capable of holding about 12 rackets, and plastered with an expensive brand name. I looked nervously at my future opponent, but my female playing partner whispered reassuringly in my ear, *"Don't worry, he's what we call, 'All the gear – no idea'"*.

And, sure enough, his playing standard was not as good as his bag had suggested and we won the match. The expression apparently originated on the ski slopes in the 1980s when big brand labels were all the rage and Gordon Gekko's *"greed is good"* philosophy was every City boy's mantra. As a nod to its origins, I have named it accordingly.

Slope's Law:
"Slope's Law specifies that the more expensive and ostentatious the branding, the less the ability of the wearer to use it."

Andre Agassi unwittingly laid down our fifth law when he was asked what made him such a superlative returner against the big servers. Agassi didn't hesitate with his response ...

Agassi's Law:
"The faster the serve, the faster the return."

These next three laws were inadvertently created by one of tennis's most revered sports commentators, the greatly missed, much lamented, Dan Maskell, who was known as "the voice of Wimbledon" for many years. One of his favourite responses to a stunning shot was not to commentate on it at all but just to burst forth with a joyous gasp of, *"Oh, I say!"* Masterful in its sincerity and simplicity. Much like the laws we honour him with here.

Maskell's First Law:
"Maskell's Law states that the higher the praise given to any featured player at any given time, the greater the complete cock-up they will make at the next given moment."

Maskell's Second Law:
"The closer a camera shall zoom in on any given person, the

more disgusting the orifice they shall pick, scratch or evacuate from."

Maskell's Third Law:
"The more vulgar the chosen orifice, the larger the live TV audience."

Dan Maskell lives on in in the memory of anyone who ever listened to his commentary, but there is also a wonderful charity that bears his name that does incredible work for disabled players up and down the country. Do check it out, it is simply called the Dan Maskell Tennis Trust.

All this talk of watching televised sport leads us neatly on to our next law. This is probably one of the most well-known of all the sporting laws, a direct cousin of Sod's Law, or Murphy's Law in Ireland, and it's one we've all experienced.

Couch Potato's First Law:
"The greater your need for the loo, the more the game will increase in excitement, drama and intensity."

Of course, the longer you try to hold out and put off your desperately needed loo break, then the more likely you are to trigger Couch Potato's Second Law.

Couch Potato's Second Law:
"All returns from the rest room are accompanied by the realisation that you have missed what the commentators are describing as the most exciting and dynamic sequence of play ever recorded."

Couch Potato's Third Law:
"The more you drink in order to try and induce Couch Potato's Second Law, the less the effect it will have."

I think Couch Potato's Third Law may also be a second cousin, once removed to the phenomena known as *Beer Goggles* and *Brewer's Droop*!

This next law doesn't strictly stem from tennis, but I'm including it for personal and nostalgic reasons as I first heard it from my uncle, Michael Newton, who won the prestigious Fastnet race in 1953. Indeed it originates from that illustrious pastime of sailing. I don't think he formulated the law himself, but I am naming after him, not so much for nepotism but more because I don't know who actually did come up with it.

I also thought it was about time that the Newton name had a new law attributed to it. After all, that spoilsport Sir Isaac Newton has been stealing the headlines with his laws for nearly four centuries now, and let's face it, people are starting to get a bit fed up with it. I mean, really, gravity is just so 1680s! How can gravitation possibly be more important than tennis?

The main reason I include it, though, is because it is just so lovely and can easily be adopted to fit just about anything from sport to business. So here, then, revealed for the first time in over four centuries, a new law from Newton ...

Newton's New Law:
"The amount and strength of wind will be exactly inversely proportional to the combined amount of experience and wisdom of the sailors on board."

In tennis terms, I guess Newton's New Law would equate to something like: *"The more dignitaries, celebrities and royalty that have gathered to watch the match, the more it will rain."*

The final few laws came about from an annual tennis holiday in the South of France, organised by the entrepreneur Richard Farleigh. Until now, he was probably best known as one of the original presenters of the TV show *Dragon's Den*, but in the financial world he's regarded as one of the most astute investors of the past thirty years, and indeed invented several trading laws and algorithms that are still used today.

All that, of course, is soon to be eclipsed with the publication of his new tennis law. The law originated in Mougins, where Richard invites a few friends out each year for a tennis-orientated holiday. Farleigh's Law is one that any long suffering tennis player, who has ever played doubles, will definitely relate to.

Pretty much every doubles match has a rally such as this at some point in the match. It's one of those points that goes on and on and develops into a marathon point. And it's not just a long rally, it's a *great* rally. One that builds incrementally and then, just when you think it's won, it's not. One impossible shot follows another impossible return, and the rally builds again, goes on even longer and reaches even greater heights. The tension mounts and expectations rise. There are audible gasps, yet still it stretches on and on. It's on target to be the longest rally ever, and then, just at the point that you least want it, that's when it happens. Farleigh's Law kicks in ...

> Farleigh's Law:
> *"The longer the rally goes on for, the greater the chance that the one person who hasn't yet played a shot, messes it up at their very first touch of the ball."*

We owe our 14th and penultimate law to that same group of friends who play out in the South of France, and, in order to protect his identity and refrain from publicly embarrassing him, we will give him a pseudonym. Let's call him Henry, although that's obviously not his real name which is Paul Pascoe. Now, I actually need to tread rather cautiously here because Pascoe's legal talents *in court* far outweigh his tennis skills *on court*, so let me phrase this very carefully ... at the time of this story, Pascoe had only recently taken up the game, and had yet to hit the peaks of the game that he has now achieved. (Phew! That should just about cover it!) During the course of the particular match in question, Pascoe had managed to take a series of what should have been easy put-away winners into a wide open court, and turned them into a sequence of horrific fluffs and hopeless errors to lose each point.

In the middle of all the ribbing and teasing, Pascoe's Law was born.

Pascoe's Law:
"The greater the gap to hit the ball into, the bigger the total cock-up will be."

The final law is actually the first law that this same group of friends stumbled upon but was previously called *"The Partner Paradox"*. It's one that a sceptical reader might assume that all the previous laws were just a ruse, randomly made up, solely so that I could slip this one in under the radar in the hope that nobody would notice that I'd shamelessly named the next law after myself. Well, oh Jaded One, you'd be right! But before you scoff dismissively at the extravagantly nepotistic self-aggrandisement of it all, just bear with me because I think you'll find it's a real corker and one that all doubles players will be painfully aware of and will have definitely been on the receiving end of.

Howgill's Law:

"This is when you're playing with someone in a game of doubles and they are fluffing easy shots, missing easy volleys, hitting the ball out, double faulting and generally just seem to be having a bit an off day. Then in the very next set, when you happen to be playing against them, inexplicably, they start to play really well, striking the ball sweetly, hitting crisp volleys, serving aces and clipping all the lines."

This, my friend, is the Partner Paradox acting out in full swing. It will live fruitfully and inexplicably as long as the game of doubles is played. No amount of wisdom can explain it and no expanse of experience can assuage it.

So try not to resort to the low tactics of Bishop's Law in order to counter-act this phenomenon as the former fluffer passes you nonchalantly down the line for a winner, just smile ruefully. You will find that just knowing that the Partner Paradox law exists will help you ease the pain and act as a soothing balm against all the hurt and searing injustice.

SECTION 16

THE FOOD AND DRINK INDUSTRY

If you're wondering how tennis can influence anything from the food and drinks industry, I'd agree that there are not many obvious links and explains why this is the shortest section in the book. So treat it like a little inter-course refresher, compliments of the chef, before diving in to one of the more substantial main courses.

A little amuse bouche, if you like.

TENNIS INVENTS AFTERNOON TEA

You may recall earlier in the book a chapter that described how the very first winner of Wimbledon, Spencer Gore, announced that he thought that this new-born game of Lawn Tennis would never catch on. Naturally, the Wimbledon tournament committee were hoping for some better press the following year.

In 1878, Frank Hadow, also a Rackets player like Gore, came through to win the second Wimbledon Championship. Surely he would throw a better light on the prospect of this burgeoning game of Lawn Tennis.

Apparently not. After his victory, Hadow commented that he saw *"no future in the game"*, and immediately retired from all racket sports and moved to Ceylon to grow tea instead.

This was to prove ironic on two fronts. Firstly, Hadow's desertion from tennis to the world of tea may have inadvertently aided to the game's allure. It seems that the rise of Lawn Tennis benefitted enormously from the post-match tea parties held afterwards, which proved almost as popular as the tennis itself.

This was mainly due to the fact that tennis provided a rare opportunity for both the sexes to get together easily and without society frowning upon it. Such a phenomenon was very rare in Victorian society, where chaperones were still deemed necessary whenever a young lady and a young gentleman socialised together. So the added benefit of the sexes being able to freely mix with each other at tea parties after the game proved an added benefit to savour, along with Hadow's finely blended leafy brews from Ceylon, of course.

In fact, the Victorian tea party proved such a popular part of tennis that many of the pictures and paintings that depict the sport in those early years often feature scenes of the accompanying tea party as well.

Two of the best-known paintings that illustrate this perfectly are John Lavery's *The Tennis Party* and Edward Brewnall's *Tea and Tennis*. Both paintings depict scenes of youths playing mixed doubles, partaking of tea, intermingling and having fun, both on and off the court.

What followed, of course, was one of Wimbledon's other great traditions – the full English cream tea, the partaking of which no Wimbledon sojourn is complete without.

The second piece of irony is that once he retired from tennis to grow tea back in Ceylon, Hadow helped another burgeoning industry to grow, that of Tasseography, a method of fortune-telling that interprets the patterns of tea leaves left over at the bottom of your cup.

If only he'd had the foresight to have a quick brew himself and check with his Tasseographer before predicting such a damning future for Lawn Tennis.

TENNIS INVENTS THE PINEAPPLE

If you are an observant tennis fan, you may well have wondered what pineapples have got to do with tennis and why the beautifully crafted Wimbledon Men's Singles Tennis trophy features a great big golden one sitting on top of its celebrated lid.

Well, the route of this exotic fruit finding its way to the top of the world's most coveted tennis trophy is a tale as sweet and delightful as the prickly podded monocot itself.

It all started in 1493, when Christopher Columbus lowered his inquisitive anchor in a lush cove off the volcanic island of Guadaloupe. As his men scurried ashore, they found a deserted Carib village. The inhabitants had fled when they saw the strange invaders embarking from their alien ship. There beneath the sun-dappled, jungle foliage, the explorers found exotic mammals, brightly coloured birds of paradise, a rich bounty of glorious tribal carvings and hastily abandoned cooking-pots filled with all sorts of wondrous things; but what most intrigued the explorers was a strange new culinary fruit that nobody had ever seen before – the pineapple.

Ananas comosus is the official name of this herbaceous perennial, which translates as excellent tufted fruit. The fruit's sweet taste and unique appearance made it an instant hit when Columbus brought it back to European shores and is the only bromeliad to bear edible fruit. However, bringing it back is exactly what we had to do for the next 200 years because it was so hard to cultivate. Being indigenous to South America it could only be pollinated by certain hummingbirds and wild bats and, despite many dogged efforts by successive horticulturists, it was nearly two centuries before they perfected the hothouse method for growing this exotic delicacy in our less than tropical climes.

Consequently, the pineapple was so rare and coveted a commodity that it was only royalty and extremely wealthy aristocrats who could afford to offer such a delicacy to their guests. Hence, the fruit itself became a badge of extreme wealth and a sign of generous hospitality for any host who could afford to offer such a luxury to welcome their guests.

Being such a distinctive shape, the Ananasian image soon found its way into 16th-century culture, featuring in everything from paintings to architecture across Europe and America. It became a popular emblem to mount on exterior façades as a symbol of welcome to visitors. That is why they often appear on the gate posts of grand manors, main reception areas of grand houses, or as finials at the bottom of staircases, mantles and the like.

It is hard for us to imagine that a fruit so easily available to us now came to be so venerated during that period, but it was such a rarity that owners often didn't eat it but rented it out to others to allow them to show it off. The tufted delicacy was considered just too valuable to eat, so was paraded from event to event, often as the main attraction.

The botanist to King Charles I described its appearance as having similar scales to an artichoke but that it smelled so fragrant and tasted so sweet, it was as if you were to combine all the finest wines with rosewater and honey all mixed together. His son, King Charles II, was so taken with the pineapple that he commissioned a portrait of himself being presented with what was purported to be the very first one to ever be grown in England. They were of such scarcity that, rather than eat them, lucky owners would rather parade the streets with one, so that they could be seen to be in possession of one, boosting their status and social standing in the community. Forget your Aston Martins, your Burberry bags or Rolex watches, if you wanted to impress your peers in those days, you'd need to stroll around with a pineapple under your arm.

In strictly financial terms, it is thought that the cost a pineapple then was about £30 to £50 and there are records that show that by the mid-1700s the price of a pineapple had risen to £150, which amounts to about £30,000 in today's money. It is little wonder then that the pineapple was recorded as one of the most stolen objects of its day and they often had to be accompanied by their own private security guards.

But there were a number of wild and exotic foods brought back from the New World in the 16th and 17th centuries, so what was it about this conical pine that so captured the public imagination and elevated it to the heady heights of prestige, luxury and status?

There are a number of theories as to what gave it its mythical quality. Firstly, it had a totally unique appearance and was like nothing else that had ever been seen. It was obviously delicious and extremely sweet, and at a time when sugar was both expensive and desirable. It was also a very rare commodity which inherently enhances its value. And yet there was much more to this barbed bromeliad than meets the tongue.

The pineapple was totally unknown in any shape or form, so it was completely free of any cultural resonances of other fruits, which enabled people to inhabit it with their own references and attribute new meanings to it.

For example, the apple already had many associations ascribed to it, from the forbidden fruit of the slippery serpent in the Bible's Garden of Eden, to the phrase about one rotten apple in a barrel. While Greek and Roman mythology is riddled with fruity illusions, from oranges to pomegranates, to the salacious innuendoes of cherries and melons.

But the pineapple's unique appearance gave it its own mythical quality. Even the circular leafed top gave it the impression of having its very own golden crown, perceived as a symbolic manifestation of its own divine right to be hailed as the king of all fruits. A fact further enhanced when it was endorsed by every king and queen in Europe, who all vied to show off the biggest and sweetest of its kind. In fact it was often called King Pine – probably because it was so 'king expensive!

But there were other reasons too. The pineapple was endowed with a plethora of health qualities as well. For instance, it is a rich source of manganese, which helps build and maintain bone strength, and it also has plenty of vitamin C to fight disease and boost immunity and even fight cancer. It is rich in beta-carotene, vitamins A and B, potassium, sodium and an excellent source of fibre. It also contains bromelain an enzyme that is often singled out by alternative medicines to combat everything from stress relief to osteoarthritis, to relieve pain and as an anti-inflammatory agent. It's also renowned as a decongestant, a digestive aid, boosts blood flow and used as a skin salve in specialist burns units. Bromelain is also the reason many people dislike pineapples, as this is the enzyme that causes that odd mouth discomfort that many feel while eating this pungent fruit.

So if you've ever been troubled by that oft-cited conundrum, what was the best thing *before* sliced bread – it was the pineapple.

So when the Wimbledon trophy was struck in 1887, the pineapple motif was at its most popular as a prestigious design element, symbolising exactly the kind of image that Wimbledon wanted to evoke, which was to welcome visitors from all around the globe to the biggest, richest, most illustrious tournament in the world. And that is how this tasty achenic ovary came to be sitting aloft one of the world's most prestigious sporting crowns.

And yet, I suspect that if the Wimbledon trophy was being struck today, a pineapple would not be the first choice of adornment, as our prickly Pitcairnial seems to have lost its allure. But why?

Well the story of how King Pine lost its star billing is a modern morality tale worthy of any Greek myth or an Aesop fable. Because, unfortunately for our prickly friend, it wasn't only royalty who took a shining to it.

By the 1950s, steam ships were pouring in with goods from the

Caribbean which meant that even your average Hoi Polloi could now afford to enjoy the glamorous delights of this exotic delicacy. But yet, there was an even more miserable fate that was about to befall this once venerated fancy – the Man from Del Monte said "Yes".

This once regal treat was now specifically bred so that it could fit inside a common tin and be fed as fodder to the masses. It was now confined to a metal cage, a prisoner of its own succulent success, now sold to the hordes by the tinny ton. King Pine's reign was over, dethroned by a new king that we all bowed down and foolishly paid homage to – commercialism.

It was to be a sorry decline for such a flavoursome deity. In the 17th century there were over fifty different varieties of this versatile fruity monopod, ranging from the pale and luscious Antiguan to the exotic Black Prince that had a unique pyramid shape giving it such a distinctive Egyptian feel that you can almost taste the juice as Cleopatra proffers up a slice to bewitch and beguile Julius Caesar. Today there are only a handful of species left and really only two that are widely available. These days, this once exalted delicacy is more likely to be seen slapped on top of a slab of soggy dough, stuffed behind a few bits of processed ham and sold as a Hawaiian Pizza. I don't know but I suspect that Columbus is not just turning in his grave but veritably spinning.

SECTION 17

TENNIS AND OTHER SPORTS

It may come as no surprise to you to learn that tennis has influenced a number of other sports, from the modern Olympics to inventing football itself.

And, whisper it quietly, tennis may even have helped England win the Football World Cup in 1966. News so shocking it's bound to make any keen soccer fan choke more than the sight of artificial grass ...

TENNIS INVENTS THE BLAG

John Mary Pius Boland may sound like a self-righteous, cross-dressing forefather of Marc Bolan's '70s pop group T. Rex, but that would have been a relatively modest lineage compared to the reality in which young Boland found himself when holidaying in Greece with his friend Manny at the turn of the last century.

Hankering for a game of his beloved tennis, Boland searched high and low to try and find a court, but the only ones near him were the newly constructed courts that had been specially built for the Olympic Games of 1896 and were not for public use.

But remembering that his friend Manny was connected to the tennis organising committee, Boland asked Manny if he could use his influence to let him get access to the courts. Having been rebuffed by the authorities, Manny came up with a sneaky plan. A plan so cunning that Baldrick himself would've been proud.

Manny advised Boland that he would be able to use the courts if he signed up to enter the Olympics as a member of the official Irish Olympic Tennis Team, that way he could pretend to be practising for the event and legally use the courts as he wished.

This would serve a double purpose because the organisers had been hard pushed to find tennis players to enter. Plus, having an official Irish entry for the struggling tournament would make the event appear much more international and successful than it actually was.

Although Boland was no slouch around the courts, he dismissed it as a ridiculous idea. He had never played competitively in an international tournament in his life. But after a little persuasion from Manny and the Olympic Committee, who were desperate to swell their tournament entries, and realising it was the only chance he was going to get to play tennis on his holiday, he begrudgingly decided to sign up.

Indeed, he was glad he did, because not only did Boland get his holiday tennis fix, he even made a few new friends from the various Olympic teams that he met on court. He particularly enjoyed practising with a German player called Fritz Traun.

But it wasn't too long before the cold reality of it all kicked in and he suddenly realised the enormity of what he had done. Here he was, a young Irish law student on holiday with his mates, about to walk out onto the world stage and represent his country in the first round of the Olympic Games tennis championships.

What is even more astonishing is that the young Irish infiltrator not only played really well but also he won his opening match! And with only about a dozen other players in the whole tournament, it wasn't long before Boland found himself deep into the tournament draw. Almost as quickly as it takes to pour a pint of Guinness, Boland had played his way into the final and was one match away from winning a gold medal for his country.

Unfortunately, the next player he was up against was the local hero, a player called Dionysus. It must have all seemed a bit surreal, but suddenly young Boland found himself in an Olympic tennis final, in Athens, playing someone named after the Ancient Greek God of wine, fertility and unrestrained consumption.

Now I don't know if Dionysus had been out the night before trying to live up to his namesake's reputation, but all I can tell you is that Boland won it in straight sets and so our accidental tourist now suddenly found himself the proud owner of an Olympic Gold Medal.

Now if that wasn't the best blag ever, and all just so that he could get a game of tennis on holiday, then just pause from pouring that celebratory pint of Guinness for just a second, hold your horse-drawn golden chariots of fire, stifle the angel from plucking her golden harp, for it seems that good things really do come to those who wait, because this Irish tale has one further twist to tell.

Remember Fritz Traun, the German player he was practising with?

Well, Fritz's doubles partner had to withdraw due to injury and he asked blag boy Boland if he would like to partner him instead.

Boland said he would love to but there was a small problem with playing for the German team – he was Irish! To top it all, he'd just contested and won a gold medal playing in the singles as an Irishman. Fritz was obviously not the sort of man to be put off by such minor details and ploughed on with the idea and quizzed Boland to see if might have had any distant German relatives, but Boland protested he didn't and continued to align himself with his original assessment of Traun's idea – in that it was absurd. But Fritz was made of sterner stuff, he didn't seem to be too deterred by such trifles, and took his request to the Olympic Committee.

He said that Boland should be allowed to partner him because Boland could actually speak a little German! The Olympic Committee weren't exactly overwhelmed with this fact, but there was a whiff of them being a little bit whelmed, so Fritz continued to fumble around trying to cook up Teutonic connections that might increase the whelm level of the committee.

Eventually Fritz found out that Boland had been to University in Bonn, and that he even knew a couple of German people. The Olympic Committee's whelming levels rose a little but didn't think that it was enough. Fritz pressed on and announced that one of the people Boland was friends with was the famous archaeologist Heinrich Schlieman.

Apparently Schlieman wasn't just an archaeologist, he was a huge international star, a sort of cross between David Attenborough and Indiana Jones. Fritz was hoping that this might sway them, but in reality he'd just delivered the dodgiest dossier since Tony Blair and George Bush put together their infamous "Weapons of Mass Destruction" one.

Now, as we all know, history has taught us that the International Olympic Committee are totally incorruptible, especially the Greek

313

ones, so how they convinced them that Boland did have some German in his blood, I don't know – maybe they gave him a bottle of Holstein Pilsner to drink; but whatever they did, it worked, and somehow Boland was sanctioned to compete as Fritz's German doubles partner.

To make matters worse, not only did Boland manage to blag his way into a second Olympic tournament under a completely new nationality but, unbelievably, he went on to mega-blag his way into winning another Gold Medal in the doubles, thus completing the greatest blag in Olympic history. It was, quite literally, an Olympic sized blag.

Now, if John Mary Pius Boland did have any self-righteous, cross-dressing forefathers that were related to Marc Bolan from T. Rex, then I'm sure they would have been very proud.

So in his honour, let's get it on and bang a gong, for our very own gold medal guru, John Boland!

TENNIS INVENTS INVISIBILITY

If you thought the fiasco of John Boland winning a brace of gold medals in the inaugural Olympic Games in Athens was chaotic, then the London Olympic Games of 1908 were not much better.

The French player Fenwick got through to the semi-finals without even playing a match. Dora Boothby lost every match she played and won a silver Olympic medal. Five players got through to the quarter-finals without even showing up, yet alone hitting a ball!

In the Ladies Lawn Tennis event, of the 13 people registered to play only 7 players showed up and 2 of those dropped out, leaving only 5. So the tournament officials had to make up a draw with "invisible" players, which they then proceeded to give byes to, just so that it looked like there was more a tournament than there really was and thus enabling them to actually put on a few matches for the public to watch.

Dora Boothby won a silver medal despite losing every match she played in, simply because she was in the lower half of the draw which the other players had pulled out of, so she got a bye straight through to the finals, which she lost. Ruth Winch also won the bronze medal despite losing her one and only match as well.

Dorothy Lambert-Chambers won the gold medal, but she had to work really hard for it, by winning three matches! It must make Andy Murray hopping mad to think of all the sweat and toil he had to put in to get his gold medal. Still, I don't suppose that Dorothy's efforts were rewarded with a letterbox painted gold in her honour, unless it was for a sport she never entered and from a town she never lived in!

TENNIS INVENTS A LOAD OF FLIM FLAM

Contrary to popular belief, and despite the fact that the China seems to hold most of the world championship titles, *Table Tennis*, or *Ping Pong*, was invented in England and is a direct descendant of tennis.

The earliest records of it are actually on picture postcards in the late 1800s, and it appears to have been invented a few years earlier by bored nobles and landed gentry, who, being hampered by the wet and windy British weather, and frustrated at not being able to go outside to play big-boys tennis, started knocking up on the dining-room table, using things like books as a net, cigar lids as bats and rounded champagne corks as the ball.

It became so popular that by the late 1880s manufacturers were producing box sets under the name Table Tennis, which came with specially made bats, nets and balls. The bats initially resembled mini tennis rackets with stretched leather skins instead of strings, but they kept the cork ball but covered it in white linen.

In 1901, a celluloid ball replaced the crude cork ball, the rackets were shortened to become bats and made from wood. Early versions were covered in fabric but soon they were all covered in a thin rubber skin, initially to reduce the noise, but latterly to increase spin and grip, two key components of the game today.

The name of *Ping Pong* caught on after the celluloid ball was introduced due to the distinctive sound the balls make. Before that *Table Tennis* had flirted with various names, many of them also reflecting the noisy sound effects. The most popular were: *Gossima, Flim-Flam, Whiff-Whaff, Pim-Pam, Bing-Bang* and *Ding-Dong*, which collectively sound less like a sport and more like a family of Pandas.

In the 1920s, several Table Tennis Federations were created and the name *Ping Pong* was no longer officially represented. But such is the power and resonance of the onomatopoeic name that it has remained in the popular vernacular and there are many clubs around the country that still bear the *Ping Pong* moniker.

Table Tennis reached new heights in the 1980s when it was officially recognised as a proper grown-up sport and made its debut at the 1988 Seoul Olympics. I'm sure if John Mary Pius Boland had still been alive, he'd have tried to enter.

TENNIS INVENTS FOOTBALL

We covered in an earlier chapter how the French word *Tenez* is thought to be the first origins of the word tennis, as the players used to call this out to alert the opposition before serving. What is intriguing, though, is that in Arnoul Gréban's passion play, written in 1448, he states that just before kick-off, footballers used to shout *Tenez* as well.

Could it be that soccer, the world's biggest sport, also has its roots in tennis? I venture here, that it does and lay out the intriguing thinking behind it.

The most commonly accepted view is that Lawn Tennis came from Real Tennis which is a direct descendant of *Jeu de paume* and *Longue paume*, ball games that were commonly played in France and England in the 11th and 12th century, which in turn comes probably comes from even earlier versions of the game like *Palla*, *Harpastum*, *Phaeninde* and *Episkyros*.

The games were a little cruder than *Jeu de paume* and, just like football, they started as fairly lawless, rough and ready games, played outside in the streets with simple chalk line marking to indicate the two sides of the territory, just as it is in tennis and football.

There are several mentions of these games throughout the centuries, not always in flattering terms, and it seems they were played in pretty rough circumstances with fights regularly breaking out in the streets, implying that large stakes were probably wagered on the outcome, all features common to the early game of football as well. There is some very appealing evidence, however, that suggests that the roots of these early games may lie further afield and date back even earlier.

Their origins may well lie in ancient China and could possibly be traced back to a man I mentioned before, the legendary Emperor called Huang-Di, who has been credited with being the father of many things, from cartography to medicine.

I explained how he used to train his troops using a game called *T'su-Chu*, but actually, you could easily re-frame *T'su-Chu* as an ancient version of keepie-uppie football as well.

So, it might be hard for us westerners to swallow, but the Emperor's early ball game may have lain down roots not only for tennis but just about every sports game you can think of, including football.

TENNIS INVENTS ENGLAND WINNING THE 1966 WORLD CUP

In the 1962 World Cup held in Chile, English football did not accredit itself well. As usual, England had made it through the group stage but were beaten as soon as they got into the knock-out phase.

Four years later, the omens were not looking much better for England as kick-off for the 1966 World Cup approached. England was all set to host the event but a few months before the start of the tournament the famous Jules Rimet golden trophy was stolen from a church hall in Westminster.

What followed was a series of false alarms, crazy theories, bungled blackmail attempts, spurious confessions, mysterious ransom demands, several botched police raids, and a handful of wrongful arrests. It was a farce worthy of an early Ealing comedy film, with Alistair Sim, Alec Guinness and Peter Sellers taking on the lead roles of spivvy suspect, incompetent detective and innocent idiot respectively.

The investigation was in a mess and going nowhere fast. There was only one thing that might just save the day – tennis.

One fine morning, Dave Corbett was out taking his dog Pickles for an early morning walk. Pickles was a 4-year-old white Collie with a penchant for chasing tennis balls. Pickles was trying to sniff an old ball out from under a bush, when his owner spotted a package wrapped up in old newspapers, hidden in the undergrowth. On closer inspection, Corbett saw something glimmering in the sunlight. He peered a little closer and saw what looked like a golden lettering with the words *Brazil*, *West Germany* and *Uruguay* engraved on it. Suddenly he realised the enormity of what he'd just found – the stolen World Cup trophy.

Corbett bundled it up and immediately handed it in to the police but it was Pickles who garnished all the attention. The scruffy little

Collie was hailed a national hero and became an overnight media sensation, appearing on chat shows, and made guest appearances on several TV programmes. He featured in films, documentaries, newspaper and magazine articles, and was even awarded Dog of the Year, not just in England but also in France, Italy and several other countries around the world.

Pickles also went on to receive various other honours and rewards including a prestigious medal from the National Canine Defence League. When England sensationally won the 1966 World Cup, Pickles was the guest of honour at the official banquet.

The tennis ball got no such recognition. It was never asked to appear on any TV shows, it just continued to lie unwanted in the woods. Eventually it started to lose it elasticity, all its hair fell out, and, to this day lies rotting and decomposing.

Fame is a fickle mistress.

SECTION 18

INDUSTRY AND COMMERCE

The world of industry and commerce has long recognised the value of tennis as a bed fellow. Tennis embodies everything that the big brands would like to be associated with; fit, young, healthy athletes who work hard, strive long and achieve greatness to live a glamorous high life of reward and riches.

It's no wonder these companies pay huge sums to sponsor the big tournaments and individual players to endorse their brand, but some completely unrelated businesses actually owe their entire existence to tennis ...

TENNIS INVENTS PLAYSTATION, NINTENDO AND XBOX

These days almost everything that can be digitalised is turned into a game, either online or as an app for your smart phone, or a video game for your TV. It's called Gamification and developers apply it to just about everything from Health & Fitness Apps to shopping. It has become the biggest growth sector of our times. The video game industry alone is expected to top $300 billion in the next few years.

Some of them were actually conceived as a game, like *Fortnite* and *Pokemon Go*, for instance. Before that there was *Candy Crush*. Preceding that, *Angry Birds*. Making it all possible were the consoles like Xbox, Nintendo with *Super Mario Bros.* Slip even further back in time, and you get games like *Space Invaders*. Before that was *Pac-Man*. And if you really want to go down Memory Lane, then how about those dreadful video games that were indigenous to end-of-pier arcades.

But did you know that the world's very first interactive digital video game, one that you could actually play and control yourself, was a game based on, what else, but tennis. I'm proud to say that I not only remember it; I actually played it. It was called *Pong*.

Thinking of it now evokes many a schoolboy memory: a friend got given one and all his mates ran over to his house to play it. But there was a small problem – first of all you had to set it up. It was a huge cumbersome thing, that came in a big old box and it had two clunky hand controllers for each player made out of cheap black plastic.

The most difficult bit was trying to figure out how to plug in all the electric wires and hook it up into the back of your parent's television set without blowing up the TV or electrocuting yourself. But, even if you managed to successfully do that, you then had to fiddle around for hours trying to tune it in, searching through every TV channel trying to find out which frequency the game was playing on. Just getting the damn thing to work was half the afternoon's entertainment.

But eventually, when you did, oh the joy. Endless hours of fun. Weekends would drift away in a black and white, square shaped haze …

Kids today, of course, wouldn't give it the time of day. Compared to today's lifelike war games, completely convincing immersive CGI global world conquest bomb and laser fests, with 3D monster slashing intergalactic space missions, where you can disappear into Virtual Reality and play an actual character within the game, or even juxtapose the two worlds of reality and games using Augmented Reality. Good old *Pong* would find it hard to compete.

It was just a white ball on a black screen. The ball drifted up and down the screen with a flat paddle at each end and you had to move the paddle from side to side to try and hit the ball back to your opponent at the other end, the first one to miss lost the point. I say that there was a ball but, in reality, the graphics were so crude that they couldn't actually make round edges to the balls, so the ball had to be square! Seriously. That's how basic the graphics were.

There was some excitement though, it would make a slight bleep sound every time you struck the ball. Cor! Be still my beating heart!

In later editions of the game, if you got into a really long rally, the ball would start to speed up. Whoa! Now you really had to be on high alert. The bleeping sound would get a little higher as well as if to crank up the already unbearable tension.

The combination made for a slightly hypnotic experience if you were concentrating really hard on playing it, or just plain annoying if you happened to be stuck nearby in the same house as the beeps got quicker and more piercing. This must have been doubly annoying if you were a parent who had been forced out of your own living room because your TV had been hi-jacked by a bunch of spotty teenagers.

And you can forget trying to get us to go to bed afterwards, we were either all high from the adrenaline rush of playing it, or totally hyper, having been electrocuted by the back of the TV trying to set it up earlier in the day.

The name *Pong* was probably fairly apt because I'm sure most kids today would say that the game stinks and walk away in disgust. But don't knock it because, without it, we would probably never have had *Minecraft*, *Tetris*, *Game Boy*, *Diablo*, *Grand Theft Auto*, *Call of Duty*, *Wii Sports*, or any of the games mentioned earlier, that we enjoy today. It was literally the Granddaddy of them all.

Bizarrely, *Pong* has enjoyed something of a comeback recently when it was reintroduced as an app, keeping its original 1970s retro feel. Today's cool hipsters probably consider it to be one of those things that is *"so lame that it's cool"*.

Hmm, I wonder, if that is the case, then maybe it's time for me to dig out my flared trousers and brightly coloured wing-collared shirts again …

TENNIS INVENTS FACEBOOK

Incredibly, it's not just video games that can be traced back to tennis, all social media websites owe a debt of gratitude to the game. These days there are myriad ways that players can connect up for a game of tennis, or any other sports or social activity. Specialist websites cater to every whim of the spectrum, from the big-name social media sites like WhatsApp, Twitter, Instagram, Snapchat, Facebook and TikTok; all of which can be tailored to create their own tennis groups dedicated to players looking for a game.

But centuries before the internet became the information superhighway that it is today, there was a much more simplistic system that also capitalised on the highway, the original highway, as used by people, horses, stagecoaches and other travellers.

In the 16th century, if you fancied a game of tennis but had no one to play with, it was customary to simply hang a tennis ball outside the court, or local tavern, signalling to all those who passed by that someone inside was up for a game. As the custom grew, local establishments would even customise their own tennis ball holders, embellishing them with eye-catching designs or just crafting them in their own unique style.

One of the best-known examples to have survived is a solid brass one in the Franeker Museum in the Netherlands, where the practice was commonplace. It has been beautifully fashioned into the shape of a bird's claw, the talons of which cleverly expand to accommodate the tennis ball. This was then hung outside the tavern or court and would have made a striking calling card.

If a passer-by saw the ball hanging from the talons, and fancied a game, then they just strolled in. So much simpler than having to log in to a social media platform, give an ID, username, fumble around the recesses of their brain trying to remember some complicated password that must incorporate

> *"at least eight digits; a minimum of 1 lower case character [a–z]; a minimum of 1 upper case character [A–Z]; a minimum of 1 numerical character, not naturally ascending or descending, or a birthday or telephone number; and have a minimum of 1 special character, not a letter or number, embedded into it!"*

No. They would simply remove the ball and go inside to find the person who was looking for a game and play. Simple.

Note to self: Remember to call Mark Zuckerberg to see if he wants to invest in my new tennis website idea, *Acebook*.

TENNIS INVENTS THE MOBILE PHONE

We take for granted the astonishing applications that exist on our mobile phones, but I doubt that many of us realise that we owe it all to an Austrian actress and her love of tennis.

The lady in question was Hedwig Eva Maria Kiesler, better known by her Hollywood stage name of Hedy Lamarr. Lamarr was so much more than the glamorous actress she was portrayed as being, and to fully understand how she came to play a pivotal role in the invention of the mobile phone, we have to go back to the very beginning of her story.

Her father was a suave, middle-class banker and her mother was a glamorous concert pianist. They met, fell in love, married and a few years later Hedy was born in Vienna in 1914, a child thrown into the horrors of the First World War. Significant to our story, both her parents had Jewish roots, making her highly sensitive to what the Nazis would later inflict.

It seems that Hedy was born glamorous and was already turning heads when, at the age of 12, she won a local beauty contest in Vienna. She had always loved the theatre and the film world, and this was soon reciprocated because the camera loved her too. Within the space of a few short years, Hedy had become of the darling of the Berlin film industry when, at the tender age of 17, she was cast in a film called *Ecstasy*. It was a Czech film in which Hedy says she was tricked by the director into doing nude scenes that he had promised wouldn't reveal anything, and worst of all tricked into having a close up on her face during an orgasm, when she was told that the camera was a long way off. It is said to be the first commercial film to ever show such a scene and it caused an international sensation.

Although the film won plaudits around the world and collected several awards in more liberal European countries, it was banned in just as many places, including the very prudish America.

Vowing never to let the film world trick or take advantage of her again, Hedy quit the movies and moved into theatre where she could choose and control the scripts more easily. With her fame, beauty and new-found notoriety, she was again an instant success and had admirers, producers and agents flooding her stage door at every performance. One such admirer was the Austrian called Friedrich Mandl. He became so obsessed with her that by today's standards he would probably be labelled a stalker and have restraining orders issued against him, but in the 1930s it was called persistence.

It probably helped his cause that there was also one other small mitigating factor in his favour, he just happened to be the richest man in Austria. Even so, Lamarr rejected his advances hundreds of times over the coming months. But, by all accounts, Mandl was very charming and persuasive, and eventually convinced her to go out with him. Swept up into a glamorous world of the European elite, he soon proposed to her, but despite warnings from her parents, the headstrong Lamarr went ahead and married him.

Big mistake. Mandl quickly banned her from working in the theatre or in films and soon banned her from even leaving the house unless she was with him. He was a totally abusive, obsessive bully and even went so far as to install a guard (that he called *"a maid"*) to ensure she stayed in the house when he went to work. Effectively, Lamarr had become a prisoner in her own home. Mandl was so paranoid that sometimes he would even take her to work with him. But remember this, as it plays a significant part in our story later on.

It was during one such meeting that Hedy, who was supposed to just sit at the back of the room and look pretty, learned all about the horrors of fascism directly from her husband and his associates, because Mandl was one of the world's leading suppliers of weapons. So amongst his closest colleagues was none other than Mussolini who had close ties with her husband through his arms dealings.

Indeed, fatefully, it was Mussolini who introduced Mandl to Adolph Hitler, to whom Mandl also ended up supplying armaments, despite the fact that this was in blatant breach of the Versailles Treaty. Lamarr soon found herself playing hostess to lavish parties attended by both Mussolini and Hitler. As Mandl's wealth grew, so did Lamarr's concerns.

Mandl's obsession, though, eventually turned to the free world's advantage. He became so fixated on not letting her out of his sight that he'd even take her to top-secret munitions meetings where she would have to sit silently in the corner while highly sensitive information was being disclosed. One such discussion, most relevant to our story, was trying to solve the problem of how to harness the use of radio waves to control the accuracy of torpedoes and rockets. But the meeting ended without resolution as they all realised that because there were 88 different frequencies of radio wave, whichever one they chose could easily be just blocked and jammed by the enemy, thus rendering the torpedoes useless. Something about the conversation stuck with Lamarr as the problem appealed to her scientific mind almost as much as it frightened her.

Lamarr knew she had to get out of this oppressive and abusive relationship, and one evening she drugged her *maid* and, taking as much of her finest jewellery that she could wear or carry, escaped by train to Paris and eventually on to London.

Her notoriety quickly drew her into the London film scene, but before she could accept any work offers, she heard that Hollywood mogul Louis B. Mayer was in town and she tried to contrive a meeting, but heard that he was leaving for New York the next day.

Hedy was a free spirit and there was nothing actually keeping her in London, so she bought a ticket on the same liner that she knew Louis B. Mayer was also on. Almost as soon as she boarded the New York bound liner, she caught the eye of the movie mogul.

Knowing exactly who she was, he immediately offered her an

exclusive contract to sign for his influential MGM studio for the then princely sum of £125 a week. She refused. Mayer was infuriated but continued to negotiate with her for the rest of the journey and by the time they docked in New York, Mayer had upped his offer to £500 a week. Lamarr was back in the movies.

It was reported that in her inaugural film for him, the audience gasped at her first close up, such was her beauty and magnetism. But Hollywood was a stereotypical workplace in the 1930s and although she became a big star she was always cast as the glamorous love interest, with nothing more to do than to extol her exotic beauty and sexuality, which, beguiling as that was, meant that she was never really given any challenging roles to play.

Lamarr quickly bored of it and turned her attentions to more important pastimes, like tennis. In fact she even became a pin-up for the sport when she was turned into a children's doll and given a tennis outfit complete with racket. It was the best-selling doll of the year.

Another of her great loves was inventing. She loved to try new things and with her Hollywood connections she ran into the aviation tycoon Howard Hawks who immediately fell under her spell. She berated Hawks and told him that the design of his planes meant that they were all too square to be aerodynamically efficient and bet him that she could design a better one. Hawk was really interested in her for his own nefarious reasons, but humoured her and gave her his own personal backing to try and prove it.

Lamarr totally surprised Hawks by going on to design a smoother rounder, more aerodynamic plane that did indeed prove to be more efficient than the ones he had. Hawks was stunned. She explained to him that she took her inspiration from studying the wing of a humming bird. Impressed, Hawks threw more money at her, gave her her own laboratory and let her invent whatever she wanted.

With Hawks' backing behind her, she was free to experiment with anything she chose and came up with all sorts of mad inventions, the most notable of which included an improved stoplight system for traffic lights, and a dissolving tablet that could be added to any plain cordial and which would instantly turn it into a carbonated fizzy drink. But it was her love of tennis that fortuitously led her to her most significant invention.

Two of her most famous doubles partners were the equally gorgeous Rita Hayworth and Ava Gardner, and the three of them were the belles of every tennis court in Hollywood. It was from one of these tennis invites that Hedy met a pianist called George Antheil, who was working on a new invention of his own, the Player-Piano or Pianola as it was later known.

Lamarr was instantly drawn to this new contraption both as an inventor and from being the daughter of a pianist mother. Lamarr's curiosity was further aroused when she asked Antheil to let her see the inner workings of his precious new invention.

Antheil opened it up and began to explain to her how, although there were 88 different keys on the keyboard, the problem was how to coordinate them all into one controlling device. Lamarr saw the scroll with all the 88 lines of differing holes punched in it that controlled each of the 88 piano keys in turn.

There was something about the number of piano keys that struck a chord with Lamarr. 88 piano keys. That was when Lamarr had her Eureka moment. She remembered the arms dealing meeting when her ex-husband was trying to solve the problem of controlling torpedoes using radio waves but couldn't work out how to do it because of the varying 88 frequencies. You could practically see the lightbulb above her head.

She posed a question to Antheil. What if you could use all the 88 radio waves to send out a mass of tiny radio signals via one controlling scroll just like the one Antheil was using to control his Pianola. Antheil pondered it a while and thought that it might work, but before they could finish their discussion they were dragged apart by others at the party and the conversation was over.

But Lamarr's creative juices were flowing. She felt inspired. She thought she might be onto something and wanted to find Antheil to continue the conversation, but couldn't find him. As she left, though, she saw Antheil's car in the driveway. She wanted to leave a note, so she looked in her handbag but had no paper or pen. No such piffling obstacle was going to stop Lamarr. She delved deeper into her bag and whipped out a tube of lipstick. And with a classic Lamarr flourish wrote her telephone number on Antheil's car in giant letters right across his windscreen in bright red, full gloss, lipstick!

What man could resist that? Sure enough, Antheil called. They set up a meeting and got together to brainstorm the problem. They came up with the idea of using a miniature version of the Pianola mechanism to synchronise radio signals in order to create a frequency-hopping system, which only used tiny parts of each of the 88 different radio frequencies for a fraction of a second, so that nobody would be able to decipher or block the frequency. They had instantly solved the problem that her husband, Mousolini, Hitler and all their cronies had failed at – how to control torpedoes with deadly accuracy using all 88 radio waves.

Ecstatic, they took their invention to the Navy but, because it didn't come from a recognised military source, the Navy disregarded it. Undeterred Hedy tried various other contacts and the army and the air force but none of them would give her the time of day. She tried all the illustrious contacts she knew from Hollywood to Capitol Hill, but none of them would take her seriously. Despite this rebuttal, Lamarr remained determined to put all her considerable talents into defeating Hitler's Nazi Germany, and offered to work at the National Inventors Council. But this time she was not just rebuffed but slighted as well. They told her that she would be of greater service to the war effort by remaining in Hollywood and using her looks and film star status to raise war bonds. Affronted at first that the country was refusing to acknowledge her intellectual talents, she eventually swallowed her pride and went on to raise an astonishing $7 million worth of bonds for the war effort.

But perhaps what was most insulting of all, was the fact that, secretly, the War Office actually had realised the true potential of her frequency-hopping system and later came back to it and putting it to deadly use during the Cuban Missile Crisis, but failed to give any credit Lamarr or Antheil. In fact their input was all but forgotten until the information was de-classified in the '70s and the significance of their invention was eventually revealed to the world.

Today, Lamarr and Antheil's frequency-hopping method led to what we now call Spread Spectrum Technology, which is the foundation of all our modern telecommunication systems, such as Bluetooth, Wi-Fi networks, laptops, tablets, GPS technology, satellite systems, computers and navigational technologies, and is the same system we all use everyday on our smart phones to connect us to the world 24/7. All from a simple invite to a tennis party.

In 1997, Lamarr and Antheil received the *Electronic Frontier Foundation Pioneer Award* and the *Bulbie Gnass Spirit of Achievement Award* for lifetime achievements in the field of inventions that have made a significant contribution to mankind. Lamarr was further recognised on several feature programmes on television, including the Science Channel, as well as several documentaries on the Discovery Channel and in BBC 4's *Revolutions* series. In 2014, Lamarr and Antheil were posthumously inducted into the National Inventors Hall of Fame.

So, the next time you're invited to a tennis party, who knows, you could still be being remembered years later, and end up being immortalised for revolutionising missile technologies and being the cornerstone of all known telecommunications around the world.

It certainly worked for me. I'm still being remembered many years later from the Slinfold Village Under 12's Tennis Tournament: To this day they still talk about me fluffing an easy volley into the net, losing in the first round and skulking off home in a huff. It's great to know that I'll always be a part of tennis history.

TENNIS INVENTS THE MASONS

Most livery companies and guilds have long been tarnished with the same suspicion that is cast upon the likes of the Masons, whose members supposedly meet up in clandestine lodges, greet each other with dodgy handshakes where the placement of the thumb and little finger indicate which position they held in the guild. They'd have strange initiation ceremonies where all the newbies have to wonder around the Lodge with their trousers half rolled up, chanting strange incantations in medieval Latin, watched by all the other members disguised in black hoods.

The mysterious mythology usually extends to people thinking that there are also a bevy of beautiful, bare-footed virgins floating around in white lace dresses, more often than not they'll think there's a chicken somewhere in the equation, a sharp knife and, at some point, the blood of a sacrificial goat. The most enduring myth is that the members are thought to hold a powerful and disturbing influence over everyone, from the police to politicians, all around the world.

Although in medieval times some of them may well have endured some strange initiations, today's guilds hold themselves to very different standards, pride themselves in their integrity, do great work for charity and are not like that at all.

What many people don't realise is that tennis had one of the earliest such guilds. Tax records show that such a guild was operating in Paris in 1292, and had probably been around for many years before that. By the mid-16th century, they had renamed the guild as Paumier-Raquetiers and they adhered to a very strict code of practice.

For instance, before being admitted as a *Paumier*, potential members had to have been a player of *Jeu de paume* for at least three years before being allowed to give a tennis lesson. They had to be well versed in the art of making tennis balls. They also had to be brilliant carpenters in order to shape and carve the rackets, as well as being able to string them. And they had to have beaten at least two well-known fellow professional players, or other *Paumiers*, in an officially recognised tennis match.

So, the next time you shake hands with your fellow players at the net after a match, pay special attention to see exactly where they place their thumb during the handshake, and on which of your knuckles they place it on. Watch also the curl of their middle finger to see if they give off any secret clues as to how high up the chain of command they are. Because you never know, they could be a secret liveryman from the ancient guild of *Paumiers*!

Of course, growing up in the back streets of Horsham town, there were none of these secret societies or clandestine guilds, we had most of the necessary materials, plenty of chickens, loads of old goats, a plethora of knives, we just fell short at the last hurdle – we could never find a dozen virgins.

TENNIS INVENTS TRAINERS

Another of the skills required of *Paumiers* before they could be inducted into the guild was making the highly specialised shoes that were worn for playing tennis.

The shoes were called *Paulaines*, originally because so many of them were imported from Poland who had cornered the market in tennis shoes in those days. Consequently the shoes had a slightly raised toe, as was the fashion of the time. They had no heel which was thought to give extra balance, feel and agility around the court, and the soles were often made from the same felt as the tennis balls themselves.

Just as the best trainers are highly sought after today, so were they by the *Jeu de paume* players. All this, seven centuries before Nike came along with their *"Just Do It"* slogan. Or *"Simplement fais-le"* as the 12th-century *Paumiers* used to say!

TENNIS INVENTS THE WASHING MACHINE

The game of *Battledore* looks a little like an early form of Badminton only it predates it by many centuries. We know it was being played in Roman times, but probably goes back even further to Ancient Greece.

The *battledore* was originally a laundry paddle that was used to stir the clothes around in soapy water, before being taken down to the river's edge where the battledore was then used to beat the clothes in order to get out the grime. It was a sort of cross between a washboard and a carpet beater.

The record books are unclear as to whether the game of *Battledore* started because some bright spark thought a washing paddle would make a good racket, or whether it was a game first and someone thought the rackets would make a good washing paddle. But if history has taught us anything, it is that necessity is the mother of invention, and it is normally something practical that is later turned into a pastime.

So, you could say that the *Battledore* tennis racket was a crude, early prototype for the modern-day washing machine.

I wonder if that's how they invented the net as well? Someone was hanging out their old underwear to dry, and some clever clogs started to play *Battledore* over the washing line.

Enough to put anyone off their volleys.

TENNIS INVENTS ALL STUFF

OK, enough of all this Tomfoolery, this is the one you've been waiting for. The big kahuna, the one that finally justifies the title of the book and explains exactly how tennis really did invent all stuff.

Manuscripts going back to the 12th century make frequent reference of the ancient art of making tennis balls, which were usually bound in fabric or leather. They were then filled with just about anything that was available, from linens and silks to cottons, wool and hair, often with a cork and sometimes even lead shot at the centre for weight.

We also know that in 12th-century France, the word for a *tennis ball* was *esteuf*, from the French word étoffer, meaning *"to fill or stuff"*. This was related to the Latin words of *stofus*, a term applied to all fabrics, like silk, wool and cotton, which were then collectively called *stuffs*.

So, there you have it, now you know how I had the nerve to entitle the book, *How Tennis Invented Everything*, because, quite literally, it invented, if not *all* stuff, then at least *stuff* itself.

And if you don't like it, well then as far as I'm concerned you can *va au étoffé*, as the ancient *Paumiers* used to say!

SECTION 19

THE TITANIC

I have to thank Robert Fuller for first bringing my attention to some of these maritime accounts. Robert is a specialist collector and highly respected tennis historian whose depth of knowledge I would often turn to when looking for a good story for *The Queen's Club Magazine*.

The sinking of the *Titanic* is one of the most well-documented events in history. The tragedy has fuelled interest for more than a century and still continues to inspire films, articles, documentaries, auctions, human interest stories and conspiracy theories to this day.

It's surprising then that so little coverage has been given to the way that the catastrophe affected the world of tennis, because on board the ship that day was not just one tennis legend, but four. And all of their stories played a pivotal part in how tennis history played out afterwards and helped shape the modern game we know and love today ...

TENNIS INVENTS TITANIC COURAGE

Richard Williams was possibly one of the most gifted players of his generation and was sailing to Newport to take part in the US Championships. The Williams family were historically significant, they were almost American royalty as his father was a direct descendant of Benjamin Franklin. In fact, they were travelling together and they were amongst the very first people to be informed that the ship had struck an iceberg.

Upon hearing the worrying news, father and son went up to the top deck to survey the damage, but could see nothing to concern themselves with and so they went back down to the on-board gym to do a spot of training. A little while later, they were both on the fixed spot exercise bikes when they noticed that the incline had become abnormally steep and, unnerved by the experience, they stopped to investigate further.

By the time they reached the top deck, the reality of what was unfolding began to sink in, and their previously calm demeanour took a very different turn. The gradient of the liner had become so pronounced that people were starting to slide off the decks and into the freezing ocean below.

As the stern of the ship continued to rise, they heard a deafening crack. The forward tunnel had split and was breaking under the strain. Suddenly it tore loose and crashed just behind Williams and his father and, because of the steep incline, started to roll towards them, indiscriminately squashing, killing or maiming everyone in its way.

Williams leapt clear just in time but his less agile father was not so lucky and was caught in its deathly path. A horrified Williams was forced to watch helplessly as his father was crushed to death right in front of him.

The funnel careered past, engulfing him in a shower of sparks and huge clouds of soot as the giant flue swept onwards, eventually plummeting into the sea, killing hordes of other people who had previously jumped ship to take refuge in the sea.

But the funnel's murderous onslaught wasn't over yet. As it plunged into the sea, the sheer weight and size of it created its own giant wave, so huge that it crashed back up across the decks of the ship sweeping hundreds of others off their feet and hurling them into the freezing seas below. One such person was Williams himself, who was thrown backwards onto the railings before being catapulted overboard.

A small collapsible boat was also swept overboard by the wave but didn't open. It did, however, float and proved robust enough for Williams and several others to be able to grab the sides of it and hang on for dear life. But, unfortunately, their gruesome ordeal was far from over.

Such was the ferocity of the freezing sea that the lower halves of their bodies quickly began to lose circulation and after about half an hour one of them gave up the ghost and just slid slowly off the craft into the sea. They all watched in silent horror as the body quietly vanished into the murky depths of the ocean below.

Everyone just stared at each other in silence, but their eyes said it all, each of them knew that the same fate was about to befall each and every one of them at any moment. Sure enough, a few minutes later a second person slid quietly off the side and faded to their icy grave. One by one, more of those who were desperately clinging to the craft slipped silently away into the dark waters.

By the time the rescue ship *Carpathia* arrived, most of those who had sought refuge from the collapsible had suffered the same fate and were long gone. Only a few of them were left, one of whom was Williams, but by the time they got him to the ship's physician, things looked grim.

The doctor saw the state of his frozen limbs and told him that the only way he could possibly survive was if he performed a double amputation immediately.

Williams, the reigning US champion, was just 21 years old.

From an early age, Williams had harboured an innate distrust of doctors and refused to give his consent. He protested that he would eventually be alright and to prove the doctor wrong insisted he should be allowed to try and stand up. Williams was helped to his feet and promptly collapsed to the floor in a crumpled heap. Both his limbs were hypothermic and his frozen muscles simply refused to respond.

The doctor insisted he risked losing his life and that a double amputation was his only chance of survival. Even so, Williams refused to give in and said he would try again in half an hour. Once more Williams was helped to his feet and once again his legs gave way.

Although the prognosis looked bleak, Williams would still not give in. After trying and failing for nearly three hours, Williams finally managed to stand for a second or two. Within a few more hours he was able to take a step as well, and, by the next day, he was able to walk, albeit tentatively.

Within months Williams had not only fully recovered, he had reached the quarter-finals of the US Open and, incredibly, actually won the doubles. The following year, he went one further and won the tournament outright. He won again in 1916, the very same year that his astonishing legs propelled him to number one in the world rankings.

But the heroic Williams's battles were not over. He went on to serve in the First World War, where he was awarded with the Croix de Guerre for his enduring courage and gallantry, as well as the Legion of Honour for bravery.

Williams documented his war efforts as totally horrific, but none of them proved as gruesome, nor more poignant, than his astonishing survival from the sinking of the *RMS Titanic*.

In later life, Williams went on to become a successful businessman and received one further sporting honour in 1957, when he was inducted into the Tennis Hall of Fame.

Thank goodness for Williams's childhood distrust of doctors, if had taken the doctor's advice, his life would have been very different and the tennis world would have lost, not just one of its greatest champions but one of its most courageous ambassadors.

TENNIS INVENTS TITANIC 88-YEAR RECORD

Our *Titanic* hero, Richard Williams, features again in this formidable tale. Richards also won the Olympic mixed doubles title at the 1924 Paris Olympics with Hazel Wightman, the woman who established the now-defunct Wightman Cup tournament.

Williams and Wightman beat fellow Americans Vincent Richards and Marion Jessup 6–2, 6–3 in the final, despite the fact that Williams suggested that that they should withdraw after he sprained his ankle in the semi-finals. But really, what's a sprained ankle to man who survived the *Titanic* and the First World War.

What marks this out as extra noteworthy, is the fact that the mixed doubles title was then dropped from the Olympics altogether and wasn't reinstated until London 2012. This decision gave rise to the peculiar anomaly in that Williams was actually the reigning Olympic mixed doubles champion for an astonishing 88 years! A record that is unlikely to ever be broken. A rather lovely and fitting tribute to one of the most extraordinary men to ever grace a tennis court.

TENNIS INVENTS TITANIC STRUGGLE

The second tennis player on board the *Titanic* that day was another American, Karl Howell Behr. A brilliant college champion who, on his Davis Cup debut, beat two Wimbledon champions. A promising tennis career beckoned then as he boarded the luxurious liner that fateful day.

Behr was on board the *Titanic* with his girlfriend and her parents, and, like Williams, his party were informed early of the collision with the iceberg. The four of them were asked if they'd like to get into one of the first lifeboats to be lowered, and they calmly accepted and got on.

It wasn't until some time later, as they watched the ensuing horror of the situation unfold, that they realised just how lucky they had been. They watched in total shock as the mighty ship reared up, split in two and sank slowly into the hungry sea.

Filled with remorse, they begged the acting skipper of the lifeboat to let them go back to pick up more survivors as they still had a few spaces left on the lifeboat. The skipper refused, knowing that if they did, they would be overloaded with desperate survivors and all of them would die. The sense of guilt, despair and culpability that overwhelmed everyone left in the boat was tangible, to the point that many of them felt physically sick. So much so, in fact, that one desolate passenger, with a rather warped sense of morality, offered Karl his gun so that he could take the more honourable way out and shoot himself along with his girlfriend and her family, rather than go home and face the criticism.

Behr graciously declined the dubiously principled proposal to murder his loved ones and instead came up with another more honourable solution. He turned to his girlfriend and asked her that, if they survived and made it home safely, whether she would marry him. She accepted. They survived the ordeal and were married in March the following year.

Behr went on to become one the stalwarts of American tennis, winning several Davis Cup ties, and although he never won a Grand Slam, he twice reached the Wimbledon finals but was runner up both times.

Not only did Behr survive the sinking of the *Titanic*, but he actually went on to meet and play another one of his fellow survivors, the aforementioned Richard Williams, in the US Open quarter-finals two years later. Newspaper headlines around the world declared it as a *Titanic* battle but one that the courageous Williams deservedly won on his way to winning the championship.

Although Williams won that particular encounter, and was rightly regarded as the superior player, Behr undoubtedly outplayed him in the field of business, going on to form, and be on the board of, many successful companies, including the Goodyear Tyre and Rubber Co.

It may have been about ten years after Williams, but Behr was eventually also inducted into the Tennis Hall of Fame in 1965. But he will probably be best remembered for that quite extraordinary and uniquely historic meeting in the US quarter-finals where these two *Titanic* survivors reminded the world what the human spirit can endure, survive and go on to achieve.

Tennis was fortunate to have Behr and Williams as its ambassadors, men that helped to build the game into the global attraction that it is today.

TENNIS INVENTS THIRD TIME LUCKY

Astonishingly, there was yet a third tennis champion on board the *Titanic* that day, Charles Eugene Williams. He was not of the Lawn Tennis variety but was the reigning World Rackets Champion who just happened to be on his way to New York to defend his title.

Like many of those who lived through the horrors of that disturbing day, Williams was so traumatised that he never spoke publicly of those harrowing events and so little is known about his story, other than the fact that he had been playing rackets on the ships rackets court before adjourning to the smoking room, where he heard the mighty crash as the ship struck the iceberg.

Williams waited on board as long as he could before jumping from the lower decks. He was fortunate enough to be plucked from the sea by a lifeboat before being hauled aboard the rescue ship *Carpathia*. Upon reaching land, Williams sent a very understated telegram to the opponent he was due to play, apologising that he was likely to be a bit late for the match, making no mention of the gruesome events that had made up the mitigating circumstances.

In true English understatement it simply read, *"Will have to postpone match. Returning next week"*.

True to his word, the low-key Williams duly returned the following week.

He probably wouldn't want me to make a big fuss about it, but he won.

TENNIS INVENTS A FEDERATION

Incredibly, there was yet one further history changing moment that the *Titanic* was still to wreak upon the tennis world, but first let me give you the background to it.

For many years, Lawn Tennis had no international governing body; until the early part of the 20th century. There were probably several political reasons why the Americans could not be persuaded to join an international body but if there was one man who might have been able to make it possible it was Duane Williams. Williams is credited as the man who actually originated the idea for an international governing body for tennis and an inaugural meeting was all set to take place on 1 March 1913. However, the sea had other plans.

Duane Williams, who should have gone down in history as the founding father, never made it. He died on the *Titanic* and so never saw his dream turned into a reality. To make matters worse, even though the meeting still went ahead, America failed to send an alternative representative to replace him.

This was a real pity as it took many years of wrangling before the Americans could yet again be persuaded to show up at the global table. They eventually signed up in 1923 to what is now known as The International Tennis Federation. This was where the four main members of England, France, Australia and the US were granted their official Grand Slam status as the four Majors of the tennis world.

So, the Americans were a bit late to join in but they got there in the end – a bit like the First and Second World Wars then!

TENNIS INVENTS TITANIC CONSPIRACY THEORY

Everyone loves a good conspiracy theory, the faked moon landings, the Kennedy assassination, Area 51, Roswell, The Twin Towers, they all have their supporters and detractors. But there is one conspiracy theory that has always intrigued me more than any other, and it is this one.

There is a very real train of thought that claims that the *Titanic* never really sank at all. If you know the theory, then you will be familiar with the idea that it was her sister ship, the *Olympic*, that struck the iceberg and sunk, not the *Titanic*. But what you may not know is that it was tennis that first ignited the rumours that led to one of the most contentious, but shockingly plausible conspiracy theories of all time.

It all starts with Paddy the Pig. No, not a children's cartoon character with a fruitful line of candy merchandising, but an Australian called Patrick Fenton. Fenton was usually dismissed as a drunken bar-fly who'd tell any stranger his *Titanic* conspiracy story if they bought him a beer. Nobody paid Paddy much attention until an Australian journalist stumbled upon him and published the story. Here's the gist of Paddy the Pig's story.

The *Olympic* was launched by the White Star Line a year before the *Titanic* and, in those days, was by far the more famous, being the first and the biggest ship of all time. But it seemed to be cursed with poor luck.

Within months of its launch in 1911, the *Olympic* experienced several minor but expensive collisions. Almost as soon as these had been repaired, she suffered another blow that proved to be far more serious. It crashed into the Royal Navy cruiser *HMS Hawke* off the coast of the Isle of Wight causing serious structural damage to the

Olympic's steel beams but, much more significantly, the collision had bent the keel.

To repair a keel in a ship of that magnitude would have been a major undertaking. It would be almost as expensive as building a whole new ship and, on top of all that, the White Star Line were denied an insurance claim on the grounds that it was said to be their fault. Because of the extensive damage, the *Olympic* was going to cost the company millions of pounds to repair, and almost as much again in lost revenue.

In today's money that would be around £300m in purely monetary terms, but it is estimated that to rebuild the *Titanic* today to the exact same spec that it was, could actually cost more like £6 billion. In reality then, the *Olympic* was a lame duck. A giant liability. Nothing more than a massive floating write-off.

To make matters worse, the White Star Line was already in financial difficulty and on the verge of bankruptcy. The *Olympic* accident meant that they were staring financial disaster in the face.

The damages forced the White Star Line to take the *Olympic* out of commission while they tried to make good the repairs. Doing this also meant that the maiden voyage of *Titanic* had to be put back from 20 March to 10 April, putting further financial pressure on the already ailing company.

So, according to Paddy the Pig, White Star came up with an emergency plan. A plan so simple in its audacity as to be brilliant. They would simply switch the lame, uninsurable *Olympic* with her sister ship, the *Titanic*, and then scuttle it, saying it was an accident, to claim the insurance. This might seem like a totally outrageous idea to us today, but in those days this fraudulent practice was rife and was the most commonly used maritime scam. Huge fortunes had been made and lost on just such a scam for centuries.

And it just so happened that the perfect opportunity to put the plan into action neatly presented itself. The *Olympic* was due to be in Belfast to have a new propeller fitted, this would mean that she would be in the same port and at the same time as the *Titanic*. They sat next to each other in the exact same dock, looking every bit like the identical twins they were.

Changing the propeller on the *Olympic* was a job that should have taken a day to do, so why then was the ship held there, sitting next to her twin, for over a week? No satisfactory explanation has ever been given by White Star for this occurrence, other than just *"a general delay"*. What was even stranger is that the *Titanic* and *Olympic* were each slipping in and out of the same dock all week, apparently *"on tests"*. The ships were so identical that half the time even the dockers themselves didn't know which ship they were working on.

As Paddy The Pig tells it, only a few people would have been allowed to know about the swap: J. Bruce Ismay and J. P. Morgan would have definitely known as they were the owners and financiers of the White Star Line, as well as Lord Pirrie and probably Thomas Andrews from Harland & Wolff. They knew that if you looked at the two ships when they were sitting beside each other you would not know which ship was which without looking at the name plates. They set about it subtly at first, by inexplicably laying a new carpet in the *Olympic* which was exactly like the *Titanic*'s one.

The cutlery and plates didn't need to be changed as they were all marked with White Star Line not *Titanic*, so that was easy. What was harder to change was the number of portholes. Closer inspection of the photographs show that when the *Titanic* was built it had 14 evenly spaced portholes, but when it left Southampton on 10 April 1912 it had 16 unevenly spaced portholes, just like the *Olympic*. Again, no good reasons have ever been given for the extra portholes.

Furthermore, the damage to the *Olympic* after its collision meant that it had a noticeable and permanent list to port. The undamaged *Titanic* had no such list and yet several of the reports noted that as the *Titanic* left Southampton that day, it also had a list to port.

There are also a few photos of the *Titanic* leaving port that show a dark patch on her bows, where it looks like paint of a slightly different hue was used. The area in question was in exactly the same place as where the *Olympic* had had its collision.

We also have the disturbing question of the cancellations. J. P. Morgan was amongst many people who cancelled his trip at the last minute as he was said to be unwell. Strange then that he was spotted in France two days later looking in perfect health. J. Bruce Ismay suddenly withdrew his entire family from the trip, citing his wife's ill health, but they had all been spotted the day before on a motoring holiday in Wales, all looking perfectly well.

There were a number of other high-profile cancellations, all wealthy businessmen and all connected to J. P. Morgan, most notably, Henry Clay Frick, Horace J. Harding and George Washington Vanderbilt. J. P. Morgan also had several very valuable pieces of his art collection removed from his cabin one hour before the ship left Southampton.

There were several arch enemies of J. P. Morgan on board as well, including John Astor, Benjamin Guggenheim and Isidor Straus, who were all rigidly opposed to J. P. Morgan's idea of creating a US Central Reserve Bank. It seems none of these men received any such forewarning and so didn't cancel their bookings. All three men died during the sinking. And Morgan got his bank.

Another matter that further fueled the conspiracy theorists was a ship named *SS Californian*, also owned by J. P. Morgan, that mysteriously left Southampton just before the *Titanic* and headed straight into the North Atlantic and seemingly stopped there as if waiting for something.

The ship would have been the perfect size to rescue about 1,500 passengers and mysteriously the ship was empty. It hadn't sold any tickets for its supposed voyage to Boston, despite the fact that there was huge demand for tickets to cross the Atlantic. A point made all the more pertinent when you consider that there was a coal strike and the cost of finding the coal would have been extortionate, so not trying to recoup the costs, and sending an empty ship, seems a strange decision, especially for a company in such dire financial straits. In fact the only goods on board was a large consignment of blankets and warm clothes. Quite a handy cargo if you were, say, picking up cold, wet passengers from a scuttled liner.

Something else that was unusual was that, when the supposed *Olympic* was taken out of service in 1935 part of the wood panelling shows the number 401 which was the ID number that was given to *Titanic*. If the paneling had been from *Olympic* the number should have been 400.

The *Northern Star* newspaper, which ran the original Fenton story, talks about an extract from a letter that was told by one of the survivors to his son, who then told Fenton directly. He says that,

> "When the surviving crew got to port they were all taken aside and met by two men, one in a high position in the company, the other man was in a very high position in the Government.
>
> "The Government man read the crew the Official Secrets Act and were told then in no uncertain terms that they were not to talk to the press or anyone about the sinking and made to sign contracts to that effect. Anyone breaching the terms of the Official Secrets Act would face a minimum of 20 years in jail, would never get a job when they got out and would not receive any of the compensation money that they were all being promised."

But it seems that some of the dockers may have spotted what was going on before the *Titanic* even set sail and tipped off their fellow workers about what was going on. This might explain why the *Titanic* struggled to find crew when, inexplicably, all but one of the entire crew resigned and refused to work on the ship at any price. This is all the more intriguing because there was a coal strike on at the time, which meant that thousands of firemen, boiler stokers and greasers were very short of work. In the end, all the vacancies were filled by inexperienced, non-local workers who had nothing to do with White Star and would not have been in the know.

Curiously, evidence from the wreck discovered by Robert Ballard in 1985 supports the switch theory. The stamp 401, the ID number used for the *Titanic*, can be seen on the ship's propeller. Although labourers from Harland and Wolff confirm that this could have been legit, as the *Titanic*'s propeller was fitted to the *Olympic* during its repair following the collision with the *Hawke* and a second propeller had to be re-cast for the *Titanic*.

Some of the Ballard photographs of the wreck appear to show the letters 'M' and 'P' on the side of the wreck. Could that be the remains of the ship's original nameplate *Olympic*? It was a characteristic of all White Star Line vessels that the ship's names were etched into the hull. Certainly the *Olympic*'s name was etched into the ship but when the *Titanic* left port it suddenly had a nameplate riveted on to the side of the hull instead. Was it covering the original etched name as part of the scam?

Other Ballard photos of the wreck show evidence of grey paint being used as an undercoat, but the *Titanic* used black paint for its undercoat, only the Olympic used grey.

Whilst it seems unlikely such a scam could be pulled off today, this was a common maritime fraud at the time and the lack of media coverage in 1912 makes it more credible. Only one newsreel survives of the *Titanic* leaving port and photographic evidence is equally rare. With the two ships as good as identical, no-one would have been able to have spotted the swap.

There are also some big question marks over why on earth the White Star Line would use Captain Smith to skipper the *Titanic*. After all he was the captain with one of the worst sea records in the fleet.

Intriguingly, he was the skipper of the *Olympic* when it had all the previously mentioned collisions. He was old, he should have been sacked or pensioned off ages ago, so why was he suddenly chosen? Did J. P. Morgan put pressure on him for maybe one final favour?

Far more importantly, of course, how does tennis fit in to all this? Well, although there doesn't seem to have been an actual full-sized tennis court on board, there was a designated facility which could be adapted so that the rackets sports of Real Tennis, Rackets, Squash and Lawn Tennis could all be practised in it.

The story is reportedly handed down from Fenton himself, who tells of a waiter who heard a tennis player talking at the bar of the great ship. The player had noticed that the court he was practising on seemed to be unusually well worn for a supposedly new court on its maiden voyage. The waiter told Fenton that he thought nothing of it until he later heard two stokers saying that the boilers were also very heavily soiled for such a supposedly new vessel.

That's when a casual comment about a tennis court started to grow from a rumour into the fully fledged conspiracy theory that we have today.

Luckily we have the technology to stop these big companies from being able to pull off such audacious frauds anymore. Now, where did I park my nice low emissions Volkswagen, I think I left my Samsung Galaxy Note 7 charging inside of it and I need to call Bernard Madoff to see how those Lehman Brothers investments he made for me are doing because my BHS pension needs topping up before I go on that Thomas Cook Holiday I booked.

Oh, dear, maybe I should've returned all those calls from that PPI firm after all ...

TENNIS INVENTS PROPAGANDA

Surprisingly for such a land-based game, there are still a few more dramatic tennis stories that took place at sea and, even though they didn't take place on board the *Titanic*, they are still worthy of a maritime mention here. This one takes place many oceans away, in Japan.

Propaganda comes from the Latin word *propagare*, meaning *to spread* which in turn gives us *propagate*. The origins of *propaganda* can be traced back as early as written records, most leaders, governments and religions have all used it to try and convince the masses of their point of view. However, it wasn't until the outbreak of the First World War that the term really started to gain traction and come into common usage, and a very early example of this was actually centred around tennis.

In 1914, Japan was a leading light in the world of tennis and their biggest name was Jiro Satoh. He was Japan's brightest star, not just in his own country, but around the world. Satoh was young, handsome and played tennis with a fearsome passion. He was a heroic competitor who was said to display the same relentless spirit of a Samurai warrior. He was renowned for taking on opponents that were bigger and stronger than him, but he would cut them down to size and conquer them with his competitive spirit. He was revered as a true Japanese hero.

Satoh was the captain of Japan's Davis Cup team, which was one of the favourites to win the title that year. However, the tournament was being staged in New York which meant that he had to sail all the way to America to play for his country. It was a highly anticipated match that had tennis fans around the world drooling in anticipation. So when news feeds started to break that Satoh had suddenly committed suicide, it made global headlines that sent shock waves around the world.

Sports fans everywhere were upset, but in Japan it was devastating news, and the whole country fell into mourning for the loss of its beloved star. In the Western world suicide was considered very shocking, especially in such a young and talented sportsman with the world at his feet. In Japan though, the act of suicide can be a most honourable act of the highest order, especially if you were sacrificing yourself for you country.

But none of this made any real sense, especially to his fellow pros who questioned the reports saying that Satoh was one of the happiest players on the tour, always joking and full of fun and life. The Japanese authorities tried to counter the growing rumours of disbelief by saying that there was a suicide note and that several heavy objects were missing from the ship, which were likely to have been used as weights to help him drown. They even issued an instruction to his fiancée to confirm the suicide theory, which she did at the time.

But none of this looked convincing to anyone in the West and, in more recent years, new information has been unearthed which may shed a different light on the Satoh story and reveal an even more moving and dramatic tale.

Satoh, you see, was also a dashingly handsome man with film-star good looks, and he had fallen head over heels in love with a young girl called Sanse Okada, herself a brilliant young tennis player. They were in the first flush of love and Satoh felt so passionately about his beloved Sanse that he asked the authorities if she could come with him on the trip as he couldn't bear the thought of sailing off to the other side of the world and being without her for many months. The authorities initially agreed to let her go with him but they were just appeasing him, and at the last minute told her that she couldn't go and she never joined him on board the ship.

The Japanese authorities insisted that Satoh had to go without her and emphasised to him what a great honour it was to represent his country. Not to do so would bring shame to himself, his family and his country, adding that Sanse would be a distraction, his country must come first. Satoh felt cheated and betrayed and it was a desolate and lovelorn Satoh that set sail that morning. In those days, there were no jet planes; he would have to travel by ship which meant he would be away from Sanse for months on end. Satoh was so distraught at the thought of being without his love for so long and, as the ship sailed further and further away from shore, he became more and more morose and anxious. There was only one thing to do. He would jump ship and swim back to her.

He leapt overboard and swam for the coast. He was young, strong, fit and a brilliant swimmer. His famous determination and Samurai spirit had carried him through adversity to win many a match and it would carry him home to his love. It was a Hollywood love story waiting to happen.

The water was freezing cold and he was many miles out. He fought ice-cold seas, wild tides, swirling undercurrents and fearsome ocean waves. But even a Samurai Warrior is no match for a force of nature like the sea, and maybe the reason that Hollywood never picked up the rights to the story was very simple – Satoh never made it to shore and tragically died.

Rather than tell the truth of Satoh's attempted swim to shore, which ended in a dishonourable failure, the Japanese authorities preferred to portray it as an honourable suicide in order to keep his legend alive.

It was a tragic love story of Shakespearean proportions. They were the Romeo and Juliet of the East. The sea may have stolen one of the world's greatest sporting heroes, but Japan had robbed us of one of the greatest love stories of all time, Satoh and Okada.

TENNIS INVENTS DRESS CODE FOR WIMBLEDON – ALL AT SEA

Fortunately, there is another great tennis story that takes place at sea, a tale that Hollywood did pick up on because it concerned one of their very own stars and had a much happier ending. It took place on board a liner almost as luxurious as the *Titanic* and one that was also sailing to New York.

It was the Roaring Twenties and amongst the many socialites, industrialists and nobility on board were two well-known celebrities from different sides of the track.

The first was one of England's finest tennis players, Henry Wilfred 'Bunny' Austin, often called the greatest player never to have won Wimbledon, although he did make it to the final twice and helped Great Britain win four consecutive Davis Cup titles. The second celebrity was one of England's finest actresses, Phyllis Konstam, probably best known for the four films she made with the master of suspense himself, Alfred Hitchcock.

Whilst Phyllis was a big star in 1929, the friend that was accompanying her was not. He was a struggling actor, who had appeared in several stage plays that year, all of which failed miserably and were very short lived. Don't get too despondent for the poor chap though, as this journey to the Americas was to change his life as well, his name was Laurence Olivier.

When Phyllis was first introduced to Bunny Austin on board the liner, the attraction was immediate. They entered into a whirlwind romance that was as tempestuous and turbulent as the seas it was born on. They became one of Britain's biggest celebrity couples, counting Charlie Chaplin, Peter Ustinov, President Roosevelt and royalty as their friends. It was a love that lasted a lifetime as they later married and had two children.

Passengers recall seeing Austin playing tennis on deck, a sight that became etched into their memories solely because of one shocking thing – he was wearing shorts. It doesn't seem unusual for us today, but in 1929 it caused quite a stir because for a gentleman to wear shorts and show off his naked legs was considered really quite scandalous, even when on holiday, especially when women were also present and doubly so to be so brazen while playing the usually respectable game of tennis.

But Austin loved playing in shorts and found he could run around much quicker without being weighed down by the traditional white flannels that were the customary attire. Austin may not have won Wimbledon but he certainly left his mark there and changed sporting history forever, because in 1932 Austin outraged tournament officials when he dared to stroll onto Centre Court wearing a pair of his favourite shorts, showing his bare legs to a shocked and stunned Wimbledon crowd.

Despite the scandal, Austin soon showed how the lighter shorts were more conducive to easier, freer, faster movement around the court and soon other players started to follow his lead and Wimbledon dress code was changed forever.

SECTION 20

FASHION

Although Bunny Austin's shorts could well have appeared in this section as a fashion that changed the world, tennis has influenced the mercurial world of fashion in many other ways as well ...

TENNIS INVENTS HIGH FASHION

Fashion houses today are often accused of creating ridiculously impractical outfits that no ordinary shopper would ever buy, but they do it to get their designs noticed on the catwalk and photographed for the media. Even in the 1530s, tennis was already leading the way in this and laying the groundwork, for the famously fey behaviour that still besets the fashion world today.

During this time, tennis was becoming incredibly popular, with royal endorsements from both the king of England and the king of France. The royal courtiers were quick to follow suit and tennis soon became so popular that it even began to influence the world of fashion, especially when endorsed by royalty.

Catherine de Medici was Queen consort of France who saw three of her sons reign as king, so she had enormous influence in France for a long period of history. She was a renowned beauty and famed as a royal trend setter. Her love of tennis extended so far as to even create a hair style dedicated to the game, the look became so popular that it was given a name, *le coiffure en raquette*. The design of the hair itself was set to mimic the strings that make up the criss-cross of the racket.

Useful, if someone was trying to lob her I guess, but these days I don't think anyone would be able to pull off such a style, unless maybe Lady Gaga takes up the sport, until then we'll just have to put it down as a bad hair day.

TENNIS INVENTS PARLIAMENTARY PANTY SCANDAL

Apart from medieval tennis players and the odd sartorially challenged superhero, underpants usually remain unseen and thankfully this was also the case in the tennis world for almost six centuries. Until, that is, a young American lady called Gussy Moran caused a worldwide sensation in 1949 when she strode out onto Wimbledon Centre Court wearing a pair of laced silk panties decorated with ruffles that were clearly on view for all to see under her very short skirt. These ruffles were certainly well named, because they ruffled quite a few feathers around the world, causing a mini rumpus with Wimbledon photographers who fought with each other as they jostled for the best position to snap shots of her saucy underwear.

Needless to say, the situation sent Wimbledon's official tournament committee into a panic and they didn't know what to do as there were no official rulings on undergarments. With the ensuing press and media coverage, the situation reached crisis point that reached out far beyond the sporting world all the way to the Palace of Westminster where the scandal even prompted a special mention by MPs in a debate in the Houses of Parliament itself.

Eventually, Moran, who was immediately dubbed "Gorgeous Gussy" by the press, was accused of bringing *vulgarity and sin into tennis* by the Committee of the All England Lawn Tennis and Croquet Club and she was forced to wear shorts to subdue them.

The man who designed them, Ted Tinling, was a well-known figure in the fashion world and an official host at Wimbledon for almost a quarter of century, but he suddenly found himself shunned by the club, and all because of Gorgeous Gussy's great gusset gaff going global.

TENNIS INVENTS MORE PANTY MAYEM

So, after six centuries with no significant panty incidents in tennis, suddenly another one emerges from the under the *hem*-isphere, if you pardon the pun.

Sure enough, in 1958, Ted Tinling, yes him again, thought it was about time he got back into women's underwear again – designing them that is, I don't want to be hit with a transvestite libel action! So Tinling decided to design a pair for the tennis player Karol Fageros, and they had the brilliant idea of debuting them at Wimbledon in an attempt to make up for the Gorgeous Gussy gusset fiasco.

What could possibly go wrong?

Well, quite a lot, apparently.

Wimbledon officials decided that Miss Fageros's perfunctory panties, being made in an especially shiny gold lamé, flaunted the Club's all white dress code, but, more than that, they also flaunted a lot more of Miss Fageros than was considered either wise or chic in the puritanical 1950s. And Tinling's gilded garbs were banned once again!

Oh dear, maybe Ted would have been better off wearing them himself after all.

TENNIS INVENTS TINDER-STYLE DATING APP

Much like London buses, where none come along for ages then three come along at once, so it is with tennis panty scandals, none for six centuries and then three come along at once.

Sure enough, only a few years after Karol Fageros and Gussy Moran had so scandalised the nation, a young American lady called Patricia Stewart found herself suddenly dumped by her boyfriend just before she set off on the tennis tour to England. In an early interview, the newly single Patricia bemoaned the fact that the players seemed to spend most of their time living out of hotel rooms making it difficult for them to meet anyone other than their fellow players.

But this was London in 1961, the Swinging Sixties, and rather than wait for someone to invent the internet and create dating sites like Tinder or Match.com, Patricia thought she would take matters into her own hands. No, don't go there, this is a family book.

In a bid to improve her social life, she wrote her telephone number in big bold print across her underpants and wore them under a racy short dress whilst playing at, where else? The Wimbledon Tennis Championships of course, sparking yet another panty controversy for the tournament committee.

The usual furore broke out in the media. It didn't improve her tennis, she was knocked out in the third round, but it worked wonders for her love life. Thanks to her bare-faced cheek, Miss Stewart's social life improved no end in the end, thanks to her end. Eagle-eyed cricketer John Eldrich spotted her saucy ad, called her up, they went out and were married a few months later. Game, set and match.

TENNIS INVENTS PANTY-MONIUM

Unbelievably, that was not the last time that a pair of ladies' smalls made a rumpus big, for there was to be one further panties incident to get the great gusset gawpers gossiping and causing the Wimbledon officials to get their knickers in a twist once more.

The year was 1975 and Margaret Court, the former champion and record 24 Grand Slam titles holder, was in the autumn of her career and was demurely going about her business, when a particularly vigorous forehand precipitated the mass undoing of all the fastenings on her dress.

As if this were not bad enough, it was at this precise moment that the elastic in her previously sturdy knickers also decided that it had had enough of being the bearer of her last bastion of dignity and decided to give up the ghost as well.

It was only the quick thinking of a Women's Royal Air Force stewardess who flew to her rescue and, along with a handful of army issue safety pins, managed to save her from any further indignity. The safety pins held up almost as well as Court that year, before she was undone in the semi-finals by Evonne Goolagong Cawley.

This brings to an end to our naughty knicker narratives from the normally demure lawns of SW19. Since then, England has been able to settle back and enjoy the last few decades relatively free from any more panty incidents. There was a short stint in the early '90s when it became fashionable to show the top of your Calvin Kleins poking out from under the waistline of your jeans, but luckily, tennis had nothing to do with this trend, which mercifully proved to be ... brief.

TENNIS INVENTS THE POSTER

OK, I may have lied about that being the last time tennis became embroiled in any more panty scandals. I had forgotten about this story, which could be said to involve a little bit of panty titillation, but all in the best possible taste, of course.

Tennis posters have a long and illustrious history, some rare items can fetch many thousands of pounds to a collector. Vintage tennis memorabilia dating from the years between the two World Wars are particularly collectable, especially posters advertising early matches at Wimbledon. The next most collectible ones are marketing posters from the past featuring tennis at luxury resorts; or advertising billboards from old ads like the Slazenger or Spalding ones.

Original Art Deco posters depicting a tennis scene also sell well, as do some of the vintage posters advertising the French Open at Roland Garros, which is famous for commissioning well-known artists each year to create posters for the event.

But, in the 1970s, the idea of posters was starting to wane and, apart from a few classic film posters, the bottom had fallen out of the market. Until, that is, a particularly pert bottom fell out from under the hem of a rather short white tennis skirt and sent stocks in tennis posters soaring again.

It was an evocatively shot slightly grainy photograph of a beautiful young woman dressed all in a pure white tennis dress with her back to us as she walked towards the net on a tennis court, her long blonde hair catching the last embers of light from a setting sun. In her right hand was a tennis racket while her left hand glanced the hem of her dress baring a tantalising glimpse of her voluptuous and bare bottom for all to see.

It was simply called *Tennis Girl* and it had an ethereal, dream-like quality to it. Etherealism, of course, being the main reason why schoolboys up and down the country had it plastered all over their bedroom walls. Apparently ethereal appreciation was in big demand that year as the image went on to sell millions of posters around the world.

Whether it was the ethereal look or the voluptuous bottom that did it is a point of contention. Either way, it didn't matter, the poster was such a success that it is said to have actually saved the ailing retail store Athena from going bankrupt in the late '70s and kept them afloat for another quarter of a century.

Despite the posters astonishing success, mystery had always surrounded the identity of the girl in the poster until, that is, the 35th anniversary of the poster. The photographer, Martin Elliot, revealed that it was his then girlfriend, Fiona Butler, who was the face behind the behind.

But for 35 years a man called Peter Atkinson has claimed that the corporeal buttocks in the picture actually belonged to his ex-wife. And for 35 years nobody believed him until, in 2015, Atkinson chanced across some tennis memorabilia being sold on eBay that he says is the missing link that proves the true identity of the girl.

In amongst the memorabilia that Atkinson had bought was a postcard featuring the photograph, but dated 1974. On closer inspection, though, he noticed that the 1974 postcard picture is of a slightly different angle to the one used in the famous poster, but the grainy, ethereal look is the same. The setting sun, the court, the golden haired girl, the dress, the bush and the tush, are all obviously identical. There seems no doubt that the buns that featured in the 1974 postcard are uncannily similar to the famous poster and must have come from the same film shoot.

But there was an anomaly, Elliot, the photographer, claimed he took the photograph of Fiona's cheeky chops in 1976, two years after the date on the postcard. Surely it was not possible for these pictures to be published two years before they were even taken. What was going on? I needed to get to the bottom of it.

It turns out that Elliot did indeed go to Athena with a set of prints from an earlier shoot that he did in 1972, and they really liked them but they thought the photographs were too grainy to blow up to poster size and told him to reshoot the pictures again with a better camera. Elliot retook the pictures, but this time used Fiona Butler as the model, but this was now several years after the original ones featuring Atkinson's ex-wife. So who's telling the truth and who's the keister shyster?

Atkinson claims that there is a simple explanation for the posterior poster mix up. It happened when Elliot returned to Athena and gave them the newer, more professional looking photographs. Athena though, had a change of heart and now decided that they liked the earlier photographs and ironically, for all the same reasons that they rejected them the first time, they now preferred the ethereal, grainy look of the original set to the clearer sharper imagery of the new shots.

Which means that it was a photograph from the first set of photos which was the one which was eventually used, the ones that featured the cheeky cheeks of Atkinson's ex-wife and not the ones of Elliot's then girlfriend.

It went on to sell literally millions of posters and went on to have a huge global impact, and not always good. In fact, several countries took such affront at the rear that the poster was banned. In the Middle East, her southern end caused such a hullabaloo that it was publicly burnt and torn to pieces as an example of Western sexual decadence.

Although Athena eventually went bust, the poster continues to sell well today in art shops and online, and is said to still produce a tidy pension for the late photographer's widow, the aptly named Noelle Bott. No, don't get me started again, I'm sure the poor lady has been the butt of enough jokes already.

SECTION 21

SCIENCE

Tennis has always been at the cutting edge of technological advances, from its early adoption of rubber for the ball to the materials used to make rackets, including wood, aluminium, titanium, carbon fibre all the way to the lightweight high modulus graphite super fibres used in rackets of today.

Here are a few of the less well-known anecdotes that link the scientific community to the tennis world.

TENNIS INVENTS THE VISUAL ILLUSION THEORY OF MOTION-INDUCED PERCEPTUAL MISLOCALISATION

Huh?

Yes, it's true. A study published by *Current Biology Magazine* revealed that the perceived position of a moving object is dependent on the object's motion coupled with the motion of other objects in the scene. This principle is in line with the relatively well-known scientific phenomenon that moving objects are misperceived by the human eye because the brain adjusts it slightly to compensate for the speed and direction of the motion.

In layman's terms then, this means that tennis players are more likely to make incorrect 'out' calls than they are to make incorrect 'in' calls. In fact, all of us are more likely to see a ball go long and make an error to call it out because of the motion-induced visual illusion that causes our brain to assimilate where the ball will bounce. This visual illusion makes the ball appear to go further than it actually does, therefore we are more likely to see a ball slightly long than short.

The study looked at over 140 player challenges during the Wimbledon championships, and more than 25% of these resulted in the umpire's call being overturned and, of those, 75% were due to errors calling it long when it wasn't, due to this very concept.

So there we have it, us tennis players are not all a bunch of short-sighted, over-competitive, unsportsmanlike, two-bit, cheating low-lifes; we're merely adhering to the scientifically proven visual illusion theory of motion-induced perceptual mislocalisation.

TENNIS INVENTS FORENSIC SCIENCE

If that all sounds a little bit complicated, let me take you back to a peaceful part of Ye Olde England, to a serene and tranquil little village of Elford, five miles from Lichfield. At the heart of the village stands an ancient stone church with a restful graveyard where you will find a small stone effigy of a young boy and, if you study it closely, you will see how it has been carefully sculpted to give the viewer their first clue in the puzzle.

The boy is cast with curly hair and is clad in a long tunic reaching to his ankles. In his left hand he clutches a small sphere, whilst his right hand is raised to his head, the fingers evidently pointing to just behind his right ear. Inscribed on the monument are the words: *Ubi dolor, ibi digitus*, meaning *Where the hurt is, there the finger points*. This is the first indication as to the cause of death and the initial hint that alerts us to the fact that something unusual happened here.

The monument is thought to depict the tragic death of Thomas Stanley, a young man who was killed whilst playing a game of tennis. The sphere in his left hand is the tennis ball that is alleged to have struck him on the head causing his death, hence the effigy's finger that is said to point to the point of impact.

Tennis balls in those days were not like the soft, rubbery ones of today, they were very hard and although most of them would have been made with a light wood or cork centre, they were often made with lead shot at the centre for weight, and then surrounded by felt. Such a ball would have been perfectly capable of rendering a fatal injury to a young boy if struck hard enough.

When you first look at the shrine it is dated 1460 and, indeed, his father Lord Stanley died a few years after the death of his son in 1474, making the dates fit well. Forensic analysis of the masonry, however, suggests something very different altogether and presents our first mystery.

Art historians examining the style of the sculpted stonework say that it looks to be correct for date on the tomb but forensic analysis discovered that the type of calcite plaster used to cast the effigy suggests that it was made about a century later than the date inscribed on the tomb. Something very odd was going on and needed further investigation. This would require a more detailed forensic analysis more akin to TV shows like *NCIS Los Angeles*, so let's take a closer look in Episode One of *NCIS Lichfield*.

There are two main theories as to why the tomb was rebuilt. The first is that it was accidentally damaged, and the second, and generally more accepted theory, is that the grave was broken into by tomb raiders and looted for the relics. A crime which was rife at the time and the scourge of graveyards up and down the country. This was because it was the customary to bury small treasures and mementos with your loved ones on passing. As the family were wealthy, they had built a large monument for their beloved son, not realising that a hundred years later such a huge monument would have stood out like a beacon to any passing tomb raider as a very lucrative prospect to target.

Following on from the tomb being burgled and so badly damaged, it would have needed to be replaced. When the tomb was reconstructed over a century after it was originally built, the family and the locals, enamoured of the tale of the boy and the tennis ball, which had now become firmly established as part of local folklore, made sure it was replaced and remodelled in the style of the period to suit the legendary story of Thomas Stanley being killed by the tennis ball.

The idea seems to have worked well because the monument remains a popular local attraction for tourists, tennis fans and forensic archaeologists alike.

The TV show *NCIS Lichfield*, however, is still awaiting commission.

TENNIS INVENTS SPACE PONG

You might have thought that a total lack of gravity, coupled with the fact that there was no playing surface, no court and no line markings, might have meant that space was not the most conducive of environments for playing a game of tennis. And, while space travel and tennis aren't the most obvious of pairings, NASA astronauts on the International Space Station just proved that you don't need any of that when you have a killer serve.

The space travellers made history in 2019 when they played the first-ever intergalactic tennis match. US astronaut Andrew Feustel, himself a keen tennis player, wanted to take the sport to new heights as part of a promotional tie-up to advertise the 2019 US Open Tennis Championships.

Prior to becoming the world's first ever celestial tennis pro, Feustel was a geophysicist who asked tennis pro Juan Martín del Potro to give him a few tips. *"I never imagined my first coaching job would be for NASA!"*, confessed the former US Open champion.

Due to the confines of the space station, and the lack of gravity to direct the balls, the astronauts could only use small tennis rackets to hit the floating ball over a make-shift net, which played out like a giant game of slow-motion Pong, the old 1970s video game.

Commander Feustel and three flight engineers, Ricky Arnold, Alexander Gerst and Serena Aunon-Chancellor were the other players. The end of the world's very first interstellar doubles match went on to prove that space tennis is no different from tennis played back on earth because, inevitably, Serena won!

TENNIS INVENTS SIBLING RIVALRY

A few years ago, I wrote an article for *The Queen's Club Magazine* about an argument that has raged throughout the scientific world for centuries, that of *Nature versus Nurture*, debating the merits of whether champions are born or bred. The article concluded that you definitely needed to have good genes to be a top athlete but that the environment plays a crucial part in how that innate talent is allowed to develop. Recent studies do tend to favour the born side of the argument. So, let's take a fresh look to see if science has moved on.

In 2016, Andy Murray and his brother Jamie both topped the ATP rankings as the number one men's singles and men's doubles players respectively. An extraordinary achievement, but you don't have to cast your mind back too far to see that tennis is brimming with sibling double acts.

Identical twins Bob and Mike Bryan, known on the circuit as the Bryan Brothers, are the most accomplished team in doubles history, dominating the doubles scene for 25 years. In the women's tour, there is Venus and Serena Williams who have been the prevailing force in both the singles and doubles since the turn of the millennium and were still contesting Grand Slam finals almost twenty years later.

But this phenomenon has apparently been going on for as long as tennis has been played. First off were identical twins Ernest and Willie Renshaw who swept all before them in the late 1890s, followed by the Baddeley brothers. Then there were the Allen twins, who were the Murray brothers of their time, carrying the Scottish flag in an all-conquering crusade. They were followed by the two that many historians regard as the greatest brother duo of all time, the indomitably doughty Doherty brothers.

Meanwhile, before Venus and Serena, Maud and Lillian Watson were the sisters who crushed all before them, swiftly followed by the Steedman sisters, Bertha and Mary. Shortly after that Annie and

Lottie Dod were a powerful force on the tour, and Lottie even won the mixed doubles championships with her brother, Tony. More recently, we've had the two Czech sisters Kristyna and Karolina Pliskova who've been going great guns.

In the late 1800s, the Roosevelt sisters, Grace and Ellen, scooped up most of the silverware, and hot on their heels the Neel brothers were stuffing their trophy cabinets as fast as you could string a racket. Just as the Roosevelt sisters hung up their long, linen dresses, then along came the Atkinson sisters, Juliette and Kathleen, who didn't let their equally demure stockings and laced up corsets prevent them from procuring silverware.

In France, the sibling sensation showed no sign of abating with les frères Vacherot thrashing any non-blood related personages who stood in their path. In the 1980s, we had John and Patrick McEnroe, the Gullikson twins, John and David Lloyd, the Amritrajs, the Austins, the Mayers, the Jordans and, more recently, Sascha and Mischa Zverev have been storming up the rankings. The list goes on and on.

I tell you, if only I'd had a brother, who knows what giddy heights I could have reached? I may well have lifted that Slinfold Village Under 12's Junior Tennis Shield after all. OK, well, maybe not won it, but maybe I would have beaten Martin Lines and at least made it through to the second round. Still it was his mum's court, so it was only polite to let him win.

But in truth, I had no chance anyway – Martin had a brother and, as we now know, in tennis terms, that's virtually cheating.

SECTION 22

MEDICAL, HEALTH AND FITNESS

Tennis players today have increasingly large teams surrounding them, many of whom will be intrinsically involved in all aspects of the player's medical health and fitness, from diet and physical training and mindfulness.

Linking tennis to health and wellbeing can be traced back to the origins of the game, including one particular ailment that even carries its name in the title ...

TENNIS INVENTS TENNIS ELBOW

At the start of the 1880s, the Renshaw twins, William and Ernest, had revolutionised the game of tennis. William was the older by just 15 minutes and was the stronger of the two. Which may not have pleased Ernest too much, but it surely cheered up Charles Darwin, as it leant weight to his *Theory of Natural Selection* that he was touting around at the time.

In reality, both brothers were spectacular players. They were the first players to have been brought up solely on Lawn Tennis, unlike most of the other competitors who had transferred over from Real Tennis or Rackets. And it showed. The Renshaws set the tennis world alight with their exciting new stroke play, fast, aggressive overhead serving and their dynamic volleying. Before the Renshaws appeared, Lawn Tennis as a competitive sport was on the wane, it was often haughtily dismissed as just *"Pat Ball"* because of its staid and gentle practice of hitting it back and forth from the baseline. Together, the Renshaw twins changed all that. They are credited with turning tennis into high drama and making it the great spectator sport that it is today. Spencer Gore was the first ever Wimbledon champion of 1877 and when he saw them playing in 1880 he said the frivolous era of *Pat Ball* tennis died that day and Lawn Tennis was born.

Although the Grand Slam system was not in operation at that time, they still won 19 major titles between them, most of those at Wimbledon. Sports stars couldn't travel as freely as they can today, otherwise they would have undoubtedly had 40 or 50 major titles between them. They were an unstoppable force, to whom every modern tennis player owes a debt of gratitude.

A few years ago, Roger Federer starting rushing to the net at unlikely times in the rally to try and distract his opponent, he hoped it would force them into rushing their shot, or changing their shot, and thus forcing an error. Even if it didn't force an error, Federer would at least catch them by surprise at the net and put away the volley. He calls it the *SABR*, a *Sudden Advance By Roger*. What Federer might not realise is that this was a tactic invented by the Renshaws a hundred and forty years ago. And it was a style of play that the crowds absolutely loved. Nobody had ever seen it before, and the crowds would cheer as they saw the brothers rushing to the net. It was so popular that the press even gave it its own name, dubbing it *The Renshaw Rush*.

Although *The Renshaw Rush* might not be talked about much today, another tactic the Renshaws employed certainly is – *The Renshaw Smash*, an overhead shot that we now just call the *smash*, the genesis of which we covered in an earlier chapter.

But there is yet a third shot credited to the twins that is also now a regular part of any tennis player's armoury – a booming first serve. This was again something that the Renshaws perfected with a new style of overhead serving to replace the more demure underarm serve that was more commonly practised. The sheer speed of the their startlingly fast serves took their opponents by surprise, but it was a real crowd pleaser and commentators of the day were quick to give this thunderous new stroke a name as well, *The Renshaw Boom*. The Boom term wasn't used again until *Boom Boom* Boris arrived on the scene. A nick-name he swears was down to his big first serve and not his off-court cupboard shenanigans. Thank you ma'am.

But, after nearly 10 years at the top of the game, the Renshaw twins were making fewer and fewer appearances, and would only show up for the Challenger Rounds or big money exhibition events, but even then, their power seemed to be diminishing and the crowds were disappointed and wanted to see more of them.

The reason was ironic and something that many of their gloating rivals may have seen as poetic justice, sweet revenge for all those years of brutal dominance. Because, unfortunately there was to be one more thing that the Renshaws were going to go down in history as making famous – tennis elbow.

Both brothers developed it, a tragic but somewhat inevitable result of decades of power play where they had to use those heavy old wooden rackets and hard rubber balls of the day. It was a cruel end to what had been two of the most dazzling athletes the world of Lawn Tennis had ever seen.

It seems ironic that today's technology has made the rackets so light that net play and touch play are becoming rarer and rarer and the game is once again drifting back to being a baseline slogging match due to the lightness of the rackets. As we all know, history repeats itself and, sadly, it seems that there is one thing that the human race is incapable of doing, and that is learning from history.

But, although many saw the Renshaws more as villains than as heroes for what some considered their ungentlemanly and brutal play, the twins had rejuvenated Lawn Tennis, transforming it from being a boring baseline slugging match, into a truly vital spectator sport, in a way that no one else had done before, and for this we must all be grateful. Hopefully there is a new breed of Renshaws waiting just around the corner.

TENNIS INVENTS THE GOAT

Every summer clubhouses all over the world will be debating who they think is worthy of the moniker GOAT, the *Greatest Of All Time*. Everyone has their own favourite. It's usually a battle between Margaret Court and Serena Williams for the ladies, but the men always stirs a more vigorous debate. Some will argue for the precocious talents of McEnroe, others Borg, there'll be a few Sampras supporters, Nadal the Spanish matador, Djokovic the Serbian terminator, and then there's probably the most popular choice, Federer, no matter what the stats say, surely his longevity should secure him the GOAT title.

Well, no, apparently not. For in truth there is a far more worthy champion. A man so great, in fact, that you could add all of the above players' titles together and he would still beat them. Hell, you could probably throw in McEnroe and Agassi's titles and this man would still have won more than all of them. So why has nobody heard of him?

The man was Jacques Barre and, when he won the Real Tennis World Championships in 1829, no one could have guessed that he would go on to do it again the following year, and then again the year after that. In fact, let me summarise this before we run out of paper and use up half the world's rain forest.

Barre not only beat Federer's 20 championship titles, he crushed it, and by some distance. Barre went on to win the Championships a record 33 times, and not only that but he won all 33 consecutively, without a single gap from 1829 to 1862. Barre eventually surrendered his title, aged 60, to a still wet-behind-the-ears young upstart called Edmund Tomkins, a sprightly 36 year old. I'm not sure what enhancements young Jacques was taking to have won 33 titles in a row, but I suspect the Russian Olympic Committee are carrying out a secret post-mortem as we speak.

BIBLIOGRAPHY

Advantages of Lawn Tennis, Henry Hall

Annals of Tennis, Julian Marshal

Banquet des Savans, Athenaios Naukratites

Beginnings of Lawn Tennis, Major Harry Gem Gibbons

Birth of Lawn Tennis, Bob Everitt and Richard Hillway

Colloquia familiaria, Desiderius Erasmus of Rotterdam

Compleat Gamester, Charles Cotton

Court Tennis, Racquets and Squash, Frederick Charles Tompkins

Daily Telegraph, various newspaper columns

Dat kaetspel ghemoralizeert, Jan van den Berghe

Deipnosophistes, Athenaeus Nokratios

Encyclopaedia of Tennis, Bud Collins

Field Magazine, sporting journal from the 19th Century

First Beautiful Game, by Roman Krznaric

George Hillyard: The Man Who Moved Wimbledon, Bruce Tarran

Game of Tennis: Its History and Description, Edouard Foumier

Great Shakespeare Hoax, Randall Barron

Guardian, various newspaper columns

Guinness Book of Sporting Blunders, Cris Freddi

Histoire de Saint-Louis, Jean de Joinville

History of Tennis, E. B. Noel and J. O. M. Clark

History of Tennis, Bud Collins

History of the Royal Game of Tennis, Albert de Luze

Odyssey, Homer

La paume et le lawn-tennis: par E. de Nanteuil, G. de Saint-Clair [et] C. Delahaye

La Maison académique, French Scientific Encyclopedia

Le Jeu de paume d'Orleans, Father Th. Cochard

Le Jeu de paume: Son histoire et sa description, Eugene Chapus

Les Jeu royal de la paume, Hulpeau

Les Jeux des anciens, Louis Becq de Fouquières

Les Jeux sportifs de pelote-paume, Julien Desees

Le Tennis à travers les âges, A. Guillaume

Language of Tennis, Ossian Shine

Lawn Tennis, Philip Heinekin

Lawn Tennis, magazine

Little History of Tennis, John Crace

Love Game, Elizabeth Wilson

Mammon, Frances Quarles

Maya Cosmos, David Freidel, Linda Schele and Joy Parker

Mystere de la passion, Arnoul Greban

New Book of Sports, London 1885

New York Times, newspaper

Old English Sports Pastimes and Customs, P. H. Ditchfield

Onomasticon, Julius Pollox, trans Teubner Hultsch

Open Tennis, Richard Evans

Pastime, magazine journal from the 19th Century

Pastimes in Times Past, London

Punch's Book of Sports, Punch Magazine

Queen's Club Magazine, various editions

Queen's Club Story, Roy McKelvie

Royal Leamington Spa: The Seeds of Lawn Tennis, W. G. Gibbons

Royal Tennis in Renaissance Italy, Cees de Bondt

Rules and Principals of Tennis, Pierre Barcellon

School for Ambassadors, M. Jusserand

Serious, John McEnroe

Sporting Fiascos, Stephen Winkworth

Sport and Society in Ancient Greece, M. Golden

Sports and Pastimes of the People of England, Joseph Strutt

Story of Tennis, Paul Stanley

Tennis: A Cultural History, Heiner Gillmeister

Tennis Cuts and Quips in Prose and Verse with Rules and Wrinkles, Julian Marshall

Tennis: Development of the European Ball Game, Roger Morgan

Tennis Miscellany, Michael Garnett

Tennis's Most Wanted, Floyd Conner

Tennis: Origins and Mysteries, Malcolm Whitman

Tennis Players, Tom Todd

Tennis Science and Technology, S. J. Haake and Andrew Coe

Tennis's Strangest Matches, Peter Seddon

Tennis: The Inner Game, Tim Gallway

Tennis Trivia, Eileen Kassower

The Times, newspaper

Trattato del Giuoco della Palla, Dr Antonio Scaino da Salo

A Treatise on Tennis, Robert Lukin

A Treatise on Tennis, S. Smith Travers

Treatise on the Royal Game of Tennis, de Manevieux

Tudor Tennis: A Miscellany, Roger Morgan

Ultimate Tennis Book, Gianni Clerici

Watchers: A Secret History of the Reign of Elizabeth I, Stephen Alford

Willis Faber Book of Tennis & Rackets, Lord Aberdare

Wimbledon Facts Figures and Fun, Cameron Brown

Wimbledon Story, Norah Cleather

Wingfield, George E. Alexander